fine
Cooking
Comfort Food

200 Delicious Recipes
for Soul-Warming Meals

Editors and Contributors of *Fine Cooking*

The Taunton Press

The Taunton Press
Inspiration for hands-on living®

The Taunton Press, Inc.
63 South Main Street
PO Box 5506, Newtown, CT 06470-5506
e-mail: tp@taunton.com

Copy editor: Valerie Cimino
Indexer: Barbara Mortenson
Cover design: Kimberly Adis
Cover photographer: Scott Phillips, © The Taunton Press, Inc.
Cover food stylist: Allison Ehri Kreitler
Interior design & layout: Kimberly Adis

Fine Cooking® is a trademark of The Taunton Press, Inc., registered in the U.S. Patent and Trademark Office.

The following names/manufacturers appearing in *Fine Cooking Comfort Food* are trademarks: Anchor Steam®, Atlas®, Beck's®, Boursin®, Cabot®, Chiquita®, Corona®, Cryovac®, De Cecco®, Delverde®, Dole®, Dos Equis®, Guinness®, Heath®, KitchenAid®, Koon Chun®, Lee Kum Kee™, Muir Glen®, Noilly Pratt®, Old Bay®, Pepperidge Farm®, Pernod®, Point Reyes Farmstead Original Blue™, Pyrex®, Quaker®, Skor®, Tabasco®, Vya®

Library of Congress Cataloging-in-Publication Data

Fine cooking comfort food : 200 delicious recipes for soul-warming meals / [by] editors and contributors of Fine cooking.
    p. cm.
 ISBN 978-1-60085-408-8
 1. Cooking, American. 2. Cookbooks. I. Taunton's fine cooking.
 TX715.F48 2011
 641.5973--dc23
                    2011026854

Printed in the United States of America
10 9 8 7 6 5 4 3 2 1

contents

Black Bean Soup
with Sweet Potatoes
(recipe on p. 5)

soups & chowders

classic tomato soup

YIELDS ABOUT 2 QUARTS;
SERVES 8

- 2 Tbs. extra-virgin olive oil
- 1 Tbs. unsalted butter
- 1 large white onion, finely chopped
- 1 large clove garlic, smashed and peeled
- 2 Tbs. unbleached all-purpose flour
- 3 cups homemade or lower-salt chicken broth
- 1 28-oz. can whole peeled plum tomatoes (with their juices), puréed
- 1½ tsp. granulated sugar
- 1 sprig fresh thyme
- Kosher salt and freshly ground black pepper
- 3 Tbs. thinly sliced fresh basil, chives, or dill (or a mix); omit if using one of the garnishes in the sidebar below

If you grew up on the soup in the red and white can, prepare to be blown away by this light, yet creamy, version.

1. Heat the oil and butter in a 5- to 6-quart Dutch oven over medium-low heat until the butter melts. Add the onion and garlic and cook, stirring occasionally, until softened but not browned, about 8 minutes. Add the flour and stir to coat the onion and garlic.

2. Add the broth, puréed tomatoes, sugar, thyme, and ¼ tsp. each salt and pepper. Bring to a simmer over medium-high heat while stirring to make sure that the flour doesn't stick to the bottom of the pan. Reduce the heat to low, cover, and simmer for 40 minutes.

3. Discard the thyme sprig.

4. Let cool briefly and then purée in 2 or 3 batches in a blender or food processor. Rinse the pot and return the soup to the pot. Season to taste with salt and pepper. Reheat if necessary. Serve warm but not hot, garnished with the herbs (or try one of the creamy garnishes in the sidebar below). *—Perla Meyers*

PER SERVING: 110 CALORIES | 3G PROTEIN | 11G CARB | 5G TOTAL FAT | 1.5G SAT FAT | 3G MONO FAT | 0.5G POLY FAT | 5MG CHOL | 430MG SODIUM | 2G FIBER

Garnishes Add a Creamy Touch

Sour cream, goat cheese, and Parmesan garnish In a small bowl, combine ½ cup sour cream with ¼ cup crumbled goat cheese. Add 1 Tbs. freshly grated Parmigiano-Reggiano, 1 Tbs. thinly sliced fresh chives, and 1 Tbs. extra-virgin olive oil. Mix thoroughly and season to taste with kosher salt and freshly ground black pepper. Add a dollop to each serving.

Crème fraîche, herb, and horseradish garnish In a small bowl, combine ½ cup crème fraîche with 1 Tbs. minced fresh dill and 1 Tbs. minced scallion. Add ½ Tbs. well-drained prepared white horseradish and mix well. Season to taste with kosher salt and freshly ground black pepper. Add a dollop to each serving.

black bean soup with sweet potatoes

YIELDS ABOUT 14 CUPS;
SERVES 8

2 Tbs. vegetable oil

2 medium yellow onions, chopped

3 medium cloves garlic, coarsely chopped

1½ tsp. ground coriander

1 tsp. ground cumin

¼ tsp. aniseed

Freshly ground black pepper

2 quarts lower-salt chicken broth or homemade vegetable broth

4 15.5-oz. or two 29-oz. cans black beans, rinsed and drained

2 medium sweet potatoes, peeled and cut into medium dice

Kosher salt

½ cup plain yogurt

8 paper-thin lime slices

The sweet potatoes in this soup contrast nicely with the tang of the yogurt and the tartness of the lime. Aniseed lends an unusual hint of licorice flavor. You can store leftovers in the refrigerator for up to 5 days.

1. Heat the oil over medium heat in a 6-quart (or larger) Dutch oven. Add the onions and cook, stirring occasionally, until starting to soften and brown slightly, about 8 minutes. Add the garlic, coriander, cumin, aniseed, and ¼ tsp. pepper and cook, stirring constantly, until fragrant, about 30 seconds. Add the broth, beans, sweet potatoes, and ¾ tsp. salt and bring to a boil over high heat; skim any foam as necessary. Reduce the heat and simmer, uncovered, stirring occasionally, until the sweet potatoes are tender, about 15 minutes.

2. Using a slotted spoon, set aside 3 cups of the beans and potatoes. Purée the remaining soup in batches in a blender. Return the solids to the soup and season to taste with salt and pepper. Serve topped with a dollop of the yogurt and a lime slice. *—Lori Longbotham*

PER SERVING: 310 CALORIES | 17G PROTEIN | 51G CARB | 6G TOTAL FAT | 1G SAT FAT | 2.5G MONO FAT | 2G POLY FAT | 0MG CHOL | 370MG SODIUM | 11G FIBER

tips for freezing soup

Many soups freeze easily, so they're great instant meals for busy nights. Follow these tips for best results.

- Chill soup thoroughly before freezing; this allows it to freeze faster. The ice crystals that form will be smaller, so your soup will have better texture and flavor.

- Freeze soup in plastic containers, leaving about ½ inch at the top to allow for expansion. Or fill plastic freezer bags about three-quarters full and squeeze out as much air as possible.

- Freeze soups in large amounts or in smaller, portion-size containers that are ready to heat and serve. The smaller the container, the quicker it will freeze and defrost.

- Before freezing, cover, label, and date your soup. As a general rule, stocks and broths can be frozen for up to 6 months; vegetable soups, about 4 months; meat, fish, or chicken soups, about 3 months; and soups with egg and cream, about 2 months.

- Keep a thermometer in the freezer to make sure the temperature remains constant at 0°F. If you're freezing a large quantity at once, turn the thermostat to its coldest setting until the soup freezes.

- Leave the soup in its container and defrost in the refrigerator, microwave oven, or under cold running water. You can also remove it from the container and reheat the frozen soup in a saucepan over low heat. A microwave oven is better for reheating small amounts of soup.

- Serve soup as soon as possible after defrosting.

- Don't be alarmed if puréed soup separates after defrosting. To fix it, just whisk it back together.

- Be aware that soups containing cream, wine, or lemon juice (or those thickened with eggs or flour) don't always freeze well. When reheating, simmer gently and whisk constantly to prevent curdling. Or better yet, add these ingredients after reheating.

chicken noodle soup with lemongrass

SERVES 4

2½ Tbs. canola oil

2 small boneless, skinless chicken breast halves (about ¾ lb.), butterflied (cut horizontally almost all the way through and then opened like a book)

Kosher salt and freshly ground black pepper

3 medium shallots (about 4 oz.), peeled and thinly sliced into rings

2 stalks lemongrass, trimmed, outer layers discarded, halved lengthwise, and smashed with the side of a chef's knife

1 Tbs. minced fresh ginger

2 tsp. packed light brown sugar

5½ cups lower-salt chicken broth

3½ oz. shiitake mushrooms, stemmed and quartered (1½ cups)

9 oz. fresh udon noodles

1 Thai bird chile (or 1 small serrano pepper), sliced into thin rings

8 large fresh basil leaves, torn; plus sprigs for garnish

1 medium lime, half juiced and half cut into wedges

1 Tbs. soy sauce; more to taste

2 medium scallions, trimmed and sliced, for garnish (optional)

1 medium carrot, cut into matchsticks, for garnish (optional)

½ cup fresh cilantro leaves, for garnish (optional)

In this cross between Vietnamese pho and Japanese udon noodle soup, fresh udon noodles are the star. Fat and bouncy in texture, they cook faster and tend to be more delicate than dried.

1. Heat 1½ Tbs. of the oil in a 5- to 6-quart Dutch oven over medium-high heat until shimmering hot. Season the chicken with ½ tsp. each salt and pepper, and cook without disturbing until it's browned and releases easily from the bottom of the pot, about 2 minutes. Flip and cook until the second side is browned and almost firm to the touch (just short of cooked through), 1 to 2 minutes more. Transfer the chicken to a cutting board to cool.

2. Add the remaining 1 Tbs. oil and the shallots to the pot. Sprinkle with ¼ tsp. salt, reduce the heat to medium and cook, stirring, until the shallots start to soften, about 2 minutes. Add the lemongrass, ginger, and brown sugar and cook, stirring, until the ginger and lemongrass sizzle and become fragrant, about 1 minute. Add the chicken broth, scraping up any browned bits from the bottom of the pot, and raise the heat to medium high. Bring the broth to a boil and then reduce to a simmer. Add the mushrooms and cook, stirring occasionally, until tender, 5 to 7 minutes.

3. Meanwhile, bring a medium pot of well-salted water to a boil and cook the noodles, stirring, until just tender, about 3 minutes. Transfer to a colander and run under cold water to cool slightly. Drain well.

4. Use your fingers or the tines of a fork to shred the chicken. Add the chicken and noodles to the broth and cook until the noodles are completely tender and the chicken is cooked through, about 2 minutes. Discard the lemongrass. Stir in the chiles, torn basil, lime juice, and soy sauce; season with more soy to taste. Divide the noodles among 4 large, deep bowls. Ladle the soup over the noodles and garnish with the basil sprigs and scallions, carrot, and cilantro, if using. Serve with the lime wedges for squeezing. —*Tony Rosenfeld*

PER SERVING: 500 CALORIES | 35G PROTEIN | 59G CARB | 15G TOTAL FAT | 2G SAT FAT | 7G MONO FAT | 3.5G POLY FAT | 45MG CHOL | 930MG SODIUM | 5G FIBER

wild mushroom soup with sherry and thyme

YIELDS ABOUT 5½ CUPS; SERVES 6

- **2** Tbs. unsalted butter
- **2** Tbs. olive oil
- **1** medium onion, cut into medium dice (to yield about 1½ cups)
- **4** cloves garlic, minced
- **¾** lb. fresh wild mushrooms, wiped clean, trimmed (stems removed from shiitakes), and thinly sliced (to yield about 4½ cups)
- **2** Tbs. plus 1 tsp. fresh thyme leaves

  Kosher salt and freshly ground black pepper
- **1** quart homemade or lower-salt chicken or vegetable broth
- **¼** cup half-and-half
- **3** Tbs. dry sherry
- **1** Tbs. soy sauce

If you like, a drizzle of white truffle oil just before serving makes this soup especially fragrant and luxurious. For the mushrooms, try a mix of half chanterelles or cremini and half shiitake.

1. Melt the butter with the olive oil in a 5-quart or larger stockpot over medium-high heat. Add the onion and cook until it's beginning to brown (resist the urge to stir too often), about 4 minutes. Stir in the garlic and cook for 1 minute. Add the mushrooms, 2 Tbs. of the thyme, and ½ tsp. each salt and pepper; cook until the mushrooms become limp, 2 to 4 minutes.

2. Add the broth, scraping up any browned bits in the pot with a wooden spoon. Bring to a boil over high heat, reduce the heat to maintain a simmer, and cook until the mushrooms are tender, 7 to 10 minutes. Remove from the heat and let cool slightly. Transfer about half of the soup to a blender and process until smooth. Return the mixture to the pot and stir in the half-and-half, sherry, and soy sauce. Add more salt and pepper to taste, if needed, and reheat. Garnish each serving with a small pinch of the remaining 1 tsp. thyme. —*Jill Silverman Hough*

PER SERVING: 160 CALORIES | 5G PROTEIN | 14G CARB | 11G TOTAL FAT | 4G SAT FAT | 5G MONO FAT | 1G POLY FAT | 15MG CHOL | 370MG SODIUM | 2G FIBER

Buying and Storing Sherry

Look for bottles labeled Jerez-Xérès or Manzanilla-Sanlúcar de Barrameda. These indicate a denomination or origin, an official designation ensuring that wines come from a defined area in and around the Spanish town of Jerez and that they meet specific standards set by a regulatory board.

It's best to store opened sherry in the refrigerator. Unlike most wines, it keeps for weeks after opening if you seal it well and put it in a uniformly cold, undisturbed spot at the back of the fridge.

french onion soup

- **2 oz. (¼ cup) unsalted butter; more for the baking sheet**
- **4 medium-large yellow onions (about 2 lb.), thinly sliced (8 cups)**
- **Kosher salt and freshly ground black pepper**
- **1 tsp. granulated sugar**
- **1 small baguette (½ lb.), cut into ½-inch slices**
- **2 quarts homemade beef broth or lower-salt beef or chicken broth**
- **1 bay leaf**
- **2 cups grated Gruyère**

Long-simmered onions and beef broth add a depth of flavor to this cheesy-topped classic.

1. Melt the butter in a 4-quart pot over medium heat. Stir in the onions and season with 1 tsp. salt and a few grinds of pepper. Reduce the heat to low. Press a piece of foil onto the onions to cover them completely, cover the pot with a lid, and cook, stirring occasionally (you will have to lift the foil), until the onions are very soft but not falling apart, 40 to 50 minutes. Remove the lid and foil, raise the heat to medium high, and stir in the sugar. Cook, stirring often, until very deeply browned, 10 to 15 minutes.

2. Meanwhile, to make the croûtes (baguette toasts), position a rack in the center of the oven and heat the oven to 350°F. Butter a rimmed baking sheet and arrange the baguette slices on the sheet in a single layer. Bake until the bread is crisp and lightly browned, turning once, 15 to 20 minutes. Set aside.

3. Add the broth and bay leaf to the caramelized onions and bring the soup to a boil over medium-high heat. Reduce the heat to medium low and simmer for 10 minutes to blend the flavors. Discard the bay leaf and season to taste with salt and pepper.

4. To serve, position a rack 6 inches from the broiler and heat the broiler to high. Put 6 to 8 broilerproof soup bowls or crocks on a baking sheet. Put 2 or 3 croûtes in each bowl and ladle the hot soup on top. Sprinkle with the cheese and broil until the top is browned and bubbly, 2 to 5 minutes. Serve immediately. —*Anne Willan*

PER SERVING: 240 CALORIES | 14G PROTEIN | 9G CARB | 16G TOTAL FAT | 10G SAT FAT | 5G MONO FAT | 1G POLY FAT | 45MG CHOL | 270MG SODIUM | 1G FIBER

cheddar and cauliflower soup

YIELDS 8 CUPS; SERVES 6 TO 8

Kosher salt

½ head cauliflower (about 1 lb.), cored and cut into 1½-inch florets

2 Tbs. unsalted butter

1 medium yellow onion, finely diced

1 medium clove garlic, minced

2 Tbs. unbleached all-purpose flour

¼ tsp. packed freshly grated nutmeg

⅛ tsp. cayenne

2 cups lower-salt chicken broth

½ cup heavy cream

3 sprigs fresh thyme

4 cups grated sharp or extra-sharp white Cheddar (about 14 oz.)

Freshly ground black pepper

Depending on how much you enjoy the intense flavor of Cheddar, choose between a sharp or extra-sharp version of the cheese for this rustic soup. To dress it up for a special occasion, garnish with a combination of 3 Tbs. of chopped toasted walnuts, 1 Tbs. of chopped fresh flat-leaf parsley, and 1½ tsp. of finely grated lemon zest.

1. Bring a large pot of salted water to a boil. Boil the cauliflower until tender, about 4 minutes. Drain and let cool slightly. Trim the stems from 18 of the cauliflower pieces and cut the crowns into mini florets about ½ inch wide; set aside. Reserve the trimmed stems with the remaining larger pieces.

2. Melt the butter in a 4-quart saucepan over medium-low heat. Add the onion and ¼ tsp. salt and cook, stirring frequently, until soft, 10 to 12 minutes.

3. Add the garlic and cook until the aroma subsides, 2 to 3 minutes. Increase the heat to medium, add the flour, nutmeg, and cayenne and cook for 3 minutes, stirring constantly. Whisk in the broth, cream, and 2 cups water. Add the thyme and bring to a simmer. Stir in the cheese until melted and simmer for 5 minutes to develop the flavors.

4. Remove and discard the thyme stems and stir in the larger cauliflower pieces and reserved stems. Working in batches, purée the soup in a blender. Return the soup to the pot, and season with salt and black pepper to taste. Add the mini cauliflower florets and reheat gently before serving.
—Tony Rosenfeld

Breaking Down Cheddar

The longer Cheddar is aged, the more pronounced and sharp its flavor becomes. In turn, it also develops a grainier (or less creamy) texture. Some prefer young, mild Cheddar for grating and melting, but for that unmistakable bite, go with sharp or aged Cheddar.

broccoli soup with bacon

SERVES 8

2 Tbs. extra-virgin olive oil

⅔ cup medium-diced onions

⅔ cup thinly sliced leeks

2 Tbs. minced garlic

Kosher salt

1¾ lb. broccoli, bottom stems trimmed, florets coarsely chopped, and stems sliced very thinly

2½ cups homemade or lower-salt chicken broth

3 Tbs. dry white wine

¼ cup heavy cream

½ tsp. freshly squeezed lemon juice; more to taste

Freshly ground black pepper

⅓ cup crumbled cooked bacon

Here's a perfect way to entice even the veggie-averse to get their greens.

1. In a 4- to 5-quart saucepan or Dutch oven, heat the olive oil over medium-low heat. When hot, add the onions, leeks, garlic, and a pinch of salt.

2. Add the broccoli, chicken broth, wine, and 2½ cups water. Stir well and bring to a simmer over medium heat. Cook, uncovered, stirring occasionally, until the vegetables are very tender and the soup is full-flavored, 10 to 20 minutes.

3. Take the pan off the heat and let the soup cool for 5 minutes. Working in batches, purée the soup in a blender (fill the jar no more than half full and vent the lid, topping it with a folded kitchen towel to prevent hot splashes). Wipe the pan clean and put the soup back into the pan.

4. Add the cream and lemon juice. Season the soup with salt and pepper. Taste the soup and adjust the seasonings with salt, pepper, or lemon juice as needed.

5. Ladle into 8 soup bowls and garnish each serving with 2 tsp. of the crumbled bacon. —*Susie Middleton*

PER SERVING: 120 CALORIES | 6G PROTEIN | 9G CARB | 7G TOTAL FAT | 3.5G SAT FAT | 3G MONO FAT | 0.5G POLY FAT | 15MG CHOL | 300MG SODIUM | 3G FIBER

chicken soup with lime and hominy

SERVES 4

12   oz. boneless, skinless chicken breasts

1   Tbs. vegetable oil

1   small white onion (8 oz.), chopped

4   medium cloves garlic, minced

1   small jalapeño, minced

1   quart lower-salt chicken broth

1   15-oz. can hominy, drained

1   tsp. dried Mexican oregano, crumbled if the leaves are large

4   to 5 Tbs. freshly squeezed lime juice

Kosher salt and ground black pepper

2½   oz. cotija or feta cheese, cut into ¼-inch cubes (½ cup)

This is a quick and easy version of sopa de lima, a comforting yet refreshing Yucatan chicken soup made tangy with fresh lime juice. Tasty garnishes include fried tortilla strips (or tortilla chips), diced avocado, and fresh cilantro.

1. Cut each chicken breast crosswise into 1½-inch-wide pieces.

2. Heat the oil in a 6-quart pot over medium-high heat until shimmering. Add the onion and cook, stirring often, until softened, about 5 minutes. Stir in the garlic and jalapeño and cook, stirring often, until fragrant, about 45 seconds. Add the broth, hominy, oregano, and chicken. Raise the heat to high and bring to a boil. Reduce the heat to medium, cover, and simmer gently, stirring occasionally and adjusting the heat as needed to maintain a simmer, until the chicken is cooked through, about 10 minutes.

3. Transfer the chicken to a plate. Using two forks, shred the meat into bite-size pieces and return to the pot. Bring the soup back to a simmer over medium heat, stir in the lime juice, and season to taste with salt and pepper. Ladle into bowls, top with the cheese, and serve immediately. —*Dawn Yanagihara*

PER SERVING: 320 CALORIES | 29G PROTEIN | 27G CARB | 12G TOTAL FAT | 4G SAT FAT | 4G MONO FAT | 3G POLY FAT | 65MG CHOL | 680MG SODIUM | 4G FIBER

classic vichyssoise

YIELDS ABOUT 6 CUPS; SERVES 6

4   medium leeks, trimmed, washed, and sliced ⅛ inch thick (about 3 cups)

2   large Yukon Gold potatoes, peeled and sliced ⅛ inch thick (about 4 cups)

2   cups whole milk

Kosher salt

1   cup heavy cream

1   Tbs. thinly sliced fresh chives, for garnish

Yukon Golds, with their rich flavor and medium starch content, are the best choice for this cold soup. Serve it as a first course or as a light lunch, accompanied by a green salad.

1. Combine the leeks, potatoes, milk, and 2 cups water in a 4-quart pot.

2. Bring to a simmer over medium-high heat. Add 1½ tsp. salt, reduce the heat to medium low, and simmer until a potato slice falls apart when you poke it with a fork, about 20 minutes. Remove from the heat, stir in the cream, and let cool briefly.

3. Purée the soup, preferably using a regular blender and working in batches, filling it only halfway each time.

4. Strain the puréed soup through a fine sieve. Let cool to room temperature, stirring occasionally (stirring prevents a skin from forming), and then refrigerate until thoroughly chilled.

5. Before serving, thin the soup with water if necessary—it should be the consistency of heavy cream. Season to taste with salt. Serve cold in chilled bowls, garnished with the chives. —*James Peterson*

PER SERVING: 300 CALORIES | 7G PROTEIN | 30G CARB | 18G TOTAL FAT | 11G SAT FAT | 5G MONO FAT | 1G POLY FAT | 65MG CHOL | 210MG SODIUM | 2G FIBER

purée of sweet potato and ginger soup with apple-mint raita

SERVES 4 TO 6

FOR THE SOUP

- 2 Tbs. unsalted butter
- 1 medium yellow onion, roughly chopped
- 2 cloves garlic, minced
- 1 oz. chunk (½ inch) fresh ginger, peeled and thinly sliced
- ¼ tsp. ground cardamom
- ½ fresh jalapeño, seeds and ribs removed, and left whole
- 2 lb. sweet potatoes (about 4 medium), peeled and cut into 1-inch cubes
- 5½ cups homemade or lower-salt canned chicken broth
- 1 tsp. kosher salt; more to taste
- 1½ cups heavy cream (optional)
- 1 Tbs. freshly squeezed lime juice
- 1 Tbs. light brown sugar

  Freshly ground white pepper

FOR THE RAITA

- ½ cup plain nonfat or low-fat yogurt
- ½ firm, sweet apple, such as Gala or Pink Lady, peeled, cored, and finely diced
- ¼ cup chopped fresh mint
- ½ tsp. finely minced fresh jalapeño; more to taste

  Kosher salt and freshly ground black pepper

Slices of fresh ginger are simmered with the soup base to gently infuse it with warmth and mellow sweetness. The raita is the perfect cooling counterpart. If you like heat, leave the ribs attached to the jalapeño half.

MAKE THE SOUP

1. Melt the butter in a soup pot over low heat. Cook the onion in the butter, stirring occasionally, until very soft but not browned, 10 to 13 minutes. Add the garlic, ginger, and cardamom and cook for another minute. Increase the heat to high and add the jalapeño, sweet potatoes, 4 cups of the broth, and the salt. Bring to a boil, reduce the heat to medium low, cover, and simmer until the potatoes are very soft, 15 to 20 minutes.

2. In a blender, purée the soup in batches until very smooth. Rinse and dry the pot and return the puréed soup to it. Add the remaining broth and the cream, if using, and bring to a simmer over medium-low heat. Add the lime juice and brown sugar, and season with salt and white pepper to taste.

MAKE THE RAITA

While the soup is simmering, combine the yogurt, apple, mint, and jalapeño in a small bowl. Season with salt and pepper to taste. Refrigerate until ready to serve.

TO SERVE

Ladle the soup into individual bowls and add a dollop of the raita.   *—Eva Katz*

PER SERVING: 250 CALORIES | 7G PROTEIN | 46G CARB | 5G TOTAL FAT | 3G SAT FAT | 1G MONO FAT | 1G POLY FAT | 10MG CHOL | 480MG SODIUM | 6G FIBER

Choosing Ginger

Ginger's aroma, texture, and flavor vary depending upon the timing of its harvest. Early harvest or young ginger (harvested after 6 months) is tender and sweet, while older, more mature ginger (harvested between 10 and 12 months) is more fibrous and spicy. The latter is usually all that's available in American supermarkets, but young ginger can often be found in Asian markets. It's easily identified by its thin, papery skin and pink-tinged tips. When cooking with young ginger, you can leave the skin on and use it in greater quantities.

Avoid ginger that looks wrinkled, discolored, or moldy. Look for ginger with a thin skin that's smooth, unblemished, and almost translucent. If you break off a knob, the texture should be firm, crisp, and not overly fibrous (making it easier to slice). It should have a fresh, spicy fragrance. Like many spices, ginger's flavor fades as it cooks. So for more gingery oomph, add some or all of the ginger at the end of cooking.

root vegetable and barley soup with bacon

YIELDS 13 CUPS; SERVES 6 TO 8

- **1** oz. dried porcini mushrooms
- **2** medium cloves garlic
  Kosher salt
- **4** slices bacon, cut in half crosswise
- **2** medium red onions, chopped
- **2** small bay leaves
- **¾** tsp. caraway seeds
- **½** tsp. dried thyme
  Freshly ground black pepper
- **2** quarts lower-salt chicken broth
- **5** medium carrots, peeled and cut into small dice
- **2** medium purple-top turnips, peeled and cut into small dice
- **2** medium Yukon Gold potatoes, peeled and cut into small dice
- **¾** cup pearl barley, picked over, rinsed, and drained
- **4** tsp. freshly squeezed lemon juice

You can store leftovers in the refrigerator for up to 2 days. If you store this for more than a day, though, the barley will absorb some of the liquid and you'll need to thin it with a little water when you reheat it.

1. In a small bowl, soak the mushrooms in 1 cup boiling water for 20 minutes. Remove the mushrooms and pour the liquid through a fine strainer to remove any grit. Reserve the liquid. Rinse the mushrooms, chop them, and set aside.

2. Chop the garlic, sprinkle it with ¾ tsp. salt, and then mash it to a paste with the side of a chef's knife. Set aside.

3. In a 6-quart (or larger) Dutch oven, cook the bacon over medium heat until crisp, about 8 minutes. Transfer to a paper-towel-lined plate, crumble when cool, and set aside.

4. Add the onion and 1 tsp. salt to the bacon fat and cook, stirring occasionally, until softened, 6 to 8 minutes. Stir in the garlic paste, bay leaves, caraway seeds, thyme, and ¼ tsp. pepper and cook, stirring constantly, until fragrant, about 1 minute. Add the chopped mushrooms, mushroom liquid, chicken broth, carrots, turnips, potatoes, barley, and 1½ cups water. Bring to a boil over high heat; skim any foam as necessary. Reduce the heat, cover, and simmer, stirring occasionally, until the barley and vegetables are tender, 20 to 25 minutes. Add the lemon juice, season with salt and pepper, and discard the bay leaves. Serve garnished with the bacon. *—Lori Longbotham*

PER SERVING: 210 CALORIES | 11G PROTEIN | 37G CARB | 3.5G TOTAL FAT | 1G SAT FAT | 1.5G MONO FAT | 0.5G POLY FAT | 5MG CHOL | 450MG SODIUM | 7G FIBER

spiced tomato and red lentil soup

YIELDS ABOUT 14 CUPS; SERVES 8

3 Tbs. vegetable oil

2 medium yellow onions, chopped

Kosher salt

2 tsp. Madras curry powder or garam masala

2 quarts lower-salt chicken broth or homemade vegetable broth

2 14.5-oz. cans petite-diced tomatoes

1 lb. (2⅓ cups) dried red lentils, picked over, rinsed, and drained

2 medium stalks celery, cut into small dice

1 medium carrot, peeled and cut into small dice

2 medium cloves garlic, peeled and chopped

⅛ to ¼ tsp. cayenne

Curry powder and garam masala are both Indian spice blends, which vary in flavor from blend to blend. Experiment to see which you prefer. You can store leftovers in the refrigerator for up to 5 days.

1. Heat the oil in a 6-quart (or larger) Dutch oven over medium heat. Add the onions and a generous pinch of salt and cook, stirring occasionally, until the onions are softened and just starting to brown, 6 to 8 minutes. Add the curry powder or garam masala and cook, stirring constantly, until fragrant, 30 seconds to 1 minute.

2. Add the broth, tomatoes and their juices, lentils, celery, carrot, garlic, cayenne, ¾ tsp. salt, and 2 cups water. Bring to a boil over high heat, stirring frequently to keep the lentils from sticking; skim any foam as necessary. Reduce the heat and simmer uncovered, stirring occasionally, until the lentils, carrots, and celery are tender, 35 to 40 minutes. Season to taste with salt.
—*Lori Longbotham*

PER SERVING: 320 CALORIES | 22G PROTEIN | 45G CARB | 8G TOTAL FAT | 1G SAT FAT | 3G MONO FAT | 2.5G POLY FAT | 0MG CHOL | 480MG SODIUM | 9G FIBER

Stock Up

With these items in your kitchen, you'll have everything you need to make a number of different kinds of soups.

In the pantry
- Canned or boxed chicken broth
- Canned diced tomatoes
- Canned beans and dried lentils
- Dried herbs and spices
- Small pasta shapes, like orzo, tubettini, acini di pepe, and ditalini
- Quick-cooking grains like rice, pearl barley, and bulgur
- Tomato paste
- Onions
- Garlic

- Potatoes
- Winter squash
- Coconut milk
- Thai curry paste
- Dried chiles
- Chile pastes, hot sauces
- Canned chipotle chiles in adobo
- Canned roasted green chiles
- Dried mushrooms
- Canned straw mushrooms
- Sun-dried tomatoes

In the fridge
- Hard cheeses like Parmigiano-Reggiano and Pecorino Romano
- Citrus fruit like lemons, oranges, and limes

- Root vegetables like carrots, parsnips, and turnips
- Celery
- Crème fraîche, sour cream, plain yogurt, and buttermilk
- Flavorful oils like chile oil, nut oils, and sesame oil

In the freezer
- Homemade vegetable, chicken, and beef broths
- Bread (for croutons or for thickening)
- Bacon
- Shrimp
- Small stuffed pastas like raviolini and tortellini
- Corn
- Peas
- Edamame

pasta e fagioli

8 slices bacon, cut crosswise into ¼-inch-wide strips

3 medium red onions, finely chopped

3 medium cloves garlic, minced

½ tsp. dried rosemary

2 quarts lower-salt chicken broth

2 15½-oz. cans chickpeas, rinsed and drained

1 14½-oz. can petite-cut diced tomatoes

4 medium carrots, peeled, halved lengthwise, and thinly sliced

3 medium stalks celery with leaves, thinly sliced crosswise

1 slender 3-inch cinnamon stick

   Kosher salt and freshly ground black pepper

1 cup tubettini (or other small pasta)

1½ tsp. red-wine vinegar; more to taste

   Grated or shaved Parmigiano-Reggiano, for garnish

This Italian soup—which has as many variations as there are cooks—is chock full of pasta, beans, and vegetables, making it a hearty one-dish meal. You can store leftovers in the refrigerator for up to 2 days.

1. In a 6-quart (or larger) Dutch oven over medium heat, cook the bacon, stirring occasionally, until partially crisp, about 7 minutes. With a slotted spoon, transfer the bacon to a paper-towel-lined plate. Add the onions to the pot and cook, scraping up any browned bits and stirring occasionally, until softened, 6 to 8 minutes. Add the garlic and rosemary and cook, stirring constantly, until fragrant, about 1 minute. Add the chicken broth, chickpeas, tomatoes and their juices, carrots, celery, cinnamon stick, ¾ tsp. salt, ½ tsp. pepper, and 1 cup water. Bring to a boil over high heat; skim any foam as necessary. Reduce the heat and simmer, stirring occasionally, until the carrots and celery are very tender, about 30 minutes.

2. Meanwhile, cook the tubettini according to the package directions and drain.

3. Discard the cinnamon stick and add the pasta. Stir in the bacon and vinegar. Season to taste with salt, pepper, and more vinegar. Serve garnished with the Parmigiano-Reggiano. *—Lori Longbotham*

PER SERVING: 370 CALORIES | 21G PROTEIN | 59G CARB | 7G TOTAL FAT | 1.5G SAT FAT | 2.5G MONO FAT | 2G POLY FAT | 5MG CHOL | 720MG SODIUM | 11G FIBER

carrot and leek soup with herbed croutons

SERVES 6

- **3 oz. (6 Tbs.) unsalted butter**
- **1 medium yellow onion, chopped**
- **2 small leeks (light-green and white parts only), sliced**
- **2 large cloves garlic, chopped**
- **Kosher salt and freshly ground black pepper**
- **3 cups lower-salt chicken broth**
- **2 lb. carrots, sliced ¼ inch thick**
- **3 fresh or 2 dried bay leaves**
- **2 sprigs fresh thyme**
- **4 oz. crusty bread, cut into ½-inch cubes (2 cups)**
- **1½ Tbs. chopped fresh chervil**
- **1 cup plain full-fat or low-fat yogurt**

Adding yogurt to the soup makes it smooth and creamy. If you can't find chervil (a relative of the carrot), use dill instead.

1. Position a rack in the center of the oven and heat the oven to 350°F.

2. In a 4- to 5-quart saucepan, melt 3 Tbs. of the butter over medium heat. Add the onion, leeks, garlic, ½ tsp. salt, and ¼ tsp. pepper; cook until softened and light golden-brown, about 10 minutes.

3. Add the broth, carrots, bay leaves, thyme sprigs, and ½ cup water; bring to a boil over medium-high heat. Reduce the heat to medium and simmer until the carrots are tender, about 15 minutes.

4. Meanwhile, melt the remaining 3 Tbs. butter in a 3-quart saucepan over medium heat. Add the bread cubes and chopped chervil and toss to coat evenly. Spread on a rimmed baking sheet, season with salt, and bake until golden, 8 to 10 minutes.

5. When the vegetables are tender, discard the bay leaves and thyme sprigs. With a regular or a hand blender, purée the soup (work in batches if using a regular blender). Stir in the yogurt. If you prefer a thinner texture, add a little water. Season to taste with salt and pepper, and serve garnished with the chervil croutons. —*Samantha Seneviratne*

PER SERVING: 290 CALORIES | 8G PROTEIN | 34G CARB | 15G TOTAL FAT | 8G SAT FAT | 3.5G MONO FAT | 1G POLY FAT | 35MG CHOL | 360MG SODIUM | 6G FIBER

What Is Chervil?

Chervil is a delicate herb that has a very mild flavor with hints of anise, pepper, and parsley. It's frequently used in French cooking, most notably as part of the fresh herb blend known as *fines herbes* (equal parts chervil, chive, tarragon, and parsley). Fresh chervil's flavor is fleeting, so it's typically added to dishes at the end of cooking.

parsnip and parmesan soup

YIELDS 5½ TO 6 CUPS;
SERVES 5 OR 6

- ¼ cup unsalted butter
- 1½ lb. parsnips, peeled, trimmed, and cut into ½-inch dice (to yield a scant 4 cups)
- 6 oz. shallots, cut into ¼-inch dice (to yield about 1¼ cups)
- 8 cloves garlic, minced
- 1 Tbs. finely chopped fresh oregano; plus tiny sprigs for garnish (optional)
- Kosher salt and freshly ground black pepper
- 4½ cups homemade or lower-salt chicken or vegetable broth
- 1½ oz. (½ cup) freshly grated Parmigiano-Reggiano
- 2 tsp. soy sauce
- 2 tsp. freshly squeezed lemon juice

Salty and savory Parmigiano-Reggiano marries well with sweet parsnips, and fresh oregano pulls it all together.

1. Melt the butter in a 5-quart or larger stockpot set over medium heat. While the butter is still foaming, add the parsnips and cook until lightly browned, 7 to 10 minutes (resist the urge to stir too often or they won't brown). Stir in the shallots, garlic, chopped oregano, 1½ tsp. salt, and ½ tsp. pepper and cook until the shallots are very limp and the entire mixture is beginning to brown, 8 to 10 minutes. Add the broth, using a wooden spoon to scrape up any browned bits in the pot. Bring to a boil, reduce the heat to maintain a low simmer, and cook until the parsnips are very soft, 6 to 8 minutes. Remove from the heat and let cool somewhat.

2. Purée the soup using a stand or immersion blender (you'll need to work in batches if using a stand blender). Return the soup to the pot and stir in the Parmigiano, soy sauce, and lemon juice. Taste and add more salt and pepper if needed. Reheat the soup and garnish each serving with an oregano sprig, if you like. —*Jill Silverman Hough*

PER SERVING: 230 CALORIES | 9G PROTEIN | 26G CARB | 11G TOTAL FAT | 6G SAT FAT | 3G MONO FAT | 0.5G POLY FAT | 25MG CHOL | 600MG SODIUM | 5G FIBER

tips for the best puréed soups

- Cut your vegetables small for faster cooking. A ½-inch dice needs no more than 10 minutes of simmering before it's soft enough to purée.

- Don't stir the vegetables too often during the sauté; once every 2 minutes or so is good. This helps them brown, and that, in turn, will flavor your soup, giving it nuance beyond simply simmered vegetables.

- Use a blender to get the smoothest soup. If you use a stand blender, be sure to let the liquid cool slightly, work in batches, and hold a towel over the lid to avoid overflowing. An immersion blender works well, too, and is even more convenient.

- Don't be afraid of salt—it can make all the difference. Taste your soup before serving and add salt to taste. The flavors will get brighter and more pronounced.

- Add an attractive garnish: It can really give the soup pizzazz. Use a sprig of an herb that's in your soup, a drizzle of a flavored oil, or a sprinkle of shredded cheese. A dollop of sour cream or crème fraîche can also enhance a simple puréed soup, making it party-fancy in both flavor and appearance.

turkey soup with dill, parsley & chive dumplings

SERVES 6

FOR THE TURKEY BROTH

2	medium carrots, cut into 2-inch pieces
2	medium stalks celery, cut into 2-inch pieces
1	medium yellow onion, cut into quarters
2	dried bay leaves
1	cup dry white wine
1	roasted turkey carcass, broken in half, plus any leftover bones

FOR THE SOUP

2	Tbs. extra-virgin olive oil
½	medium yellow onion, finely diced
4	medium carrots, quartered lengthwise and cut into ½-inch pieces
4	medium parsnips, quartered lengthwise, cored, and cut into ½-inch pieces
1½	cups small-diced celery root
	Kosher salt and freshly ground black pepper
1	14½-oz. can diced tomatoes with juice
½	cup dry white wine
1	dried bay leaf
3	cups medium-diced roast turkey
2	cups chopped Swiss chard leaves (ribs removed)

FOR THE DUMPLINGS

3	oz. (6 Tbs.) unsalted butter
2	tsp. kosher salt
3⅜	oz. (¾ cup) unbleached all-purpose flour
3	large eggs
1	Tbs. chopped fresh dill
1	Tbs. chopped fresh flat-leaf parsley
1	Tbs. chopped fresh chives

A roasted turkey carcass produces rich broth that makes for a delicious turkey soup. This version incorporates airy herb-flecked dumplings. You'll have extra turkey broth, which you can use to make the Turkey Bolognese on p. 84.

MAKE THE BROTH

In a 10-quart pot, combine the carrots, celery, onion, bay leaves, wine, carcass, and bones. Add 7 quarts of water and bring to a simmer over medium-high heat. Reduce the heat and simmer gently until the broth is rich and flavorful, 4 to 6 hours. Strain the broth through a fine sieve and discard the solids. Let cool; then skim off and discard the fat on the surface. The broth may be refrigerated for up to 2 days or frozen for up to 2 months.

MAKE THE SOUP

1. Heat the oil in a heavy-duty 6- to 8-quart pot over medium-high heat. Add the onion and cook until starting to brown, about 2 minutes. Add the carrots, parsnips, and celery root and cook until the vegetables start to color, about 4 minutes. Season with salt and pepper.

2. Add the tomatoes, wine, and bay leaf and bring to a boil. Add 2 quarts of the turkey broth and return to a boil. Reduce the heat and simmer until the vegetables are tender, 10 to 15 minutes. Season to taste with salt and pepper.

3. Add the turkey and Swiss chard and simmer until the chard is wilted, about 5 minutes. (The soup may be cooled and refrigerated for up to 2 days. Bring to a simmer before continuing.)

MAKE THE DUMPLING BATTER

1. In a 3-quart saucepan, bring ¾ cup water and the butter and salt to a boil over medium heat. When the butter melts, remove the pan from the heat and stir in the flour until thoroughly combined. Return the pan to medium heat and stir until the mixture pulls away from the sides of the pan.

2. Scrape the dough into a large bowl. With a sturdy wooden spoon, beat in the eggs, one by one, until the batter is smooth. Fold in the chopped herbs. (The batter may be covered and refrigerated for up to 1 day.)

FINISH THE SOUP WITH THE DUMPLINGS

Using two ½-tsp. measures, drop spoonfuls of batter into the simmering soup until all of the batter is used. After the dumplings rise to the top, cover the pan and steam the dumplings until they have puffed up to double their size, about 4 minutes. Serve hot. *—Maria Helm Sinskey*

PER SERVING: 530 CALORIES | 27G PROTEIN | 44G CARB | 26G TOTAL FAT | 11G SAT FAT | 10G MONO FAT | 3G POLY FAT | 180MG CHOL | 1,360MG SODIUM | 7G FIBER

roasted hubbard squash soup
with hazelnuts and chives

**YIELDS ABOUT 10 CUPS;
SERVES 8 TO 10**

- 3 Tbs. extra-virgin olive oil
- 3 large cloves garlic, peeled
- 1 Tbs. coriander seeds
- 1½ tsp. fennel seeds
- 1½ tsp. dried sage
- 1 small (5½- to 6-lb.) Hubbard squash, halved lengthwise and seeded
- 2 Tbs. unsalted butter
- 1 large leek (white and light green parts only), halved lengthwise and thinly sliced crosswise
- 2 medium carrots, peeled and cut into small dice
- Kosher salt
- 5 cups homemade or lower-salt chicken or vegetable broth
- 1 bay leaf
- 2 tsp. freshly squeezed lemon juice
- Freshly ground black pepper
- ½ cup hazelnuts, toasted, skinned, and chopped
- 2 Tbs. thinly sliced chives
- Several small pinches of piment d'Espelette or cayenne

If you can't find piment d'Espelette, use just a pinch of cayenne instead. The soup keeps for 3 days in the refrigerator or 2 months in the freezer.

1. Position a rack in the center of the oven and heat the oven to 400°F. Line a heavy-duty rimmed baking sheet with parchment.

2. In a mortar and pestle, pound the oil, garlic, coriander seeds, fennel seeds, and sage until they resemble a coarse paste. Rub the spice mixture on the flesh of the squash halves. Set them cut side down on the prepared pan and roast until tender when pierced with a fork, about 1 hour. Let cool, cut side up. When cool enough to handle, scrape the flesh away from the rind—you'll need about 5 cups.

3. Melt the butter in a 5- to 6-quart Dutch oven over medium heat. Add the leek, carrots, and a big pinch of salt and cook, stirring occasionally, until the leek is softened, 8 to 10 minutes. Add the squash, broth, bay leaf, and 1 tsp. salt and bring to a boil over high heat. Reduce the heat to a low simmer, cover, and cook for 30 minutes to develop the soup's flavor.

4. Remove the bay leaf and let the soup cool slightly. Purée the soup in batches in a blender. Return the soup to the pot and add the lemon juice; season to taste with salt and pepper. Garnish with the chopped hazelnuts, chives, and piment d'Espelette or cayenne. *—Ivy Manning*

PER SERVING: 240 CALORIES | 9G PROTEIN | 29G CARB | 13G TOTAL FAT | 3G SAT FAT | 7G MONO FAT | 2G POLY FAT | 5MG CHOL | 180MG SODIUM | 7G FIBER

All about Hubbards

Probably the largest squash you'll find at the market, these teardrop-shaped behemoths are often sold in manageable chunks, so you can buy only what you need. Hubbards have thick skin that ranges from dark green to bluish gray and a dense orange flesh with a rich pumpkin flavor. Hubbards sweeten with age and can be stored whole in a dry place at a cool room temperature for up to 5 months before using.

More ways to cook with Hubbard squash Roast bite-size pieces of Hubbard tossed with chopped fresh rosemary, olive oil, salt, and pepper in the same pan with a whole chicken or turkey breast. Or roast squash halves with toasty spices like coriander, fennel, cumin, nutmeg, or curry powder and then mash the flesh.

garlicky tortellini, spinach & tomato soup

SERVES 2 OR 3

- 2 Tbs. unsalted butter
- 6 to 8 cloves garlic, chopped
- 1 quart homemade or lower-salt chicken broth
- 6 oz. fresh or frozen cheese tortellini
- 1 14-oz. can diced tomatoes, with their liquid
- 10 oz. spinach, washed and stemmed; coarsely chopped if large
- 8 to 10 leaves fresh basil, coarsely chopped

  Freshly grated Parmigiano-Reggiano

If you have tortellini in your freezer, a hunk of Parmigiano-Reggiano in the fridge, and a can of diced tomatoes on the shelf, all you'll need to do is pick up a bag of triple-washed spinach and a bunch of basil on the way home for this terrific soup. It takes just minutes to pull it all together.

1. Melt the butter in a large saucepan over medium-high heat. Add the garlic and sauté until fragrant, about 2 minutes. Add the broth and bring to a boil. Add the tortellini and cook halfway, about 5 minutes for frozen pasta, less if using fresh. Add the tomatoes and their liquid, reduce the heat to a simmer, and cook just until the pasta is tender.

2. Stir in the spinach and basil and cook until wilted, 1 to 2 minutes. Serve sprinkled with the grated Parmigiano-Reggiano. —*Joanne McAllister Smart*

PER SERVING: 270 CALORIES | 15G PROTEIN | 22G CARB | 15G TOTAL FAT | 9G SAT FAT | 3G MONO FAT | 1G POLY FAT | 35MG CHOL | 560MG SODIUM | 6G FIBER

creamy seafood chowder with bacon, thyme & jalapeño

SERVES 4

- 4 slices bacon, cut crosswise into ¼-inch strips
- 1 medium shallot, minced
- 1 large jalapeño, seeded and very finely chopped (about 2 Tbs.)
- 2 Tbs. unbleached all-purpose flour
- 2 6½-oz. cans chopped clams, clams and juice separated (about 1 cup juice)
- 2 8-oz. bottles clam juice
- 1 cup heavy cream
- 8 to 10 oz. unpeeled red potatoes (about 2 medium), scrubbed and cut into ½-inch dice
- ½ tsp. dried thyme
- ¾ lb. skinless haddock or cod fillets

  Kosher salt and freshly ground black pepper

Cream cuts the jalapeño's heat, but you can still taste its bright, fresh flavor.

1. In a 4-quart Dutch oven or heavy saucepan, cook the bacon over medium heat, stirring occasionally, until browned and crisp, about 8 minutes. Transfer the bacon to a small dish lined with paper towels, leaving the fat behind in the pan.

2. Add the shallot and 1 Tbs. of the jalapeño to the bacon fat and cook over medium heat, stirring occasionally, until the shallots are softened, about 2 minutes. Add the flour and cook, stirring, for 1 minute. Gradually stir in all the clam juice (from the cans and bottles). Add the cream, potatoes, and thyme; bring to a simmer over medium-high heat, stirring occasionally. Reduce the heat as necessary and simmer, stirring occasionally, until the potatoes are tender, about 10 minutes. Add the whole fish fillets and cook for 3 minutes. Stir in the clams and continue stirring until the fish has broken into chunks. Cook until the fish is cooked through and the clams are heated, about another 2 minutes.

3. Season the soup with salt and pepper to taste. Serve sprinkled with the reserved bacon and the remaining jalapeño. —*Joanne McAllister Smart*

PER SERVING: 410 CALORIES | 28G PROTEIN | 16G CARB | 25G TOTAL FAT | 15G SAT FAT | 8G MONO FAT | 1.5G POLY FAT | 160MG CHOL | 1,220MG SODIUM | 1G FIBER

baked potato and leek soup with cheddar and bacon

YIELDS ABOUT 6 CUPS;
SERVES 4

- 2 medium russet potatoes (about ½ lb. each)
- ¼ cup unsalted butter
- 2½ cups sliced leeks (about 2 medium leeks; white and light green parts), rinsed well
- 2 medium cloves garlic, minced
- Kosher salt and freshly ground black pepper
- 2 cups homemade or lower-salt chicken broth
- 4 thick slices bacon, cut into ½-inch dice
- ½ cup milk
- ½ cup sour cream
- 1 cup grated sharp Cheddar (about ¼ lb.)
- 2 Tbs. thinly sliced scallion greens or fresh chives

With a couple of potatoes on hand, you can create this filling soup—it's like a baked potato in a bowl.

1. Heat the oven to 375°F. Scrub the potatoes in water, pat dry, and pierce in several places with a fork. Set them directly on an oven rack and bake until very tender when pierced with a fork, about 1 hour. Let cool completely on a wire rack.

2. Melt the butter in a soup pot over medium-low heat. Add the leeks and garlic, season with salt, and cook, stirring occasionally, until softened, about 10 minutes. Add the broth and 2 cups water. Bring to a simmer over medium heat and cook until the leeks are very tender, about 20 minutes.

3. Meanwhile, put the bacon in a skillet and cook over medium heat, stirring occasionally, until browned and crisp, 8 to 10 minutes. Transfer the bacon bits with a slotted spoon to a saucer lined with paper towels to drain and cool.

4. When the potatoes are cool, cut one of them in half lengthwise. Use a large spoon to scoop the flesh in one piece from each half. Cut the flesh into ½-inch cubes and set aside. Coarsely chop the potato skin and the entire remaining potato and add to the pot with the leeks. Purée the contents of the pot in a blender until very smooth (you'll need to work in batches).

5. Return the puréed soup to a clean soup pot and reheat over medium low. In a small bowl, whisk the milk and sour cream until smooth and then whisk this into the soup, along with ½ cup of the Cheddar. Stir in the diced potato. The soup should be fairly thick, but if it seems too thick, thin it with a little water. Season to taste with salt and pepper. Serve garnished with the remaining Cheddar, the bacon bits, and the scallions or chives. —*Jennifer Armentrout*

PER SERVING: 470 CALORIES | 15G PROTEIN | 30G CARB | 32G TOTAL FAT | 20G SAT FAT | 9G MONO FAT | 2G POLY FAT | 85MG CHOL | 850MG SODIUM | 3G FIBER

curried zucchini soup

YIELDS 8 CUPS; SERVES 6 TO 8
AS A FIRST COURSE

- 6   Tbs. olive oil
- 5   zucchini (about 2 lb. total), trimmed and sliced into half-moons
- 3   medium onions (about 1 lb. total), peeled and thinly sliced
- 3   large apples (about 1½ lb. total), halved, cored, and thinly sliced
- 1   medium carrot, peeled and thinly sliced
- 3   cloves garlic, finely chopped
- 1   tsp. chopped fresh ginger
- 1   or 2 serrano chiles, seeded and finely chopped

    About 10 stems fresh cilantro

- 2   Tbs. mild curry paste (or 1½ tsp. curry powder)
- 5   to 6 cups homemade or lower-salt chicken or vegetable broth
- 2   tsp. freshly squeezed lemon juice; more to taste

    Kosher salt

Garnish this soup with a swirl of crème fraîche or sour cream flavored with lime juice and zest.

1. In a large saucepan, heat the olive oil over medium heat. Add the zucchini, onion, apples, and carrot and cook without browning until the onion is soft and translucent, about 15 minutes. Add the garlic, ginger, chiles, cilantro stems, and curry paste. Continue cooking, stirring often, until all the ingredients are tender, about 20 minutes.

2. Add the broth and bring to a boil over high heat. Reduce to a simmer and cook uncovered until the vegetables and the apples begin to fall apart, about 20 minutes. Add the lemon juice and 2 tsp. salt.

3. Remove the soup from the heat to cool slightly and then purée in a blender or food processor—in batches if necessary—until very smooth. Reheat the soup just before serving. Season to taste with salt. —*Loretta Keller*

PER 1 CUP: 200 CALORIES | 4G PROTEIN | 24G CARB | 11G TOTAL FAT | 2G SAT FAT | 8G MONO FAT | 1G POLY FAT | 0MG CHOL | 570MG SODIUM | 5G FIBER

All about Zucchini

Green zucchini is medium or dark green with tiny gold flecks; its skin is smooth or lightly ridged. Cousa, also called Lebanese, Middle Eastern, Magda, and Kuta, is shorter and plumper than its darker relative, with a blunt, rounded bottom end. This pale green squash has thin, tender skin and meltingly creamy flesh. Golden zucchini is sunny yellow and shaped like its green cousin. Don't confuse it with yellow straightneck summer squash.

How to choose Zucchini, like all summer squash, tastes best when picked young; if squash is allowed to grow too big, it gets watery, tough, and tasteless. Whether you're choosing from the garden or the produce counter, pick small, firm squash that are plump and brightly colored. The skin should be free of blemishes and should have a smooth, glossy sheen. Zucchini is best when it's no more than 6 inches long.

   If you see squash with fresh-looking blossoms still attached, buy them. This is a sure sign that the squash was picked and handled carefully on the way to the market.

How to prep After a gentle scrub under the faucet, zucchini is ready to cut. There's no need to peel it. Besides adding nutrients, the skin helps the vegetable hold together better when cooked.

How to store Keep squash in a plastic bag in the refrigerator's crisper drawer. It will last for 4 to 7 days, depending on its freshness when purchased.

winter vegetable soup with coconut milk and pears

YIELDS ABOUT 8 CUPS;
SERVES 6 TO 8

- 3 Tbs. unsalted butter
- 1½ cups thinly sliced onion
- 1 cup medium-diced carrot
- 1 cup medium-diced parsnip
- 1 cup medium-diced turnip
- 1 cup medium-diced parsley root or celery root
- ½ cup finely chopped inner stalks of celery, with leaves
- 1 cup thinly sliced Savoy cabbage
- 1 Tbs. peeled, minced fresh ginger
- 1 tsp. fresh thyme leaves; more leaves lightly chopped, for garnish
- 1 medium clove garlic, finely chopped

  Kosher salt and freshly ground black pepper
- 1 13½- or 14-oz. can coconut milk (do not shake)
- 2 cups homemade or lower-salt chicken broth; more as needed
- 3½ cups ½-inch-diced butternut squash (from a 2-lb. squash)
- 2 medium firm-ripe Bosc pears, peeled, cored, and cut into ½-inch pieces (1 ¼ cups)

Tossing pears into the mix of vegetables adds another layer of flavor and a wonderful texture.

1. Melt the butter in a 5- to 6-quart Dutch oven over medium heat. Stir in the onion, carrot, parsnip, turnip, parsley or celery root, and celery and cook, stirring occasionally, until the vegetables begin to soften, about 8 minutes. Stir in the cabbage, ginger, thyme, garlic, ¾ tsp. salt, and ¼ tsp. pepper and cook, stirring occasionally, until the cabbage begins to soften, about 3 minutes.

2. Scoop ¼ cup of coconut cream from the top of the can and set it aside in a small bowl at room temperature. Add the remaining coconut milk, broth, and the squash and pears to the vegetables. Bring the mixture just to a boil over medium heat, stirring to scrape up any browned bits. Reduce the heat to low, cover, and cook at a bare simmer, stirring occasionally, until the squash is very soft, 20 minutes.

3. Purée with an immersion blender in the Dutch oven or in batches in a regular blender. Pour the soup through a large coarse strainer set over a large glass measure or bowl. If the soup is too thick, add more chicken broth until thinned to your liking. Season to taste with salt and pepper.

4. If necessary, reheat the soup in a clean pot. Ladle the soup into bowls, drizzle with the reserved coconut cream, and sprinkle with the lightly chopped thyme. *—Lori Longbotham*

PER SERVING: 220 CALORIES | 4G PROTEIN | 23G CARB | 15G TOTAL FAT | 12G SAT FAT | 1.5G MONO FAT | 0.4G POLY FAT | 10MG CHOL | 310MG SODIUM | 6G FIBER

What Is Coconut Milk?

What's the difference between coconut water, coconut milk, coconut cream, and "lite" coconut milk? At 4 months old, the young coconut (also called a jelly or green coconut) contains a delicate, clear, slightly sweet liquid called coconut water. Coconut milk, however, is white and thick and is made by blending grated mature coconut with hot water and then straining the liquid. Coconut cream is the thick substance that floats to the top of the coconut milk and may be spooned off. Reduced-fat or "lite" coconut milk is just regular canned coconut milk with water added.

thai hot and sour shrimp soup

YIELDS ABOUT 8 CUPS; SERVES 4

- 1 Tbs. vegetable oil
- 1 tsp. finely chopped garlic
- ½ tsp. chile paste
- ½ tsp. crushed red pepper flakes
- 3 thin slices fresh or frozen galangal (or 2 thin slices peeled fresh ginger)
- 1 stalk lemongrass, bruised with the side of a knife and cut into 1-inch pieces on the diagonal
- 6 cups homemade or lower-salt chicken broth
- 2 Tbs. fish sauce
- 4½ tsp. granulated sugar
- 2 wild lime leaves, cut in half (optional)
- ½ cup drained canned straw mushrooms (or 3 oz. white mushrooms, quartered)
- 2 plum tomatoes, seeded and chopped
- ½ lb. raw shrimp, shelled and deveined
- ¼ cup freshly squeezed lime juice
- 1 scallion (white and green parts), coarsely chopped
- 5 fresh basil leaves, chopped
- 5 sprigs fresh cilantro, chopped

Chile paste, made from ground red chiles, garlic, and vinegar, is sold in Asian markets and some supermarkets.

1. In a saucepan, heat the oil over moderate heat. Add the garlic, chile paste, and red pepper flakes. Stir until fragrant, about 1 minute. Add the galangal and lemongrass; stir until lightly browned, about 2 minutes. Add the broth and simmer for 15 to 20 minutes.

2. Bring the soup to a boil. Add the fish sauce, sugar, wild lime leaves, mushrooms, and tomatoes. Add the shrimp and cook until they just turn pink, about 2 minutes. (The shrimp will continue to cook in the hot broth.) Remove the pan from the heat and add the lime juice, scallion, basil, and cilantro. Serve immediately. —*Mai Pham*

PER SERVING: 150 CALORIES | 15G PROTEIN | 12G CARB | 5G TOTAL FAT | 1G SAT FAT | 3G MONO FAT | 1G POLY FAT | 85MG CHOL | 860MG SODIUM | 1G FIBER

What Is Lemongrass?

Evergreen in warm climates, lemongrass is a sharp-bladed, perennial, blue-green grass that grows in 3- to 6-foot-tall cascading clumps. Its ethereal aroma—redolent of tropical flowers, ginger, and all things citrus—is like a delicate perfume for food. Lemongrass is particularly good with seafood, chicken, and pork and also has an affinity for coconut milk. Its most iconic use is in Thai curry pastes, where it's puréed with

chiles, shallots, ginger, garlic, and spices to become an aromatic flavor base for all types of curries.

Much of lemongrass's flavor is concentrated in its lower, cane-like stalks, which is why most markets sell them already trimmed of their leafy tops, leaving just a few short, spiky blades still attached. Look for firm, pale green stalks with fat, bulbous bottoms and reasonably fresh-looking tops (they may be a little dry but shouldn't be desiccated or yellowed). To store, wrap in plastic and refrigerate for 2 to 3 weeks, or freeze for up to 6 months.

cinnamon beef noodle soup

SERVES 6 TO 8

- 1 tsp. peanut or vegetable oil
- 3 cinnamon sticks (about 3 inches each)
- 6 scallions, cut into 1½-inch pieces
- 6 cloves garlic, smashed
- 2 Tbs. minced fresh ginger
- 1½ tsp. aniseed
- 1½ tsp. Asian chile paste
- 1 quart homemade or lower-salt chicken broth
- ½ cup soy sauce
- ¼ cup rice vinegar
- 2½ lb. boneless beef chuck, trimmed and cut into ¾-inch cubes
- 9 oz. fresh udon noodles (or 6 oz. dried)
- 1 1- to 1½-lb. bunch bok choy, bottom trimmed, stalks washed and cut into 1-inch pieces
- ½ cup fresh cilantro leaves

Packaged stewing beef is often made up of irregularly shaped pieces from different cuts, so cut your own stew meat from a boneless chuck roast or two ¾-inch-thick chuck steaks.

1. Heat the oil in a heavy soup pot or Dutch oven over medium heat. When very hot, add the cinnamon, scallions, garlic, ginger, aniseed, and chile paste; cook, stirring, for 1 minute. Add 7 cups water, the broth, soy sauce, and vinegar; bring to a boil over high heat. Add the meat and bring to a vigorous simmer. Lower the heat to maintain a gentle simmer and cook, partially covered, until the meat is very tender, about 1½ hours, checking to be sure that the soup doesn't boil or stop simmering.

2. Shortly before the soup is done, bring a large pot of water to a boil. Cook the noodles according to the package directions until just tender. Drain and rinse under cold water.

3. When the meat is tender, remove the cinnamon sticks. Add the bok choy to the soup and simmer until the stalks are crisp-tender and the greens are very tender, 5 to 10 minutes. Stir in the noodles and let them warm through. Serve immediately, garnished with the cilantro leaves. —*Eva Katz*

PER SERVING: 490 CALORIES | 31G PROTEIN | 25G CARB | 29G TOTAL FAT | 11G SAT FAT | 13G MONO FAT | 2G POLY FAT | 100MG CHOL | 1,360MG SODIUM | 2G FIBER

colombian chicken soup (ajiaco)

SERVES 8

FOR THE SOUP

- 3 lb. cut-up chicken, skin removed
- 1 large white onion, peeled and quartered
- 1 leek (white and light green parts), cut into 1-inch rings, rinsed thoroughly
- 1 green bell pepper, seeded and cut into 1-inch pieces
- 2 ears fresh corn, cut into quarters
- 2 stalks celery, cut into 1-inch pieces
- 2 large carrots, peeled and cut into 1-inch pieces
- ¾ lb. Yukon Gold potatoes, peeled and cut into 1-inch cubes
- ¾ lb. Idaho potatoes, peeled and cut into 1-inch cubes
- ¾ lb. small red potatoes, peeled and cut into 1-inch cubes
- 6 cloves garlic, peeled
- ½ cup fresh cilantro leaves
- 2 chicken bouillon cubes

  Kosher salt and freshly ground black pepper

FOR THE AJI

- 4 scallions (white and light green parts)
- 1 medium tomato, peeled and seeded
- 1 small white onion, peeled
- 2 fresh Scotch bonnet or habanero chiles or 2 fresh hot red chiles, stemmed and seeded
- 3 Tbs. fresh cilantro leaves
- 3 Tbs. white vinegar
- ¼ tsp. kosher salt

Aji, a Colombian hot sauce, is traditionally made with chiles that haven't been seeded, but you'll probably find it plenty spicy without the seeds. The soup and aji can be made a day ahead. If the soup is too thick after it's reheated, thin it with water.

MAKE THE SOUP

1. Put the chicken in a large stockpot and add 8 cups water. Bring to a boil over high heat and then reduce the heat to a vigorous simmer. Simmer for 10 minutes, frequently skimming off the foam that floats to the surface.

2. Add all the vegetables, garlic, cilantro, and bouillon cubes, along with 1 Tbs. salt and ½ tsp. pepper. Stir a few times and submerge as many of the solids as possible. When the broth returns to a gentle boil, partially cover the pot and simmer, stirring once or twice, for 1½ hours. Taste for salt.

3. Using tongs or a slotted spoon, transfer the chicken pieces to a large plate. Stir the soup with a large spoon, breaking up some of the potatoes to thicken the soup slightly. Keep hot if serving soon or let cool and refrigerate.

4. When the chicken is cool enough to handle, pull the meat off the bones and shred it by hand. Discard the bones and tendons, and put the shredded chicken in a serving bowl.

MAKE THE AJI

In a food processor, pulse all the aji ingredients until finely minced. Transfer to a serving bowl.

SERVE THE AJIACO

Put the avocados, sour cream, capers, and cilantro in small bowls and set them on the table along with the bowls of shredded chicken and aji. Reheat the soup if necessary and ladle it into large soup bowls, putting a quarter ear of corn in each bowl. Let guests add the garnishes and the aji to their own servings. *—Tania Sigal*

PER SERVING: 440 CALORIES | 26G PROTEIN | 46G CARB | 19G TOTAL FAT | 6G SAT FAT | 8G MONO FAT | 3G POLY FAT | 70MG CHOL | 1,300MG SODIUM | 8G FIBER

FOR THE GARNISHES

2   ripe avocados, cut into ½-inch
    cubes

1   cup sour cream or crème
    fraîche

½   cup nonpareil or other small
    capers (or large capers,
    coarsely chopped), rinsed
    and drained

½   cup chopped fresh cilantro
    leaves

Chiles and Colombian Cuisine

Colombian cuisine isn't as spicy as some others in the region (think Mexican), but it does use its share of chiles, most often in aji sauces. Scotch bonnet and habanero chiles are commonly employed, but be warned: They can be intense. The heat level of an average habanero is hot but varies immensely; typically, it ranges between 80,000 and 150,000 Scoville units. (The Scoville scale measures the amount of heat in chiles.) To give some perspective, that means a habanero is 20 to 50 times hotter than a jalapeño. In any case, if you're not hot on heat, use fewer of these chiles and add more cilantro to the aji.

tunisian chickpea soup

1½ cups dried chickpeas, washed and picked over

2 bay leaves

1 Tbs. cumin seeds

2 Tbs. olive oil (the fruitier the better)

1 cup coarsely chopped onion

4 cloves garlic, crushed or minced

1 Tbs. harissa or hot sauce; more or less to taste

Kosher salt

1½ to 3 Tbs. lemon juice or white-wine vinegar

4 medium stale pita or other flatbread, torn or cut into 4 cups

¼ cup large capers, soaked, rinsed, and drained

2 Tbs. finely chopped flat-leaf parsley

Extra-virgin olive oil, for drizzling

8 lemon wedges (optional)

Harissa is a hot pepper paste you'll find in most Middle Eastern markets. One dollop turns up the heat in this make-ahead soup.

1. Soak the chickpeas overnight in about 6 cups water. Drain and transfer them to an ovenproof casserole, along with the bay leaves and enough water to cover the chickpeas by 1½ inches. Bake uncovered at 325°F until you can pierce the chickpeas easily with a knife, about 2 hours; most should stay intact. (During baking, add more water if needed.) Set aside.

2. While the chickpeas are cooking, toast the cumin seeds in a heavy skillet over medium heat until fragrant but not brown, about 5 minutes. Grind them to a fine powder with an electric spice grinder or a mortar and pestle. Set aside.

3. In a large, heavy saucepan over medium heat, warm the oil until fragrant. Cook the onion, stirring, until tender but not browned, 5 to 7 minutes. Stir in the garlic and cook for 1 minute. Add the harissa and ground cumin; cook briefly, just until fragrant. Add the cooked chickpeas, their liquid, and 1 Tbs. salt; simmer until the onions have disintegrated, about 1 hour. Remove the pan from the heat; season with the lemon juice or vinegar to taste. Remove and discard the bay leaves, taste, and adjust the seasonings.

4. Portion the pita into heated soup bowls. Spoon the chickpeas over the bread with equal portions of the liquid. Sprinkle with the capers and parsley, and add more harissa to taste. Just before serving, drizzle a bit of olive oil over each bowl. Serve lemon wedges on the side if you like extra tartness.
—Robert Wemischner

PER SERVING: 620 CALORIES | 22G PROTEIN | 85G CARB | 23G TOTAL FAT | 3G SAT FAT | 14G MONO FAT | 4G POLY FAT | 0MG CHOL | 2,260MG SODIUM | 12G FIBER

creamy tomato soup with basil coulis

YIELDS ABOUT 6½ CUPS;
SERVES 6

FOR THE BASIL COULIS

- **1 cup packed fresh basil leaves**
- **1 clove garlic, crushed and peeled; more to taste**
- **Sea salt or kosher salt**
- **¼ cup fruity extra-virgin olive oil; more if needed**

FOR THE SOUP

- **3 Tbs. extra-virgin olive oil**
- **1 medium yellow onion, finely chopped**
- **1 stalk celery, finely chopped**
- **½ red bell pepper, finely chopped**
- **3 cups homemade or lower-salt chicken broth**
- **1 28-oz. can whole peeled plum tomatoes, drained and coarsely chopped (reserve the juice)**
- **1 large sprig fresh thyme**
- **Kosher salt and freshly ground pepper**

Canned tomatoes make a soup loaded with flavor. The coulis adds an extra punch.

MAKE THE COULIS

1. Have ready a medium bowl of ice water. In a small saucepan, bring 1 quart water to a boil. Add the basil and blanch for 30 seconds. Remove from the water with a strainer or slotted spoon and plunge into the ice water.

2. When the basil is cool, squeeze it with your hands to remove excess water. Put the basil in a blender or food processor and add the crushed garlic and a pinch of salt. With the machine running, slowly add the oil. If the mixture clings to the side of the bowl, add another 2 Tbs. olive oil. Purée until smooth, scraping down the sides of the bowl as needed.

3. Transfer the coulis to a squeeze bottle or a jar. (The coulis can be made 2 or 3 days ahead and stored in the refrigerator. Let it come to room temperature before using.)

MAKE THE SOUP

1. In a 5- to 6-quart Dutch oven, heat the oil over medium-low heat. Add the onion, celery, and red pepper and cook, stirring occasionally, until the vegetables are quite soft, about 10 minutes. Add the broth, tomatoes, thyme, ¼ tsp. each salt and pepper, and 1 cup water. Bring to a simmer over medium-high heat. Reduce the heat to low, cover, and simmer for 40 minutes.

2. Discard the thyme sprig. Let cool briefly and then purée the soup in 2 or 3 batches in a blender or food processor. Rinse the pot and return the soup to the pot. If it's too thick, add some of the reserved tomato juice. Reheat the soup if necessary and season to taste with salt and pepper. Top each serving with a little of the basil coulis. —*Perla Meyers*

PER SERVING: 250 CALORIES | 4G PROTEIN | 13G CARB | 21G TOTAL FAT | 3G SAT FAT | 15G MONO FAT | 2.5G POLY FAT | 0MG CHOL | 460MG SODIUM | 4G FIBER

bouillabaisse

SERVES 10

- 4 lb. mixed filleted, skinned fish, such as Pacific rockfish, monkfish, sea bass, or halibut

  Salt (use sea salt if possible)

- ½ cup extra-virgin olive oil

- 2 large leeks, chopped

- 1 large bulb fennel, chopped

- 2 large potatoes, peeled and chopped

  Pinch of saffron (about 20 threads)

- 3 bay leaves

- 1 tsp. dried thyme

  Freshly ground black pepper

- 8 large ripe tomatoes (or one 28-oz. can tomatoes), peeled, seeded, and chopped; juice strained and reserved

- 4 quarts homemade fish or seafood stock

- 1 lb. small clams, rinsed

- 1 lb. small mussels, scrubbed and rinsed

- ¾ lb. thin-fleshed squid, cleaned and cut into ringlets

- 2 Tbs. chopped fresh flat-leaf parsley

- 10 slices sourdough bread, toasted or grilled and rubbed with garlic

  Rouille (recipe facing page)

Remember that you can use whatever combination of fish and shellfish you like, provided you don't include oily fish such as salmon, mackerel, or tuna.

1. Locate the bones running vertically down the rockfish and other fish and make a cut on either side of the bones and take them out; use them for the stock, if you like. Cut all the fish fillets into 2- to 3-inch pieces, keeping the different varieties of fish separate. Sprinkle them with salt and toss them gently to distribute the salt; set aside.

2. Warm ¼ cup of the olive oil in a large soup pot; add the leeks, fennel, potatoes, saffron, bay leaves, thyme, 1 Tbs. salt, and a little pepper. Stir the mixture well and cook slowly over medium-low heat until the leeks are completely soft but not browned and the potatoes are tender, about 30 minutes. Add the tomatoes, strained tomato juice, and fish stock. Taste and add more salt as needed. Bring to a rapid simmer.

3. Add the fish and the remaining ¼ cup olive oil to the simmering broth, raise the heat to high, and boil for about 10 minutes. Next add the clams and mussels and cook for another 5 minutes. In the last minute, add the squid and parsley. Taste and add salt if needed. Remove the soup from the heat, cover, and let stand for 15 minutes.

4. Put a slice of the toasted garlic bread in the bottom of wide-rimmed serving bowls and ladle the soup on top. Serve with a spoonful of the rouille.
—Paul Bertolli

PER SERVING: 740 CALORIES | 59G PROTEIN | 39G CARB | 35G TOTAL FAT | 6G SAT FAT | 23G MONO FAT | 5G POLY FAT | 170MG CHOL | 1,040MG SODIUM | 5G FIBER

All about Saffron

The stigma of a little purple perennial crocus flower, saffron must be gathered by hand during a harvest that lasts just a couple of weeks in the fall, and there are only three stigmas per blossom. It takes about 75,000 flowers to yield a pound of saffron. Fortunately, a pinch (about 20 threads) is usually all it takes to impart saffron's distinctive yellow color and vaguely metallic, dried alfalfa hay and bittersweet wildflower-honey flavor.

How to choose Buy saffron in threads. Powdered saffron can contain other products, and it's hard to know if you're buying the pure spice. Look for saffron that contains short, deep red threads. Lesser grades of saffron include threads with some yellow areas (which is the style part of the flower). This isn't a bad thing, but the yellow part doesn't have the same coloring and flavoring power as the red stigmas, so the saffron isn't as potent.

How to store Stored in a sealed container in a dark place, saffron should last a couple of years before the flavor starts to diminish.

rouille

YIELDS ABOUT 1¾ CUPS

- ½ **cup soft white breadcrumbs**
- ¼ **cup homemade fish or seafood stock**
- 2 **large red bell peppers, roasted, peeled, seeded, and chopped (reserve any juice)**
- 2 **fresh serrano or other small hot chiles**
- 2 **to 3 cloves garlic**
-    **Pinch of saffron (about 20 threads)**
-    **Freshly ground black pepper**
- 1 **tsp. red-wine vinegar**
-    **Table salt**
- ½ **cup fruity extra-virgin olive oil**

In a bowl, combine the breadcrumbs with the fish stock and any juices reserved from the roasted peppers; mix well. In a mortar, pound the chiles, garlic, and saffron to a paste. Add the red pepper, a bit at a time, and work to an even consistency. Add the breadcrumbs; stir and grind the mixture until it resembles a fine porridge. Grind a little black pepper into the sauce, add the vinegar, salt to taste, and stir in the olive oil.

PER 1 TBS: 45 CALORIES | 0G PROTEIN | 1G CARB | 4G TOTAL FAT | 0.5G SAT FAT | 3G MONO FAT | 0.5G POLY FAT | 0MG CHOL | 25MG SODIUM | 0G FIBER

minestra di pasta e piselli

1½ oz. slice of prosciutto (about ¼ inch thick), roughly chopped

¼ cup lard (or 2 Tbs. butter and 2 Tbs. olive oil)

1 medium onion, roughly chopped

1 large clove garlic, roughly chopped

12 large fresh basil leaves

2 quarts homemade or lower-salt chicken broth

½ cup stelline, orzo, acini di pepe, or other tiny soup pasta

½ cup peas

½ cup finely diced carrot

½ cup finely diced fennel

Kosher salt and freshly ground black pepper

Lemon wedges

Freshly ground Parmigiano-Reggiano, for garnish

This Italian vegetable soup is thinner than minestrone and thickened with tiny pasta.

1. In a food processor, blend the prosciutto, lard, onion, garlic, and basil until all the pieces are minuscule, scraping down the sides occasionally. Alternatively, chop everything very finely with a knife. Put this mixture (called a battuto) in a large saucepan and cook over medium heat until the onions are soft and everything looks mushy, 8 to 10 minutes, stirring frequently.

2. Add the chicken broth. Bring to a boil, reduce to a simmer, and add the pasta. Simmer for 5 minutes. Add the peas, carrot, and fennel, simmering until both the pasta and the vegetables are just tender, about another 5 minutes. Season with salt and pepper to taste. Ladle into bowls, add a squeeze of lemon, sprinkle on some Parmigiano, and serve immediately.
—*Clifford A. Wright*

PER SERVING: 300 CALORIES | 14G PROTEIN | 22G CARB | 17G TOTAL FAT | 7G SAT FAT | 7G MONO FAT | 2G POLY FAT | 25MG CHOL | 840MG SODIUM | 3G FIBER

Keep Pasta Firm in Soup

For the best-tasting soup, it's crucial that the pasta stay firm and doesn't get mushy. But pasta naturally soaks up water, and it will continue to soak up whatever broth it's sitting in, even after the soup is done. There are a few ways to minimize this.

Before you add the pasta, make sure the soup is almost done. Everything else in the soup should finish cooking in about the same short time that the pasta needs to cook. The best way to check is by tasting. If there are beans in the broth, be sure that they're almost completely tender before adding the pasta. Then, once the pasta is cooked, take the soup off the heat and serve it right away.

When freezing the soup to eat another time, cook the pasta only halfway. Or, omit the pasta until you're ready to reheat the soup, which you should do gently to cook the pasta. If you need to thin the soup, just add a little water until it's the consistency you like.

minestrone with green beans and fennel

**YIELDS ABOUT 2 QUARTS;
SERVES 4 TO 6**

- **3** Tbs. extra-virgin olive oil
- **2** medium cloves garlic, smashed
- **½** lb. green beans, trimmed and cut into 1-inch pieces
- **1** small fennel bulb, quartered, cored, and cut into ¼-inch dice

  Kosher salt
- **1** quart homemade vegetable broth
- **1** 14½-oz. can diced tomatoes
- **1** 15½-oz. can cannellini beans, rinsed and drained
- **½** cup dried ditalini pasta or small elbows
- **½** cup freshly grated Parmigiano-Reggiano; more for sprinkling
- **6** large fresh basil leaves, coarsely chopped

  Freshly ground black pepper

Plump, creamy-white cannellini beans lend a mellow, earthy flavor to this soup. If you have the time, swap in dried beans for an even more excellent result.

1. Heat the oil and garlic in a medium saucepan over medium heat until the garlic begins to brown, 2 to 3 minutes; discard the garlic. Raise the heat to medium high, add the green beans, fennel, and ¾ tsp. salt, and cook, stirring, until the beans and fennel begin to soften and brown in places, 5 to 7 minutes. Add the broth and the tomatoes with their juices and bring to a boil. Add the cannellini beans and pasta and return to a boil. Reduce the heat to a simmer, cover, and cook until the pasta and green beans are completely tender, 10 to 12 minutes.

2. Stir in the cheese and basil and season to taste with salt and pepper. Serve sprinkled with more cheese. —*Tony Rosenfeld*

PER SERVING: 220 CALORIES | 10G PROTEIN | 27G CARB | 9G TOTAL FAT | 1.5G SAT FAT | 5G MONO FAT | 1.5G POLY FAT | 0MG CHOL | 510MG SODIUM | 6G FIBER

What Is Fennel?

Fennel has a pleasantly sweet licorice-like flavor. There are two forms of edible fennel. One is strictly an herb whose leaves, stalks, and seeds are used as flavorings. The other, often called Florence fennel, is the vegetable we find in the market.

In talking about fennel, we refer to the bulb, but that swollen portion is really the thickened, succulent stem of the plant growing in tight layers above the ground. Fennel thrives in cool weather; its seasons are spring and fall, though as with many vegetables, it's usually available year-round. Grocers sometimes label it as anise, a misnomer.

When choosing fennel, look for clean, firm bulbs with no sign of browning. When you get it home, refrigerate it tightly wrapped in a plastic bag for up to 5 days. It's easier to get it in the fridge if you cut off the stalks first.

french farmers' soup

YIELDS 10 CUPS

- **8 oz. (1¼ cups) dried flageolets or baby lima beans, picked over and rinsed**
- **1 medium clove garlic, smashed and peeled**
- **1 bay leaf**
- **Kosher salt**
- **2 Tbs. extra-virgin olive oil**
- **¼ lb. bacon, pancetta, or sausage (optional)**
- **1½ cups chopped shallots and leeks**
- **Freshly ground black pepper**
- **4 tsp. chopped fresh thyme**
- **1 Tbs. tomato paste (optional)**
- **1 cup peeled carrots, cut into ¼-inch-thick half-moons**
- **1 cup peeled celery root, cut into ½-inch dice**
- **1 cup peeled turnips, cut into ½-inch dice**
- **5 to 6 cups homemade or lower-salt chicken broth or homemade vegetable broth**
- **1 to 2 tsp. white-wine vinegar**
- **1 cup croutons (recipe facing page)**
- **⅓ cup chopped fresh flat-leaf parsley**

This hearty soup makes the most of root vegetables, paired with baby lima beans.

1. Put the beans in a large bowl and add enough cold water to cover the beans by 3 inches. Soak for 4 to 12 hours.

2. Drain the beans, rinse them, and transfer to a 3- to 4-quart saucepan. Add the garlic clove, bay leaf, and 6 cups cold water. Partially cover to limit evaporation and simmer gently, stirring every 20 to 30 minutes, until the beans are tender and almost creamy inside, without being mealy or mushy, 45 minutes to 1 hour. When the beans are about three-quarters done, season with ¾ tsp. salt. If at any time the liquid doesn't cover the beans, add 1 cup fresh water. Drain the beans, reserving the cooking liquid, and discard the bay leaf. You can cook the beans 1 day ahead.

3. Heat the olive oil in a 4- to 5-quart soup pot or Dutch oven over medium heat. Add the bacon, pancetta, or sausage (if using) and cook until it browns. Pour the meat and fat into a small strainer set over a bowl and set the meat aside. Spoon 2 Tbs. of the fat back into the pot and return it to medium heat. Add the shallot and leek to the pot, season with a pinch of salt and pepper, and cook until they begin to soften but not brown, 4 to 6 minutes. Stir in the thyme and tomato paste (if using) and cook for 1 minute.

4. Add the carrots, celery root, turnips, and 2 cups of the broth. Partially cover and simmer until the vegetables are just barely tender, 10 to 20 minutes. Add the beans and 3 cups of the broth, plus 1 cup of the reserved bean-cooking liquid. If you have less than 1 cup of bean liquid, adjust the broth for a total of 4 cups liquid. Return the cooked meat to the pot, if using. Stir and simmer, partially covered, for 10 minutes. Add the vinegar and salt and pepper to taste. Top each serving with a small handful of croutons and a sprinkle of parsley.
—*Molly Stevens*

PER SERVING: 300 CALORIES | 16G PROTEIN | 40G CARB | 9G TOTAL FAT | 2G SAT FAT | 5G MONO FAT | 1.5G POLY FAT | 5MG CHOL | 470MG SODIUM | 9G FIBER

Quick-Soak Beans

If you don't have at least 4 hours to soak beans, you can quick-soak them. In a saucepan, add enough cold water to cover the beans by 2 inches, bring quickly to a boil, remove from the heat, and let soak for 1 hour. The results tend to be less consistent than those you'd get from a cold-water soak, but it's a good trick in a pinch.

croutons

YIELDS 2 TO 3 CUPS

3   **Tbs. unsalted butter or extra-virgin olive oil**

1   **large clove garlic, crushed and peeled**

4   **oz. (2 to 3 cups) bread cubes**

½   **tsp. kosher salt**

Homemade croutons make good soup even better.

Heat the oven to 350°F. In a small skillet, melt the butter or heat the oil over medium-low heat. Add the garlic clove, mashing and breaking it up slightly with a wooden spoon, and raise the heat to medium. Cook until the garlic just begins to brown, 1 to 2 minutes. Remove the skillet from the heat and discard the garlic clove. Put the bread cubes in a mixing bowl, drizzle the melted butter or oil all over, sprinkle on the salt, and toss to distribute evenly. Spread the cubes in a single layer on a rimmed baking sheet and bake until golden all the way around, turning once or twice with a spatula, 15 to 20 minutes. Let cool.

PER ¼ CUP: 80 CALORIES | 1G PROTEIN | 7G CARB | 5G TOTAL FAT | 3G SAT FAT |
1G MONO FAT | 1G POLY FAT | 10MG CHOL | 220MG SODIUM | 0G FIBER

rustic bean and farro soup

SERVES 6 AS A MAIN DISH,
8 AS A FIRST COURSE

- 3 Tbs. olive oil
- ¾ cup chopped pancetta
- 1 medium onion, chopped
- 2 medium carrots, peeled and chopped
- 2 medium stalks celery, chopped
- 4 large cloves garlic, minced
- 2 tsp. chopped fresh sage, marjoram, or thyme, or a mix
- 1¼ cups dried chickpeas or cannellini beans (or a combination), picked over, soaked overnight, and drained (or 3½ cups canned chickpeas, cannellini beans, or a combination)
- 1½ cups canned diced tomatoes
- 2 quarts homemade or lower-salt chicken broth or water

  Kosher salt and freshly ground black pepper
- 1¼ cups uncooked whole-grain farro

  Extra-virgin olive oil, for garnish

  Freshly grated Parmigiano-Reggiano, for garnish

The farro can get soft if it sits in the soup overnight, so cook it separately and add it only to the amount of soup you're serving.

1. Heat the olive oil in a soup pot set over medium heat. Add the pancetta and sauté until golden brown, about 5 minutes. Add the onion, carrots, celery, garlic, and herbs and sauté until the vegetables soften, about 5 minutes.

2. If using dried beans, add the soaked, drained beans to the soup pot, with the tomatoes, the broth or water, and 2 tsp. salt, and bring to a boil. Reduce the heat, cover, and simmer until the beans are tender, 1 to 2 hours. (If using canned beans, drain and rinse them, add the tomatoes, broth or water, and 2 tsp. salt to the soup pot and bring to a boil. Reduce the heat, add the beans, and simmer for about 20 minutes.) Season with salt and pepper. For a creamier soup, purée 1 cup of the bean mixture and stir it back into the pot.

3. In a saucepan, bring 6 cups salted water to a boil. Add the farro, reduce the heat, and simmer until it's just al dente and chewy, 10 to 30 minutes. Drain the farro, add it to the soup, and simmer for another 10 to 15 minutes to let the flavors meld and to finish cooking. Stir to prevent scorching. Ladle into bowls and garnish with a swirl of olive oil, grated cheese, and pepper. —*Joyce Goldstein*

PER SERVING: 330 CALORIES | 16G PROTEIN | 43G CARB | 12G TOTAL FAT | 2G SAT FAT | 7G MONO FAT | 2G POLY FAT | 10MG CHOL | 820MG SODIUM | 7G FIBER

What Is Farro?

Farro is an ancient variety of wheat cultivated in Italy that has caught the attention of cooks in the United States. It has a nutty flavor and a firm, chewy texture that resembles barley more than wheat. Italians put farro in soups, salads, and stuffings.

Buying tips Don't confuse whole-grain farro with the cracked form, which looks like bulgur, has a very different texture, and cooks much faster. You can buy whole-grain farro in specialty food shops or by mail order.

Cooking basics Many farro recipes say to soak it for 2 hours to shorten the cooking time, but we in the *Fine Cooking* test kitchen find it unnecessary. Simmer 1 part whole-grain farro in about 5 parts salted water until it's pleasantly toothy and chewy but no longer hard and then drain any excess water. Unsoaked, it cooks in 15 to 30 minutes. Cooked farro will keep in the refrigerator for 5 days; reheat it in broth or water.

tomato bisque & cheese toasts

SERVES 2

FOR THE BISQUE

- 2 Tbs. olive oil
- 1 small onion, diced
- 1 clove garlic, minced
- 3 hearty sprigs fresh thyme
- 1 28-oz. can crushed tomatoes in purée
- 1½ cups lower-salt chicken broth
- 3 Tbs. honey
- 1½ tsp. coarse salt; more to taste
- ¼ tsp. finely ground black pepper; more to taste
- ⅓ cup heavy cream
- 2 Tbs. chopped fresh flat-leaf parsley (optional)

FOR THE TOASTS

- 4 slices country bread, about ½ inch thick
- 1 Tbs. Dijon mustard
- 4 to 6 slices Gruyère
- 1 Tbs. grated Parmesan

Tomato soup with grilled cheese is a comforting classic; Gruyère and Parmesan toasts make this a more refined version.

1. In a medium pot, heat the oil. Add the onion and cook over medium heat, stirring frequently, until tender and lightly browned on the edges, about 7 minutes. Add the garlic and thyme; stir until fragrant, about 1 minute. Add the tomatoes, broth, honey, salt, and pepper. Bring to a boil over high heat. Reduce the heat and simmer, stirring frequently, until reduced by a quarter and thickened, about 15 minutes. Using a stand or immersion blender, purée about half the soup; it will be still be chunky and thick. Return it to the pot and stir in the cream. Heat gently and adjust the seasonings.

2. Arrange an oven rack to the highest rung and heat the broiler on high. Line a baking sheet with foil. Put the bread on the foil and toast each side until golden brown. Spread the mustard evenly on one side of each toast, cover with the Gruyère, and sprinkle with the Parmesan. Slide the toasts back under the broiler and cook until bubbling and lightly browned on top, about 2 minutes. Cut each toast in half. Ladle the soup into bowls, sprinkle with the parsley if using, and serve immediately with the toasts. —*Abigail Johnson Dodge*

PER SERVING: 950 CALORIES | 35G PROTEIN | 100G CARB | 51G TOTAL FAT | 23G SAT FAT | 21G MONO FAT | 3G POLY FAT | 120MG CHOL | 2,820MG SODIUM | 13G FIBER

spicy noodle soup with shrimp and coconut milk

SERVES 4

FOR THE SOUP BASE

- 1   small onion, roughly chopped
- 1   2-inch piece fresh ginger (about 1 oz.), peeled and sliced into disks
- 5   cloves garlic, crushed
- 2   to 3 fresh serrano chiles, stemmed and roughly chopped
- 2   stalks lemongrass, trimmed and roughly sliced
- 1   Tbs. freshly ground coriander seeds
- 1   tsp. freshly ground cumin seeds
- ½   tsp. ground turmeric
- ¼   cup fish sauce
- 2   tsp. light brown sugar
- 2   Tbs. peanut or vegetable oil

    Shells from the shrimp (below)
- 2   cups homemade or lower-salt chicken broth
- 1   14-oz. can coconut milk
- ¼   cup freshly squeezed lime juice

    Kosher salt

FOR THE SOUP

- 6   to 7 oz. wide rice noodles
- ¼   English (seedless) cucumber
- 1   cup mung bean sprouts, rinsed and dried
- 1   fresh chile (serrano, jalapeño, or Thai), stemmed and sliced into thin rounds (optional)
- ½   cup fresh cilantro leaves, roughly chopped or torn
- ½   cup fresh mint leaves, roughly chopped or torn
- 1   lb. shrimp (31 to 40 per lb.), shells removed and reserved; deveined
- 4   lime wedges, for garnish

Don't be intimidated by the long list of ingredients—this soup comes together in under an hour. The result is otherworldly: rice noodles bathed in a silky, spicy coconut broth and capped with a crunchy, cooling garnish.

MAKE THE SOUP BASE

1. Put the onion, ginger, garlic, chiles, lemongrass, coriander, cumin, turmeric, fish sauce, and brown sugar in a food processor. Purée to make a paste, scraping down the sides as needed.

2. Heat the oil in a heavy soup pot or Dutch oven over medium heat until hot but not smoking. Add the paste mixture and sauté, stirring often, until it softens, becomes very aromatic, and deepens in color, about 8 minutes. Stir in the shrimp shells and cook until they turn pink, about 2 minutes. Add the chicken broth, 3 cups water, coconut milk, lime juice, and 1 tsp. salt and bring to a boil. Lower the heat so that the broth simmers gently for 30 minutes.

3. Strain the broth through a fine sieve and discard the solids. Clean the pot; return the broth to the pot, season with salt to taste, and return to a simmer.

WHILE THE SOUP BASE IS SIMMERING

1. Bring a large pot of water to a boil and then remove from the heat. Put the rice noodles in the water and let sit until tender, 5 to 10 minutes. Drain, rinse, and distribute among 4 large, shallow soup bowls.

2. Slice the cucumber into ¼-inch rounds, stack the rounds, and slice into thin matchsticks. Put the cucumber sticks in a medium bowl and toss with the bean sprouts, sliced chiles (if using), and herbs.

3. Just before serving, add the shrimp to the broth and gently simmer until they're just cooked through, about 3 minutes. Ladle the hot soup over the noodles. Arrange a mound of the cucumber and bean sprout mixture in the center of the bowl, top with a lime wedge, and serve immediately.   *—Eva Katz*

PER SERVING: 560 CALORIES | 24G PROTEIN | 55G CARB | 30G TOTAL FAT | 20G SAT FAT | 5G MONO FAT | 3G POLY FAT | 135MG CHOL | 2,100MG SODIUM | 4G FIBER

poultry stocks

Turkey and chicken stocks are the foundation for so many dishes, from soups and stews to sauces and risottos. Although these require several hours of simmering, you can assemble the ingredients in about 15 minutes.

turkey stock

YIELDS ABOUT 9 CUPS

2 Tbs. vegetable oil

Carcass from a 12- to 16-lb. turkey (plus bones and wings, if saved)

1 large onion (unpeeled), halved

2 stalks celery, scrubbed and coarsely chopped

1 large carrot, scrubbed and coarsely chopped

¼ cup brandy

1 1-inch chunk fresh ginger, peeled and sliced

1 bay leaf

1 sprig fresh thyme

10 peppercorns

1. Position a rack in the center of the oven and heat the oven to 425°F. Pour the oil into a large flameproof roasting pan. Break or chop the turkey carcass into 3 or 4 pieces and put it in the roasting pan, along with the onion, celery, and carrot. Roast for 30 minutes, stirring 2 or 3 times to ensure even browning.

2. Transfer the turkey and vegetables to a large stockpot. Pour off and discard any fat from the roasting pan, set the pan over medium heat, and add the brandy. Stir with a wooden spoon, scraping up all the browned bits. When the mixture is bubbling, pour the drippings into a stockpot. Add the ginger, bay leaf, thyme, and peppercorns to the pot.

3. Add about 12 cups cold water (or enough to almost cover the turkey pieces). Bring to a simmer, skim any foam that rises to the top, and then reduce the heat to a very slow simmer. Simmer for 2 hours (if you used more than 12 cups water, you may need to boil it down a bit further for flavor). Strain through a fine sieve into a large bowl, let cool, and refrigerate. The next day, skim the fat. —*Jennifer McLagan*

PER 1 CUP: 20 CALORIES | 2G PROTEIN | 1G CARB | 0.5G TOTAL FAT | 0G SAT FAT | 0.5G MONO FAT | 0G POLY FAT | 0MG CHOL | 40MG SODIUM | 0G FIBER

chicken stock

YIELDS ABOUT 3 QUARTS

8 lb. chicken bones, trimmed of fat (necks and backs work well)

2 onions, coarsely chopped

2 carrots, coarsely chopped

2 stalks celery, coarsely chopped

2 cloves garlic, peeled

1 tsp. black peppercorns

4 sprigs fresh thyme or 1 tsp. dried

1 bay leaf

Combine all the ingredients in a large stockpot and add 5 quarts water. Bring to a boil, reduce the heat, and simmer uncovered for 4 hours, skimming occasionally. Strain through a fine sieve. Taste and reduce for flavor if necessary. Chill immediately in an ice bath or in the refrigerator. When chilled, skim the fat. —*Irving Shelby Smith*

PER 1 CUP: 90 CALORIES | 6G PROTEIN | 8G CARB | 3G TOTAL FAT | 1G SAT FAT | 1.5G MONO FAT | 0.5G POLY FAT | 5MG CHOL | 0MG SODIUM | 0G FIBER

Stock vs. Broth

Bones make a stock a stock and not a broth. With little to no meat on them, bones lend gelatin to the stock, giving it "body." Stock may also contain aromatics, like vegetables or herbs.

Broth, on the other hand, is made from meat, vegetables, and aromatics. Though it's sometimes made with meat still on the bone, broth's distinguishing flavor comes from the meat itself. Compared with stock, it has a lighter body and a more distinctly meaty (or vegetal) flavor. Broth is more or less ready to eat, whereas stock typically needs some enhancement for further cooking.

vegetable stock

YIELDS ABOUT 1 QUART

1½ Tbs. unsalted butter
   or olive oil

2 cups large-diced yellow onion

2 cups large-diced outer
  stalks celery

1 cup large-diced leek tops

1 cup large-diced fennel tops
  or bulbs

¾ cup large-diced carrot

1 head garlic, halved crosswise

8 stems fresh parsley

2 sprigs fresh thyme

For dishes where vegetables are the star, or when cooking for vegetarians, vegetable stock is a better choice than chicken stock because of its lighter, sweeter flavor. Avoid using onion skins and carrot tops as they'll make the stock bitter; trimming or peeling other vegetables is optional. Scrub or rinse all vegetables well, especially if they're not peeled.

1. Heat the butter or oil over medium-low heat in a large stockpot. Add the onion, celery, leeks, fennel, carrot, and garlic. Cook uncovered, stirring frequently, until the vegetables have softened and released their juices, about 30 minutes (don't let them brown). Add enough cold water to just cover the vegetables, about 4 cups. Tie the parsley and thyme in a cheesecloth bundle and add it to the stock. Bring to a gentle simmer, cover, and cook without stirring until the stock is flavorful, about 45 minutes (adjust the heat to maintain a gentle simmer).

2. Strain the stock immediately through a fine sieve, pressing gently on the vegetables. Let cool to room temperature and then refrigerate for up to a week, or freeze for up to 6 months. —*Irving Shelby Smith*

PER 1 CUP: 50 CALORIES | 2G PROTEIN | 2G CARB | 4.5G TOTAL FAT | 2.5G SAT FAT | 1G MONO FAT | 0G POLY FAT | 10MG CHOL | 0MG SODIUM | 0G FIBER

Add Flavor with a Bouquet Garni

Bouquets garni (pronounced boo-kay gahr-nee) are little bundles of herbs and spices tied together with twine or wrapped in cheesecloth. These packets can be added to soups, stocks, sauces, braises, or any other dish with a lot of liquid and a long simmer. A bouquet garni keeps all of the herbs together, making them a cinch to remove before serving. Parsley, thyme, and bay leaf are the standard trio—use 4 or 5 parsley stems, a sprig or two of thyme, and a bay leaf.

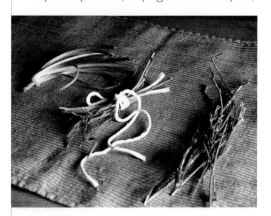

You can tie a bouquet garni with twine, but if you're using small spices like peppercorns or cloves, or if you're worried about thyme leaves getting into a clear soup, you should bind everything in cheesecloth.

SOUPS & CHOWDERS **43**

fish stock

YIELDS ABOUT 3 QUARTS

- **3 cups crisp, acidic dry white wine, such as Sauvignon Blanc**
- **5 lb. white fish bones, cut into 5-inch pieces (lobster, shrimp, or crab shells may be used, too, but avoid fatty fish like salmon)**
- **2 onions, coarsely chopped**
- **2 carrots, coarsely chopped**
- **2 stalks celery, coarsely chopped**
- **2 cloves garlic, peeled**
- **1 tsp. black peppercorns**
- **4 sprigs fresh thyme or 1 tsp. dried**
- **1 bay leaf**

Fish stock is one of the fastest stocks to make (less than an hour) and adds distinctive flavor to chowders and other fish stews. As with other stocks, the foundation is bones, but you can also eke flavor out of shells from lobster, shrimp, or crab. Be sure the fish bones and shells are clean by rinsing under cold water before starting. Overcooked fish stock can taste bitter, so keep an eye on the pot.

Combine all the ingredients in a large stockpot and add 3 quarts water. Bring to a boil, lower the heat and simmer uncovered for 30 minutes, skimming occasionally. Strain through a fine sieve. Taste and reduce for flavor if necessary. Chill immediately in an ice bath or in the refrigerator. When chilled, skim the fat. —*Irving Shelby Smith*

PER 1 CUP: 80 CALORIES | 4G PROTEIN | 2G CARB | 1.5G TOTAL FAT | 0G SAT FAT | 0G MONO FAT | 0G POLY FAT | 0MG CHOL | 0MG SODIUM | 0G FIBER

beef stock

YIELDS ABOUT 3 QUARTS

- **8** lb. beef or veal bones, or a mix
- **2** onions, coarsely chopped
- **2** carrots, coarsely chopped
- **2** stalks celery, coarsely chopped
- **2** cloves garlic, peeled
- **1** tsp. black peppercorns
- **4** sprigs fresh thyme or 1 tsp. dried
- **1** bay leaf

Homemade beef stock brings a richness to any soup or stew with meat, but it also adds complexity to simple classics like French onion soup. The key is to roast the bones before simmering.

1. Position a rack in the center of the oven and heat the oven to 450°F. Spread the bones in large shallow roasting pans and roast until well-browned, about 40 minutes. Turn the bones, add the onions, carrots, and celery, and roast for another 20 minutes. Transfer the roasted bones and vegetables to a large stockpot. Pour off the fat from the roasting pans and deglaze them with 2 cups water. Add this to the pot, along with 4½ quarts water, the garlic, peppercorns, and herbs.

2. Bring to a boil, reduce the heat to low, and simmer uncovered for 5 to 6 hours, skimming occasionally. Strain through a fine sieve. Taste and reduce for flavor if necessary. Chill immediately in an ice bath or in the refrigerator. When chilled, skim the fat. —*Anne Willan*

PER 1 CUP: 40 CALORIES | 5G PROTEIN | 1G CARB | 1.5G TOTAL FAT | 0G SAT FAT | 0.5G MONO FAT | 0G POLY FAT | 0MG CHOL | 15MG SODIUM | 0G FIBER

Defatting Broth Easily

A fat separator—a cup with a spout at the bottom that lets you pour off fat-free liquid once the fat has risen to the top—has one drawback: Some fat always gets in the spout, too. Oxo offers a neat solution: A rubber stopper in the spout keeps the fat in the cup and out of the spout. You can buy this at www.oxo.com.

Texas Beef Chili with
Poblanos and Beer
(recipe on p. 68)

stews & chilis

beef stew with root vegetables

SERVES 6 TO 8

3 lb. boneless beef chuck

Kosher salt and freshly ground black pepper

3 Tbs. olive or vegetable oil; more as needed

2 large or 3 medium onions, diced

3 large cloves garlic, minced (about 1 Tbs.)

2 bay leaves

2 tsp. dried thyme leaves

3 Tbs. unbleached all-purpose flour

1 cup full-bodied red wine

3 cups mixed carrots and turnips (both peeled and cut into bite-size pieces)

½ lb. small red or new potatoes, halved if large, parboiled in salted water until tender (optional)

1 cup frozen green peas, thawed

3 Tbs. coarsely chopped fresh flat-leaf parsley, for garnish

The key to the success of this stew is to keep the meat moist using a heavy-based pot with a tight-fitting lid made with heavy-duty foil. This is great with mashed potatoes.

1. Position a rack in the lower middle (but not the bottom) of the oven and heat the oven to 450°F.

2. Pat the beef dry with paper towels, trim away any thick pieces of fat, and cut into 1-inch cubes. Season generously with salt and pepper. Heat 2 Tbs. of the oil over medium-high heat in a heavy-based Dutch oven that's 9 to 10 inches in diameter. As soon as the oil is very hot, add a quarter of the beef cubes, taking care not to crowd the pan. Sear the beef until two sides form an impressive dark-brown crust, 8 to 10 minutes. Transfer the beef to a bowl and continue to sear the remaining beef in batches, adding more oil to the pan if needed. It's fine for the pan bottom to darken, but if it smells like it's burning, lower the heat just a little. Set all the seared beef aside in a bowl.

3. Reduce the heat to medium and add the onions and garlic to the empty pot, adding another 1 Tbs. oil if the pan is dry. Cook, stirring frequently, until soft, about 5 minutes.

4. Add the bay leaves and thyme and continue to cook, stirring, until fragrant, 30 seconds to a minute. Season with salt and pepper. Stir in the flour and then the red wine and 2 cups water. Return the beef and any accumulated juices back to the pot.

5. Lay a large sheet of heavy-duty foil over the pot and, using a potholder or a thick towel, press it down in the center so that it almost touches the stew. Crimp the foil around the pot's rim for a tight seal. Cover snugly with the pot's lid. Turn the burner to medium high until you hear the juices bubble. Put the pot in the oven and cook for 1 hour. Check the stew: If the meat is fork-tender, it's done; if not, cook for another 15 minutes, adding a little more water to the pan if it looks dry.

6. Meanwhile, in a large sauté pan, heat enough oil to cover the bottom of the pan. Sauté the carrots and turnips over medium heat until just tender, about 15 minutes. Add the potatoes (if using) and brown them lightly. Add the thawed peas and cook until warmed through.

7. Remove the pot from the oven, carefully remove the foil, and stir in the cooked vegetables. Remembering that the pot and lid are hot, cover again with the foil and the lid. Let stand so that the meat rests and the vegetables marry with the stew, about 15 minutes. When ready to serve, the stew juices might need thinning to achieve a thin gravy texture. If so, stir in water—¼ cup at a time—as needed. Season with salt and pepper to taste; discard the bay leaves. Gently reheat, if necessary, and serve garnished with the parsley.
—*Pam Anderson*

PER SERVING: 480 CALORIES | 34G PROTEIN | 15G CARB | 28G TOTAL FAT | 10G SAT FAT | 14G MONO FAT | 1G POLY FAT | 110MG CHOL | 700MG SODIUM | 4G FIBER

transylvanian goulash

SERVES 4

- 2 Tbs. lard or extra-virgin olive oil
- 1 large red onion, finely chopped
- 2 lb. pork butt, cut into ¾-inch cubes
- 1 green bell pepper, cored, seeded, and sliced
- 1 tsp. paprika
- 1 small tomato, peeled and sliced
- 2 tsp. red pepper paste (recipe below) or 1 tsp. kosher salt

  Freshly ground black pepper
- 1½ lb. sauerkraut, rinsed and drained
- 1½ cups sour cream; more for garnish

It's all right for the meat used in this dish to be slightly on the fatty side. Sliced Hungarian sausage can also be added with the pork. Because of the sauerkraut, Alsatian wines, such as Gewürztraminer or Riesling, go particularly well with this dish.

In a deep pot, heat the lard or oil and then add the onion and sauté until light brown. Add the pork and brown it. Stir in the green pepper, paprika, tomato, red pepper paste or salt, a pinch of black pepper, and enough water to cover the bottom of the pan. Cover and cook for about 45 minutes, stirring occasionally and adding a little water if needed. Mix in the sauerkraut and a little water (or some of the sauerkraut juice if it isn't too tart). Continue cooking until the meat is tender. Taste for salt and then mix in the sour cream. Don't boil at this point or the sour cream will curdle. Serve topped with a spoonful of sour cream and accompanied by Hungarian bread.
—*Maria and Lorant Nagyszalanczy*

PER SERVING: 600 CALORIES | 48G PROTEIN | 16G CARB | 38G TOTAL FAT | 18G SAT FAT | 14G MONO FAT | 3.5G POLY FAT | 185MG CHOL | 1,520MG SODIUM | 6G FIBER

red pepper paste

- 2 lb. red bell peppers
- 8 oz. sea salt

Clean the peppers and cut them in pieces. Purée the peppers to a paste in a food processor. Mix in the salt, put into jars, and refrigerate. It will keep indefinitely. Use it with soups, goulashes, and paprikás dishes instead of salt.

lamb stew with parsnips, prunes & chickpeas

SERVES 4 TO 6

FOR THE LAMB

- **3** lb. boneless leg of lamb, cut into 1-inch cubes

  Kosher salt and freshly ground black pepper

- **2** medium carrots, cut into 3-inch pieces

- **1** medium yellow onion, peeled and stuck with 1 whole clove

- **1** 3-inch cinnamon stick

- **1** bay leaf

FOR THE STEW

- **2** Tbs. unsalted butter or olive oil

- **1** large yellow onion, cut into small dice

  Kosher salt and freshly ground black pepper

- **4** medium cloves garlic, roughly chopped

- **1** Tbs. paprika

- **2** tsp. cumin seed, toasted and ground

- **2** tsp. coriander seeds, toasted and ground

- **½** tsp. cayenne

- **2** cups cooked chickpeas, rinsed and drained if canned

- **18** pitted prunes, halved

- **¼** cup tomato purée

- **1** lb. medium parsnips, peeled, cored (see how on p. 86), and cut into 2-inch pieces

- **1** Tbs. chopped fresh cilantro or flat-leaf parsley

North African in spirit, this hearty sweet and savory stew is perfect in winter. Serve it with couscous or good crusty bread.

PREPARE THE LAMB

1. Position a rack in the center of the oven and heat the oven to 350°F.

2. Season the lamb with 2 tsp. salt and ½ tsp. pepper. In a 5- to 6-quart Dutch oven, combine the lamb, carrots, onion, cinnamon, bay leaf, and enough water to cover. Cover and braise in the oven until the meat is very tender, about 2½ hours. Strain the mixture through a fine sieve over a large bowl. Discard the vegetables and spices. (The recipe may be prepared to this point up to 2 days ahead. Cool the lamb and broth, and refrigerate separately. Skim the fat from the broth before continuing.)

MAKE THE STEW

1. In a 5- to 6-quart Dutch oven, heat the butter or oil over medium-high heat. Add the onion, a pinch of salt, and a few grinds of pepper and cook, stirring occasionally, until softened and lightly browned, about 8 minutes. Add the garlic, paprika, cumin, coriander, and cayenne and cook, stirring occasionally, until fragrant (don't let the garlic burn), 1 to 2 minutes.

2. Stir in the chickpeas, prunes, tomato purée, and a pinch of salt. Add the reserved lamb and 4 cups of the broth and bring to a boil. Boil for 5 minutes and then turn the heat to low. Cover and simmer for 10 minutes. Add the parsnips and cook until tender, about 10 minutes. Season to taste with salt and pepper, and serve sprinkled with cilantro or parsley. —*David Tanis*

PER SERVING: 560 CALORIES | 54G PROTEIN | 52G CARB | 16G TOTAL FAT | 6G SAT FAT | 5G MONO FAT | 2G POLY FAT | 155MG CHOL | 950MG SODIUM | 12G FIBER

southwestern spiced chicken and black bean stew

SERVES 4 TO 6

- **2** Tbs. extra-virgin olive oil
- **3** thick slices bacon
- **6** bone-in, skinless chicken thighs (about 2¼ lb.), large pieces of fat trimmed

  Kosher salt and freshly ground black pepper
- **1** large yellow onion, diced
- **1** red bell pepper, cored, seeded, and finely diced
- **2** tsp. chili powder
- **1** tsp. ground cumin
- **¾** cup beer
- **1** can (15½ oz.) black beans, rinsed (about 2 cups)
- **1** dried chipotle chile (optional)
- **2** cups homemade or lower-salt canned chicken broth; more if needed
- **1** lime
- **3** Tbs. chopped fresh cilantro leaves

  Sour cream, for garnish

  Fried tortilla strips (optional)

It's well worth the effort to find a dried chipotle, which gives the broth a wonderful smoky spice. To make fried tortilla strips, cut corn or flour tortillas into long strips and fry in 350°F oil until they start to brown, about 2 minutes.

1. Heat the oil in a large Dutch oven or heavy pot over medium heat. Add the bacon and cook until it renders much of its fat and crisps slightly, about 7 minutes. Transfer the bacon to a plate lined with paper towels. Season the chicken well with salt and pepper. Add half of the thighs to the pan and brown them well on both sides, 2 to 3 minutes per side. Transfer to a plate. Brown the remaining thighs and reserve with the rest.

2. There should be 2 to 3 Tbs. fat left in the pan; if there's more, spoon out and discard the excess. Add the onion and bell pepper, season well with salt, and cook, stirring often, until the onion softens and caramelizes slightly, about 7 minutes. Raise the heat to high, add the chili powder and cumin, and cook, stirring, for 30 seconds. Add the beer and cook until it's almost completely reduced, about 3 minutes. Add the beans, the chipotle (if using), and the chicken broth. When the mixture comes to a boil, adjust the heat to maintain a simmer and cook for 5 minutes. Transfer 2 cups of the beans and broth (but not the chipotle) to a blender, purée, and then mix it back into the rest of the broth.

3. Return the thighs to the pot, cover with the lid slightly ajar, and simmer until the chicken is cooked through (check by slicing through the bottom of one of the thighs to the bone), about 30 minutes. If the stew is too thick, thin it with more chicken broth. Discard the chipotle. Crumble the reserved bacon. Juice one half of the lime; cut the other half into wedges. Stir the bacon, lime juice, and 2 Tbs. of the cilantro into the stew and season well with salt and pepper. Ladle some of the beans and chicken into each bowl. Sprinkle each serving with the remaining cilantro and a small dollop of sour cream. Serve with lime wedges and fried tortilla strips, if you like. *—Tony Rosenfeld*

PER SERVING: 350 CALORIES | 22G PROTEIN | 20G CARB | 20G TOTAL FAT | 6G SAT FAT | 10G MONO FAT | 3G POLY FAT | 70MG CHOL | 390MG SODIUM | 6G FIBER

artichoke ragoût
with shallots and fennel

SERVES 6

FOR THE RAGOÛT

16 baby artichokes, trimmed and halved, or two 10-oz. packages frozen artichokes, thawed, well drained, and patted dry

1 lemon, halved (if using fresh artichokes)

2 sprigs fresh rosemary, plus 1 tsp. chopped

2 large sprigs fresh thyme

2 bay leaves

¼ cup extra-virgin olive oil; more for drizzling

3 cloves garlic, slivered

8 shallots (root ends intact), peeled and quartered

1 fennel bulb, trimmed and cut into 1-inch pieces

8 small fingerling potatoes (about 1 lb. total), scrubbed and cut into 1-inch pieces

2 Tbs. unbleached all-purpose flour

Kosher salt and freshly ground black pepper

¾ cup dry white wine

1½ cups homemade or lower-salt vegetable broth

FOR THE PERSILLADE

3 Tbs. coarsely chopped fresh flat-leaf parsley

1 large clove garlic

1 tsp. grated lemon zest

To prepare fresh baby artichokes, trim them as shown below. If you can't find fresh baby artichokes, good-quality frozen ones will do.

MAKE THE RAGOÛT

1. If using fresh artichokes, rub the cut surfaces with the lemon to prevent browning.

2. Tie the rosemary sprigs, thyme sprigs, and bay leaves into a bouquet (see p. 43).

3. In a large Dutch oven, heat the oil with the garlic and the herb bouquet over medium-high heat. Add the shallots and fennel. Cook, stirring frequently, until the vegetables are nicely browned, about 10 minutes. Add the artichokes and potatoes; sprinkle the flour over them and stir well. Cook, stirring, another 5 minutes, until the vegetables' edges are browned. Add 1 tsp. salt, a bit of ground pepper, and the wine. Simmer vigorously, scraping the browned bits off the bottom of the pan, until the wine is reduced by half. Add the broth, bring to a boil, and cover the pot. Reduce the heat to low and simmer until the vegetables are tender when pierced with a knife, about 40 minutes, stirring occasionally. Stir in the chopped rosemary. Remove the herb bouquet and adjust the seasonings, if needed.

PREPARE THE PERSILLADE AND SERVE

Chop the parsley and garlic together until finely textured; add the lemon zest. Ladle the ragoût into soup plates, sprinkle some of the persillade onto each plate, and serve. —*Deborah Madison*

PER SERVING: 230 CALORIES | 6G PROTEIN | 32G CARB | 9G TOTAL FAT | 1G SAT FAT | 7G MONO FAT | 1G POLY FAT | 0MG CHOL | 500MG SODIUM | 8G FIBER

how to trim baby artichokes

Break off the outer leaves by pulling downward. Keep pulling until you get to the core of pale green leaves.

Trim the stem with a sharp paring knife. Shave off rough areas around the base.

Cut off the top ½ inch of the artichoke. Halve it and rub cut areas with lemon to prevent browning.

eggplant stew with tomatoes and chickpeas

SERVES 4 TO 6

- **1½ lb. eggplant**, preferably plump round ones
- **2 Tbs. olive oil**; more for brushing the eggplant
- **1 large red onion**, cut into ½-inch dice
- **1 large bell pepper**, red or yellow, cored, seeded, and cut into 1-inch pieces
- **2 plump cloves garlic**, thinly sliced
- **2 tsp. paprika**
- **1 tsp. ground cumin**
- **Generous pinch of cayenne**
- **2 Tbs. tomato paste**
- **5 plum tomatoes**, peeled, quartered lengthwise, and seeded
- **1 15-oz. can chickpeas** (preferably organic), rinsed and drained
- **Kosher salt**
- **¼ cup coarsely chopped fresh flat-leaf parsley**
- **Freshly ground black pepper**

Broiling the eggplant first helps it keep its shape in the stew.

1. Heat the broiler. Cut the eggplant crosswise into ¾-inch rounds, place on a baking sheet, and brush both sides with olive oil. Broil until light gold on each side, about 2 minutes per side. Let cool and cut into 1-inch pieces.

2. In a medium Dutch oven, heat the 2 Tbs. olive oil over medium-high heat. Add the onion and bell pepper; sauté until the onion is lightly browned, 12 to 15 minutes. In the last few minutes of browning, add the garlic, paprika, cumin, and cayenne. Add the tomato paste and stir for 1 minute. Add ¼ cup water and boil; stirring the juices up from the bottom of the pan. Add the tomatoes, eggplant, chickpeas, 1 cup water, and 1 tsp. salt. Bring to a boil and then simmer, covered, until the vegetables are tender, about 25 minutes, stirring once or twice. Stir in the parsley, add salt and pepper to taste, and serve.
—*Deborah Madison*

PER SERVING: 220 CALORIES | 6G PROTEIN | 32G CARB | 8G TOTAL FAT | 1G SAT FAT | 5G MONO FAT | 1G POLY FAT | 0MG CHOL | 550MG SODIUM | 8G FIBER

gumbo ya ya

SERVES 8 AS A MAIN COURSE, 12 AS FIRST COURSE

3 Tbs. plus ¾ cup vegetable oil

2½ lb. bone-in, skinless chicken thighs

Kosher salt and freshly ground black pepper

1 cup unbleached all-purpose flour

1 medium bunch celery, cleaned and thinly sliced (5 cups)

4 large onions, diced (8 cups)

4 green or red bell peppers, diced (4 cups)

2 Tbs. minced garlic

½ to 1 tsp. cayenne

¾ tsp. dried oregano

¾ tsp. dried basil

¾ tsp. dried thyme

4 bay leaves

8 cups homemade or lower-salt chicken broth or water

1½ lb. andouille sausage or other spicy smoked sausage, cut into ½-inch chunks

1 Tbs. filé powder

6 cups cooked white rice

Chopped scallions, for garnish

Tabasco® sauce

This South Louisiana favorite comes in many versions; this one calls for sausage and chicken in a broth thickened with filé powder.

1. In a heavy-based soup pot, heat 3 Tbs. of the oil over high heat until almost smoking. Season the chicken generously with salt and pepper, dust it with ¼ cup of the flour, and shake off the excess. Sear the chicken until golden brown, turning once to brown both sides, 4 minutes on each side. Set aside.

2. Let the oil reheat for a minute, then reduce the heat to medium high and add the celery, onions, and peppers. Cook, stirring, until soft, 15 to 18 minutes. Remove the vegetables and any liquid from the pan and set aside. Add the remaining ¾ cup oil to the pot and let it heat up for a minute over medium heat. Slowly add the remaining ¾ cup flour and cook, stirring constantly, until the mixture is the color of chocolate, 20 to 30 minutes. Stir carefully, being sure to scrape the sides and bottom of the pot to prevent burning the roux; if you do burn it, you'll need to start over.

3. When the roux has reached a good mahogany brown, return the cooked vegetables to the pot, along with the garlic, cayenne, oregano, basil, thyme, and bay leaves. Stir to scrape the bottom of the pot and cook until well combined, 3 to 5 minutes. Season with salt and pepper.

4. Slowly add the broth while stirring until smoothly blended. Add the chicken and sausage. Bring to a simmer and skim off excess fat. Simmer uncovered for 2½ hours, skimming any foam or fat that rises to the surface. When the chicken meat falls from the bones, remove the bones from the pot and discard.

5. Return the gumbo to a boil and stir in the filé powder, stirring vigorously to avoid clumping, until the filé powder is dissolved. Add salt and pepper to taste. Remove the bay leaves. Serve the gumbo in bowls over the cooked white rice, garnished with the chopped scallions and Tabasco to taste. *—Jamie Shannon*

PER SERVING: 910 CALORIES | 35G PROTEIN | 83G CARB | 47G TOTAL FAT | 11G SAT FAT | 17G MONO FAT | 15G POLY FAT | 95MG CHOL | 1,020MG SODIUM | 4G FIBER

three steps to good gumbo

First make a roux with approximately equal weights of oil and flour. Use a heavy-based pan, stir with a wooden spoon, and go slow.

Cook the roux until it's glossy and a rich dark brown. It should smell toasty and nutty, not burnt.

Add the vegetables carefully—brown roux is extremely hot. The "holy trinity"—celery, onion, and bell pepper—gives the gumbo a true Creole flavor.

beef, barley & butternut squash stew
with blue cheese croutons

SERVES 6

1¾ lb. boneless beef chuck, trimmed and cut into 1-inch cubes

Kosher salt and freshly ground black pepper

5 Tbs. unbleached all-purpose flour

4½ Tbs. unsalted butter (1½ Tbs. softened)

1 Tbs. extra-virgin olive oil

2 large leeks (white and light green parts only), halved and thinly sliced

2 medium carrots, cut into 1-inch pieces

2 medium ribs celery, chopped

1 cup dry white wine, such as Sauvignon Blanc

6 cups lower-salt chicken broth

⅔ cup pearl barley

3 dried bay leaves

1 Tbs. finely chopped fresh sage

1 tsp. freshly grated nutmeg

1 small butternut squash (about 1½ lb.), peeled, seeded, and cut into ½-inch cubes (about 3⅓ cups)

¼ cup chopped fresh flat-leaf parsley

¼ cup half-and-half

3 oz. blue cheese, crumbled (about ¾ cup)

3 Tbs. finely chopped walnuts

18 ½-inch-thick baguette slices

Top this satisfying stew with the salty blue cheese and walnut croutons, breaking them up into the stew as you eat.

1. Position a rack in the center of the oven and heat the oven to 350°F.

2. Season the beef with 1 tsp. salt and ¼ tsp. pepper and then toss in a large bowl with 2 Tbs. of the flour. Heat 1 Tbs. of the butter and the oil in a 5½- or 6-quart Dutch oven over medium-high heat. Cook half of the beef until browned on several sides, about 5 minutes. Using a slotted spoon, transfer the beef to a plate. Repeat with the remaining beef.

3. Melt 2 Tbs. of the butter in the pot. Add the leeks, carrots, celery, and a pinch of salt, reduce the heat to medium and cook, stirring occasionally, until softened, about 10 minutes. Add the wine and cook, scraping up any browned bits with a wooden spoon, until evaporated, 7 to 8 minutes. Stir in the remaining 3 Tbs. flour and cook for 1 minute.

4. Whisk in 5 cups of the broth. Stir in the barley, bay leaves, sage, nutmeg, ½ tsp. salt, and the beef along with any accumulated juices. Bring to a boil. Cover the pot snugly with foil and then a tight-fitting lid and braise in the oven until the beef is almost tender, about 1 hour. Stir in the squash and the remaining 1 cup broth. Cover with the foil and lid and continue braising until the beef and squash are very tender, about 30 minutes more.

5. Remove and discard the bay leaves from the stew, and then stir in the parsley and half-and-half. Season to taste with salt and pepper. Keep hot.

6. In a small bowl, combine the 1½ Tbs. softened butter with the blue cheese, walnuts, and ½ tsp. pepper. Spread the mixture evenly onto the baguette slices. Transfer to a baking sheet.

7. Position a rack about 8 inches from the broiler element and heat the broiler on high. Broil the croutons until deep golden-brown and crisp, 2 to 3 minutes. Serve the stew with the croutons. —*Liz Pearson*

PER SERVING: 690 CALORIES | 34G PROTEIN | 54G CARB | 36G TOTAL FAT | 16G SAT FAT | 13G MONO FAT | 3.5G POLY FAT | 95MG CHOL | 750MG SODIUM | 9G FIBER

Buying Beef Chuck

Although quite flavorful, chuck requires a long, moist cooking method to turn this otherwise tough cut into a tender piece of meat. For stew, look for trimmed chuck and cut it into uniformly sized cubes for even cooking. Keep in mind that a small amount of marbling is good, but too much makes for a fatty stew.

brazilian chicken and shrimp stew

SERVES 4

- 3 cloves garlic, chopped

  Kosher salt

- 1 large white or yellow onion, coarsely chopped (3 cups)

- 2 large ripe plum tomatoes, peeled, seeded, and coarsely chopped (1 cup)

- ½ cup coarsely chopped fresh cilantro stems and leaves, plus ½ cup whole leaves, for garnish

- ¼ cup freshly squeezed lime juice

- 4 fresh Thai bird chiles, coarsely chopped, or jarred malagueta peppers, drained

- 1 Tbs. minced fresh ginger

  Freshly ground black pepper

- 4 bone-in, skinless chicken thighs (1½ lb.)

- 1 lb. jumbo shrimp (21 to 25 per lb.), shelled and deveined

- 2 Tbs. plus ⅓ cup lightly salted cashews, toasted

- 3 Tbs. olive oil or well-shaken dendê and soy oil blend

- ¾ cup well-stirred canned coconut milk

  Hot cooked white rice, for serving

This is a take on xim-xim, a traditional stew from Brazil by way of West Africa. Xim-xim relies on a specific set of ingredients: dendê oil (the Brazilian name for palm oil), coconut milk, and nuts. You can substitute olive oil for the dendê oil.

1. Sprinkle the garlic with 1 tsp. salt, and with the side of a heavy chef's knife, mash to a paste. Transfer to a food processor and add the onion, tomatoes, chopped cilantro stems and leaves, lime juice, chiles, ginger, and ¼ tsp. black pepper. Pulse until finely chopped and almost smooth. Put the chicken and shrimp in a large bowl, add the onion mixture, and turn to coat well. Cover and refrigerate for 1 to 2 hours.

2. Meanwhile, pulse 2 Tbs. of the cashews in a spice grinder just until finely ground; do not let them form a paste.

3. Remove the chicken from the marinade, brushing excess marinade back into the bowl. Pat the chicken dry with paper towels. Season on both sides with ¼ tsp. salt. Heat 2 Tbs. of the olive or dendê oil in a 5- to 6-quart Dutch oven over medium heat. Add the chicken and cook, turning once, until very lightly browned on both sides, about 4 minutes per side. Transfer the thighs to a plate as they are browned.

4. Remove the shrimp from the marinade and set them aside. Put the marinade in the Dutch oven, add the coconut milk and ground cashews, and cook over medium heat, stirring and scraping the bottom of the pan, for 3 minutes to cook off the raw onion flavor.

5. Return the chicken to the Dutch oven, turn the heat to low, cover, and simmer, stirring occasionally and turning the chicken halfway through cooking, until the chicken is tender and cooked through, about 25 minutes total.

6. Increase the heat to medium, stir in the shrimp, and cook, stirring constantly, just until the shrimp are bright pink and nearly opaque throughout, 2 to 3 minutes; they will continue to cook after they're removed from the heat. Off the heat, stir in half the remaining cashews and half the whole cilantro leaves. Season to taste with salt.

7. Transfer the chicken to a large deep platter and pour the shrimp and sauce over it. Drizzle with the remaining 1 Tbs. dendê or olive oil, top with the remaining cashews and cilantro leaves, and serve hot with the white rice.
—*Lori Longbotham*

PER SERVING: 490 CALORIES | 36G PROTEIN | 13G CARB | 33G TOTAL FAT | 13G SAT FAT | 14G MONO FAT | 4G POLY FAT | 215MG CHOL | 650MG SODIUM | 3G FIBER

cod stew with chorizo, leeks & potatoes

SERVES 4

- 2 small leeks (or 1 large)
- 6 oz. chorizo
- 1 lb. red potatoes (4 to 5 medium), scrubbed and cut into ¾-inch cubes
- Kosher salt and freshly ground black pepper
- 1 Tbs. olive oil
- 3 cloves garlic, minced
- 1 28-oz. can diced tomatoes, with their juices
- ½ cup dry white wine
- ¼ cup chopped fresh flat-leaf parsley
- 1 lb. cod fillet, cut into 4 equal portions

The mildness of the cod gets a wonderful punch from spicy chorizo.

1. Trim off the root, the dark greens, and most of the light green parts of the leeks. Chop the leeks into ½-inch pieces and rinse thoroughly to remove all the grit. Cut the chorizo in half lengthwise and slice into half-moons about ⅛ inch thick.

2. Put the potatoes in a large saucepan and cover with cold water by 1 to 2 inches. Salt the water, cover partially, and bring to a boil over high heat. Reduce the heat as needed and boil until the potatoes are tender, 10 to 15 minutes; drain. While the potatoes cook, heat the oil in a large pot (choose one that's wide enough to hold the fish in a single layer) over medium heat for 1 minute. Add the chorizo and leeks and cook, stirring occasionally, until the chorizo has browned slightly and the leeks are soft, about 6 minutes. Add the garlic and cook for 1 minute.

3. Stir in the tomatoes and their juices, the wine, 1½ cups water, and ½ tsp. salt. Bring to a boil over high heat. Partially cover the pot, reduce the heat to medium, and simmer for 15 minutes. Add the potatoes, season with salt and pepper, and stir in half of the parsley. Season the cod with salt and pepper, set the fillets on top of the stew, cover, and simmer until just cooked through, 6 to 8 minutes.

4. Using a wide spatula, carefully transfer the cod to shallow soup bowls (the fillets may break apart). Spoon the stew over the cod and serve immediately, garnished with the remaining parsley. —*Eva Katz*

PER SERVING: 490 CALORIES | 37G PROTEIN | 38G CARB | 21G TOTAL FAT | 7G SAT FAT | 11G MONO FAT | 2G POLY FAT | 85MG CHOL | 1,340MG SODIUM | 6G FIBER

Choosing Chorizo

Chorizo is a spicy pork sausage that hails from Spain, though many countries with a history of Spanish colonization have their own versions as well. Consisting primarily of pork, pimentón, and garlic, this dry-cured sausage adds a meaty note to stews, pastas, and eggs. Some hard and dry chorizos are fully cured and ready to eat. Others are meant to be cooked before eating, like the links in the cod stew above. When shopping, take a look at the label. If there are cooking instructions, it's likely that the chorizo shouldn't be eaten raw. Also note its position in the store. If it's in the cheese or deli case, it's probably ready to eat. If it's in the meat case, it's probably meant to be cooked.

spicy sausage, escarole & white bean stew

SERVES 3 OR 4

- 1 Tbs. extra-virgin olive oil
- 1 medium yellow onion, chopped
- ¾ lb. hot Italian sausage, casings removed
- 2 medium cloves garlic, minced
- 2 15-oz. cans cannellini beans, rinsed and drained
- 1 small head escarole, chopped into 1- to 2-inch pieces, washed, and lightly dried
- 1 cup homemade or lower-salt chicken broth
- 1½ tsp. red-wine vinegar; more to taste

  Kosher salt

- ¼ cup freshly grated Parmigiano-Reggiano

Escarole is a member of the chicory family, and cooking it for a short amount of time tames its bitter edge.

1. Heat the oil in a heavy 5- to 6-quart Dutch oven over medium heat. Add the onion and cook, stirring occasionally, until tender, 5 to 6 minutes. Add the sausage, raise the heat to medium high, and cook, stirring and breaking up the sausage with a wooden spoon or spatula until lightly browned and broken into small (1-inch) pieces, 5 to 6 minutes. Add the garlic and cook for 1 minute, then stir in the beans. Add the escarole to the pot in batches; using tongs, toss with the sausage mixture to wilt the escarole and make room for more.

2. When all the escarole is in, add the chicken broth, cover the pot, and cook until the beans are heated through and the escarole is tender, about 8 minutes. Season to taste with the vinegar and salt. Transfer to bowls and sprinkle each portion with some of the Parmigiano. —*Joanne McAllister Smart*

PER SERVING: 390 CALORIES | 20G PROTEIN | 40G CARB | 17G TOTAL FAT | 5G SAT FAT | 8G MONO FAT | 3G POLY FAT | 25MG CHOL | 1,079G SODIUM | 13G FIBER

What Is Escarole?

Escarole is a broad-leaved chicory, with wide succulent stems and leaves that look more crumpled than curly. Like all chicories, it has a bitter flavor, though somewhat less so than curly endives. Other names are common chicory, broad chicory, and Batavian endive.

When choosing escarole, avoid heads with especially thick or tough-looking outer leaves. Escarole can be quite sandy, so wash leaves in a few changes of water before using.

beer-braised sirloin tip stew with mushroom sauce

SERVES 4

- **1** tsp. dry mustard
- **1** tsp. light brown sugar
- **½** tsp. dried thyme leaves, crushed
- **½** tsp. ground ginger
- **½** tsp. sweet paprika
- Kosher salt
- **1½** lb. sirloin tip steaks, ¾ to 1 inch thick
- **½** lb. fresh mushrooms, preferably a mix of half shiitake and half cremini
- **2** Tbs. olive oil or vegetable oil
- **2** Tbs. unsalted butter
- **4** scallions, thinly sliced, white and light green parts separated from dark green parts (save both)
- **1** cup dark ale or porter beer (such as Beck's® Dark)
- **2** tsp. Worcestershire sauce

Sirloin tips are a great choice for a quick braise, as they're full of flavor and will have a pleasantly chewy texture after 20 minutes of cooking (further cooking would toughen them). Some grocers mistakenly label tri-tip steak as sirloin tips. You'll recognize real sirloin tips (also called loin flap meat) by the marbling. If the cut looks lean, ask your butcher if it's truly loin flap meat.

1. In a small bowl, mix the mustard, brown sugar, thyme, ginger, paprika, and 1 tsp. salt. Coat both sides of the steaks with the spice mix.

2. Remove and discard the stems from the shiitake, if using, and trim the stem ends from the cremini. Wipe all the mushrooms clean and slice them ¼ inch thick.

3. Heat the oil in a large skillet over medium-high heat. When the oil is shimmering, add half the steaks and sear them until nicely browned, 2 to 3 minutes per side (the steaks will brown quickly because of the sugar in the spice mix). Transfer to a plate and repeat with the remaining steaks.

4. Reduce the heat to medium, add 1 Tbs. of the butter to the pan, and let it melt. Add the mushrooms, the scallion whites, and ¼ tsp. salt and cook, stirring occasionally with a wooden spoon, until the mushrooms soften and brown, 4 to 6 minutes. Pour in the beer and Worcestershire. Scrape the bottom of the pan with the spoon, raise the heat to medium high, bring to a boil, and cook, uncovered, until the liquid is reduced by half, about 4 minutes.

5. Return the steaks and any accumulated juices to the pan, cover tightly with a lid or foil, and reduce the heat to a low simmer. Braise, turning the steaks after 8 minutes, until tender and just cooked through (they should be easy to slice with a paring knife), about 16 minutes total. Transfer the steaks to a cutting board and slice them thinly. Cut the remaining 1 Tbs. butter into 4 pieces and swirl them into the sauce. Stir in the scallion greens and taste for seasoning. Serve the steak slices topped with the sauce. *—Molly Stevens*

PER SERVING: 400 CALORIES | 38G PROTEIN | 12G CARB | 20G TOTAL FAT | 7G SAT FAT | 10G MONO FAT | 1G POLY FAT | 120MG CHOL | 620MG SODIUM | 2G FIBER

Picking the Perfect Braising Pan

Ideally, you want to choose a pan for braising that will hold all the pieces of meat in a snug but not overlapping layer; this helps everything stay moist as the braise cooks and concentrates all the flavors. A deep 10- or 12-inch skillet (2½ to 4 inches deep) is usually perfect. If it comes with a lid, great; otherwise, use foil. But if the pan is just right for braising, it might be too tight for searing all the meat at once—the pieces need some elbow room while searing or they'll steam rather than brown.

moroccan vegetable ragoût

SERVES 3 OR 4

- 1 Tbs. extra-virgin olive oil
- 1 medium yellow onion, thinly sliced (about 1¼ cups)
- 1 3- to 4-inch cinnamon stick
- 1½ tsp. ground cumin
- 2 cups peeled and medium-diced (½-inch) sweet potatoes (about ¾ lb.)
- 1 14- to 16-oz. can chickpeas, rinsed and drained
- 1 14½-oz. can diced tomatoes, with their juices
- ½ cup pitted green Greek or Italian olives
- 6 Tbs. orange juice, preferably freshly squeezed
- 1½ tsp. honey
- 2 cups lightly packed very coarsely chopped kale leaves (from about ½ lb. kale)

  Kosher salt and freshly ground black pepper

Kale, chickpeas, and sweet potatoes combine for a unique sweet-savory flavor in this unusually spiced stew. Serve with a green salad and couscous studded with toasted almonds.

1. Heat the oil in a 5- to 6-quart Dutch oven or other heavy pot over medium-high heat. Add the onion and cook, stirring frequently, until soft and lightly browned, about 5 minutes. Add the cinnamon stick and cumin and cook until very fragrant, about 1 minute. Add the sweet potatoes, chickpeas, tomatoes and their juices, olives, orange juice, honey, and 1 cup water; bring to a boil. Reduce the heat to medium low and simmer, covered, stirring occasionally, until the sweet potatoes are barely tender, about 15 minutes.

2. Stir in the kale. Cover and continue cooking until wilted and softened, about another 10 minutes. Season with salt and pepper to taste. *—Kate Hays*

PER SERVING: 290 CALORIES | 9G PROTEIN | 52G CARB | 6G TOTAL FAT | 1G SAT FAT | 4G MONO FAT | 1G POLY FAT | 0MG CHOL | 1,030MG SODIUM | 8G FIBER

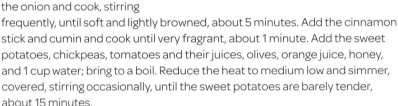

All About Kale

Kale is a little peppery and a bit sweet, with a slight mineral edge. Its blue-green leaves have substantial texture that doesn't get mushy. Kale is also a nutritional powerhouse, with high levels of beta-carotene and vitamins A, C, and K, as well as iron and calcium.

How to choose Kale is usually sold in bundles. Choose deeply colored leaves, with no signs of yellowing or bruising. If it's secured by a twist-tie or band, check around it for slime.

How to prep Remove the tough stems and central ribs from all but the smallest leaves by cutting them out with a knife or simply tearing the leaf away from the rib.

  Wash kale in a deep sink or a very large bowl of cold water, gently swirling to encourage any soil

to float off. Kale can harbor little insects such as aphids, so always take a look on the back side of the leaves to be sure all critters have washed away. Lift out the leaves and shake off the excess water. For most preparations, it's fine to leave some droplets clinging to the kale.

How to store Store kale unwashed in an unclosed plastic bag in the refrigerator's crisper drawer, where it will keep for several days. If you need to store it longer, wrap the bundle in slightly damp paper towels before putting it in a plastic bag to help prolong its freshness. But try to use kale within 5 to 7 days, because the longer you keep it, the stronger its flavor will become and the more its nutrients will fade.

shrimp stew with coconut milk, tomatoes & cilantro

SERVES 6 TO 8

- **3** lb. jumbo shrimp (21 to 25 per lb.), peeled and deveined

  Kosher salt
- **2** Tbs. extra-virgin olive oil
- **1** large red bell pepper, sliced into very thin 1½-inch-long strips
- **4** scallions, thinly sliced, white and green parts kept separate
- **½** cup chopped fresh cilantro
- **4** large cloves garlic, finely chopped
- **½** to 1 tsp. crushed red pepper flakes
- **1** 14.5-oz. can petite-diced tomatoes, drained
- **1** 13.5- or 14-oz. can coconut milk
- **2** Tbs. freshly squeezed lime juice

This spicy shrimp stew is a great cold-winter-night dinner for company. Best of all, it takes less than 20 minutes to cook.

1. In a large bowl, sprinkle the shrimp with 1 tsp. salt; toss to coat, and set aside.

2. Heat the oil in a 5- to 6-quart Dutch oven over medium-high heat. Add the bell pepper and cook, stirring, until almost tender, about 4 minutes. Add the scallion whites, ¼ cup of the cilantro, the garlic, and the pepper flakes. Continue to cook, stirring, until fragrant, 30 to 60 seconds.

3. Add the tomatoes and coconut milk and bring to a simmer. Reduce the heat to medium and simmer to blend the flavors and thicken the sauce slightly, about 5 minutes.

4. Add the shrimp and continue to cook, partially covered and stirring frequently, until the shrimp are just cooked through, about 5 minutes more. Add the lime juice and season to taste with salt. Serve sprinkled with the scallion greens and remaining ¼ cup cilantro. *—Pam Anderson*

PER SERVING: 270 CALORIES | 29G PROTEIN | 6G CARB | 15G TOTAL FAT | 10G SAT FAT | 3G MONO FAT | 1G POLY FAT | 250MG CHOL | 580MG SODIUM | 1G FIBER

soupe au pistou with lamb shanks

**SERVES 8 WITH PLENTY
OF LEFTOVERS**

FOR THE SOUP

3 cups shell beans (if fresh, try
half cranberry beans and half
another white variety; if dried,
try cannellini or another white
runner variety)

2 lamb shanks (about 2 lb. total)

2 Tbs. olive oil

Kosher or sea salt

6 large cloves garlic, crushed

2½ lb. ripe tomatoes (a mix of red
and yellow if possible), peeled
and coarsely chopped (about
6 cups)

2 cups peeled, seeded, and
cubed butternut or other
winter squash

3 yellow onions, diced

2 carrots, peeled and diced
(about 1 cup)

1½ lb. fresh green or yellow beans,
or a mix

½ lb. green zucchini (1 large),
quartered lengthwise and
sliced ¾ inch thick

1 cup small or medium dried
pasta (riso, ditalini, penne)

FOR THE PISTOU

4 medium cloves garlic

2 tsp. kosher or sea salt

2 cups packed fresh basil leaves

⅓ cup freshly grated
Parmigiano-Reggiano

½ cup extra-virgin olive oil

*This medley of beans, vegetables, and lamb is named for the Provençal version
of pesto called* pistou.

MAKE THE SOUP

1. If using dried beans, rinse and soak them overnight in cold water. Drain.
Cover with cold water by 2 inches, bring to a boil over medium heat, simmer
15 minutes, drain, and set aside.

2. In a stockpot that's wide enough to fit the lamb shanks on their sides, brown
the shanks well in the olive oil on all sides. Add 3 quarts cold water. Bring to
a boil, uncovered, and thoroughly skim the foam from the surface. Add 2 to
3 Tbs. salt, the garlic, and about 2 cups of the tomatoes. If using dried shell
beans, add them now. Adjust the heat to a simmer and cook for 45 minutes.
Add the squash, onions, carrots, green beans, zucchini, the remaining 4 cups
tomatoes, and the shell beans, if using fresh. Bring the pot to a boil. Lower the
heat and simmer until the lamb meat is very tender, the beans are soft, and
the soup has developed a velvety texture, another 2 to 2½ hours. Remove the
shanks and pull the meat from the bones. Cut the meat into small pieces and
return them to the soup.

MAKE THE PISTOU

With a mortar and pestle (or in a food processor), mash the garlic and salt.
Add the basil and work to a paste. Work in the Parmigiano. Slowly mix in the oil.
Taste for salt.

TO SERVE

Bring the soup to a boil and add the pasta. Cook at a light boil until the pasta is
tender, about 10 minutes. The soup should be thick, but if too thick, add hot
water. Taste for salt and serve with a dollop of pistou stirred into each bowl.
—Alice Waters

PER SERVING: 310 CALORIES | 17G PROTEIN | 39G CARB | 11G TOTAL FAT | 2G SAT FAT |
7G MONO FAT | 1G POLY FAT | 15MG CHOL | 1,030MG SODIUM | 10G FIBER

quick chicken chili

SERVES 6 TO 8

- 2 Tbs. vegetable oil
- 1 large onion, cut into medium dice
- 2 Tbs. ground cumin
- 2 tsp. dried oregano
- 3 medium cloves garlic, minced
- 1 3½- to 4-lb. store-bought rotisserie chicken, meat removed and chopped
- 1 jar or can (about 4 oz.) diced mild green chiles, drained
- 1 quart lower-salt chicken broth
- 2 15.5-oz. cans white beans, drained
- 1 cup frozen corn

If you like, serve the chili with any combination of the following: tortilla or corn chips, shredded sharp cheese, thinly sliced scallions, cilantro leaves, sliced pickled jalapeño chiles, red or green hot sauce, sour cream, guacamole, red or green salsa, and lime wedges.

1. Heat the oil over medium-high heat in a 5- to 6-quart Dutch oven. Add the onion and cook, stirring, until tender, 4 to 5 minutes. Add the cumin, oregano, and garlic and cook until fragrant, about 1 minute longer. Stir in the chicken and chiles and then add the broth and 1 can of beans. Bring to a simmer. Reduce the heat to low and simmer, partially covered and stirring occasionally, until the flavors blend, about 20 minutes.

2. Meanwhile, purée the remaining can of beans in a food processor. Stir the puréed beans into the chicken mixture along with the corn. Continue to simmer to blend the flavors, about 5 minutes longer. Ladle into bowls and serve.
—*Pam Anderson*

PER SERVING: 590 CALORIES | 69G PROTEIN | 32G CARB | 20G TOTAL FAT | 5G SAT FAT | 7G MONO FAT | 5G POLY FAT | 175MG CHOL | 270MG SODIUM | 7G FIBER

brisket and bean chili

SERVES 4 TO 6

FOR THE BEANS

- 1 **cup dried pinto or kidney beans**
- 1 **large yellow onion, chopped**
- 2 **large cloves garlic, minced**
- 1 **tsp. dried oregano**
  Kosher salt

FOR THE CHILI

- 3 **Tbs. olive oil**
- 2 **large yellow onions, chopped**
- 4 **large cloves garlic, minced**
- 3 **Tbs. ancho chile powder**
- 1 **Tbs. dried oregano**
- 1 **Tbs. ground cumin**
- ¼ **tsp. cayenne**
  Kosher salt and freshly ground black pepper
- 1 **28-oz. can diced tomatoes**
- 1 **12-oz. bottle lager beer (such as Corona®)**
- 1 **6-oz. can tomato paste**
- 1 **lb. leftover brisket (recipe p. 119), cut into ½-inch dice (about 4 cups), plus 1½ cups leftover brisket juices**
  Dash of balsamic or red-wine vinegar (optional)

> If you can't find ground ancho chile powder, use regular chili powder instead and reduce the oregano and cumin to ½ tsp. each. Add cayenne to taste.

Chunks of leftover brisket make this chili much more interesting than one made with ground beef. If you don't have time to cook beans, skip that step and use 3 cups drained and rinsed canned beans instead.

PREPARE THE BEANS

1. In a medium bowl, soak the beans in enough water to cover by at least 2 inches, and refrigerate overnight.

2. Drain the beans and put them in a medium saucepan. Cover with fresh cold water by about 1 inch. Add the onion, garlic, and oregano. Bring to a boil over high heat, lower the heat to a simmer, and cook for 30 minutes. Add 1 tsp. salt and continue to simmer until tender, about 30 minutes more. Drain and set aside.

MAKE THE CHILI

1. Heat the oil in a heavy-based 6-quart pot over medium heat. Add the onions and cook, stirring occasionally, until soft and pale gold, about 15 minutes. Add the garlic, chile powder, oregano, cumin, cayenne, 1 tsp. salt, and 1 tsp. black pepper and cook for 1 to 2 minutes. Stir in the tomatoes and their juices, beer, and tomato paste.

2. Add the brisket and its juices, bring to a boil, and then reduce the heat to low. Simmer, covered, until the meat is meltingly tender and the sauce is flavorful, about 30 minutes. Season to taste with salt, pepper, and vinegar, if the chili needs some acidity for balance.

3. Serve the beans on the side, or stir them into the chili and simmer for about 15 minutes before serving. —*Joyce Goldstein*

PER SERVING: 460 CALORIES | 35G PROTEIN | 45G CARB | 16G TOTAL FAT | 3G SAT FAT | 8G MONO FAT | 2.5G POLY FAT | 40MG CHOL | 1,240MG SODIUM | 12G FIBER

texas beef chili with poblanos and beer

3 Tbs. olive oil; more as needed

2 large sweet onions, diced (about 4 cups)

2 large fresh poblano peppers (or green bell peppers), stemmed, seeded, and diced (about 1½ cups)

5 cloves garlic, minced

1 tsp. kosher salt; more to taste

4½ lb. boneless beef chuck, cut into 1-inch cubes

2 bay leaves

2 cinnamon sticks, 3 to 4 inches long

3 Tbs. New Mexico chile powder (or 2 Tbs. ancho chile powder)

1 Tbs. chipotle chile powder

1 Tbs. ground cumin

⅛ tsp. ground cloves

1 12-oz. bottle amber ale, such as Shiner Bock (made in Shiner, Texas), Dos Equis® Amber, or Anchor Steam® Liberty Ale

1½ quarts homemade or lower-salt beef broth

FOR THE GARNISH

2 14-oz. cans kidney beans, rinsed and drained

1 medium red onion, chopped

3 medium tomatoes, cored, seeded, and chopped

⅓ cup coarsely chopped fresh cilantro

12 oz. sour cream or whole-milk plain yogurt

This chili has a pleasant kick. It thickens as it sits overnight, and the flavors round out and deepen. It's best with chipotle and New Mexico chile powders, but ancho, another pure chile powder, is a good substitute for New Mexico. Both ancho and chipotle powders are available in most grocery stores.

1. In a 12-inch skillet, heat 2 Tbs. of the oil over medium-high heat. Add the onions and sauté until softened, translucent, and starting to brown, 8 to 10 minutes. Add the poblanos, reduce the heat to medium, and cook, stirring occasionally, until the poblanos soften, another 8 to 10 minutes. If the pan seems dry, add a little more olive oil. Add the garlic and 1 tsp. salt and sauté for another 5 minutes. Set aside.

2. Meanwhile, heat the remaining 1 Tbs. olive oil in an 8-quart or larger Dutch oven (preferably enameled cast iron) over medium-high heat. Sear the beef cubes until browned and crusty on two sides, working in batches to avoid crowding the pan. With tongs or a slotted spoon, transfer the browned beef to a bowl. During searing, it's fine if the pan bottom gets quite dark, but if it smells like it's burning, reduce the heat a bit. If the pan ever gets dry, add a little more oil.

3. Once all the beef is seared and set aside, add the onions and peppers to the pan, along with the bay leaves, cinnamon sticks, chile powders, cumin, and cloves and cook, stirring, until the spices coat the vegetables and are fragrant, 15 to 30 seconds. Slowly add the beer while scraping the pan bottom with a wooden spoon to dissolve the coating of spices. Simmer until the beer is reduced by about half and the mixture has thickened slightly, 5 to 7 minutes. Add the beef, along with any accumulated juices, and the beef broth. Bring to a simmer and then reduce the heat to medium low. Simmer, partially covered, for 3 hours, stirring occasionally. Test a cube of meat—you should be able to cut it with a spoon. Discard the cinnamon sticks and bay leaves.

4. If not serving immediately, chill overnight. The next day, skim any fat from the top, if necessary, before reheating.

5. To serve, heat the chili gently if necessary. Using a slotted spoon, transfer about 2 cups of the beef cubes to a plate. Shred the meat with a fork and return it to the pot. (The shredded meat will help create a thicker texture.) Taste and add more salt if needed. Heat the beans in a medium bowl covered with plastic in the microwave (or heat them gently in a saucepan). Arrange the beans, chopped red onion, tomatoes, cilantro, and sour cream in small bowls to serve as garnishes with the chili. —*Paula Disbrowe and David Norman*

PER SERVING: 590 CALORIES | 58G PROTEIN | 20G CARB | 29G TOTAL FAT | 11G SAT FAT | 13G MONO FAT | 2G POLY FAT | 175MG CHOL | 900MG SODIUM | 6G FIBER

The Tradition of Texas Chili

Texas chili is all about the beef—think of it as a spicy beef stew. The broth gets its oomph from pure chile powders, while plenty of sweet onions and fresh poblano chiles, which lend aroma and flavor, also help temper the dried spices. A bottle of dark beer lends deep flavor. True to Texas tradition, there are no beans in this chili but rather served on the side.

When you see a spice jar labeled simply "chili powder," it's actually a mix of ground chiles with several spices like oregano, garlic powder, and cumin. Blending ground chiles with these spices gives chili powder a balanced flavor and a measure of convenience—it's easier to simply stir chili powder into a dish rather than open up six or seven spice jars.

But when you're looking to add a more nuanced hit of flavor and heat, pure chile powders—ones ground solely from a specific type of chile—are just the thing. You may even already have one in your spice rack: Cayenne is a pure chile powder. You can find this and other chile powders in the spice section at your local market.

| Pasilla | Ancho | New Mexico | Chipotle | Cayenne |

cornbread with scallions and bacon

YIELDS ONE 10-INCH
ROUND BREAD; SERVES 8

- 4½ oz. (1 cup) unbleached all-purpose flour
- 1 cup yellow cornmeal, preferably stone-ground
- 2 tsp. baking powder
- 1 tsp. table salt
- 1¼ cups low-fat milk
- 2 Tbs. honey
- 1 large egg
- ⅓ cup corn oil
- 8 scallions (white and light green parts only), trimmed and thinly sliced

    Freshly ground black pepper

- 3 thick slices bacon

This cornbread has a moist, tender crumb. It gets a nice crisp crust in a cast-iron skillet.

1. Heat the oven to 400°F. In a large bowl, whisk the flour, cornmeal, baking powder, and salt. In a medium bowl, whisk the milk, honey, egg, oil, scallions, and 2 grinds of black pepper until well combined. In a 10-inch ovenproof skillet (preferably cast iron), cook the bacon over medium heat until crisp. Transfer to paper towels to drain. Spoon off all but about a tablespoon of the bacon fat from the skillet. Add the milk mixture to the dry ingredients and stir with a rubber spatula until the ingredients are just blended. Crumble the bacon and fold it in; don't overmix.

2. Pour the batter into the hot skillet and bake until the top is golden brown, firm, and springy to the touch, 20 to 25 minutes; a toothpick inserted in the center should come out clean. Let cool in the pan for 5 minutes. Turn out onto a rack or serve in the pan, warm or at room temperature.
—*Paula Disbrowe and David Norman*

PER SERVING: 260 CALORIES | 6G PROTEIN | 33G CARB | 12G TOTAL FAT | 2G SAT FAT | 3G MONO FAT | 6G POLY FAT | 30MG CHOL | 510MG SODIUM | 2G FIBER

chicken and pinto bean chili

YIELDS 10 CUPS; SERVES 8

- **8** dried red chiles, such as New Mexico red, stemmed and seeded
- **1** Tbs. cumin seeds
- **1½** Tbs. fresh oregano leaves or 2 tsp. dried
- **1** lb. dried pinto beans, soaked overnight and drained
- **3** medium yellow onions, chopped
- **2** large carrots, chopped
- **6** cloves garlic, chopped
- **3** fresh jalapeños (preferably red), cored, seeded, and chopped
- **2** lb. bone-in, skinless chicken thighs

  Kosher salt

  Shredded sharp Cheddar or cotija cheese, for garnish

New Mexico red chiles are common dried chiles found in many grocery stores. You can also use a couple of chilcostle chiles or tiny cascabels in place of some of the New Mexico red chiles for a more complex flavor.

1. Cover the chiles with about 4 cups boiling water and steep until soft, about 15 minutes. Reserve 2 cups of the soaking liquid and then drain the chiles. In a blender, purée the chiles with the reserved liquid.

2. Meanwhile, toast and grind the cumin seeds and toast the fresh oregano (if using dried oregano, don't toast). Put the beans in a stockpot and cover them with 7 cups water. Add the chile purée, toasted ground cumin, toasted (or dried) oregano, onions, carrot, garlic, jalapeños, and chicken thighs. Bring to a boil, reduce the heat, and simmer, skimming any foam. Remove the chicken thighs when cooked, 25 to 30 minutes. When the chicken is cool enough to handle, pull the meat from the bones into large pieces and set aside; discard the bones. Continue cooking the beans until tender, another 1 to 1½ hours.

3. Return the chicken to the pot to heat it thoroughly. Season with salt to taste. Serve in bowls topped with the grated cheese. —*Ben Berryhill*

PER SERVING: 470 CALORIES | 41G PROTEIN | 48G CARB | 13G TOTAL FAT | 7G SAT FAT | 3G MONO FAT | 2G POLY FAT | 115MG CHOL | 1,990MG SODIUM | 16G FIBER

How to Toast Oregano

Heat a small, heavy skillet over medium-high heat. Add fresh oregano, giving the pan an occasional shake. Remove the leaves after they've begun to dry out but before they lose all of their green color, about 3 minutes.

tex-mex chili

- 1   Tbs. cumin seeds
- 1½   tsp. coriander seeds
- 2   Tbs. fresh oregano leaves or 1 Tbs. dried
- 3   Tbs. vegetable oil
- 3   lb. beef chuck, cut into ½-inch cubes
- ½   large yellow onion, chopped
- 8   cloves garlic, chopped
- 5   fresh jalapeños (preferably red), stemmed, seeded, and chopped
- 3   Tbs. masa harina
- 2   Tbs. ground pasilla powder
- 2   lb. tomatoes (fresh or canned), seeded and chopped
- 1   dried chipotle chile, seeded
- 1   dried New Mexico red chile
- 1   12-oz. bottle dark beer, such as Negra Modelo
- 1   oz. unsweetened chocolate
- 4   cups water or homemade or lower-salt canned chicken stock

Pasilla powder, made from toasted and ground pasilla chiles, and masa harina, a dried corn flour, are available at specialty grocery stores.

1. Toast and grind the cumin and coriander, and toast the fresh oregano as described on the facing page (don't toast dried oregano).

2. In a large, heavy-based skillet, Dutch oven, or stockpot, heat the oil until very hot. Brown the meat in the oil in batches (add more oil to the pan as needed), being careful not to crowd the pan or the meat will stew in its own juices and not brown. Transfer the browned meat from the pan to a plate lined with paper towels. Don't clean the skillet after browning the meat.

3. To the same skillet, add the onion, garlic, jalapeños, masa harina, pasilla powder, the toasted ground cumin and coriander, and toasted (or dried) oregano. Stir over medium-high heat until the onion begins to soften, 5 to 8 minutes. Return the meat to the skillet; add the tomatoes, whole dried chiles, beer, chocolate, and water or stock. Simmer until the meat is fork-tender, about 1½ hours. Remove the whole chiles before serving.
—*Ben Berryhill*

PER SERVING: 750 CALORIES | 80G PROTEIN | 32G CARB | 31G TOTAL FAT | 12G SAT FAT | 13G MONO FAT | 6G POLY FAT | 235MG CHOL | 230 MG SODIUM | 7G FIBER

Chile Peppers Are the Heart of Chili

Chipotle A smoke-dried jalapeño with a sweet, smoky flavor.

Cascabel Small with a rich woodsy flavor and a tannic heat.

Chilcostle Medium heat with an orangy sweetness and color.

New Mexico red Also known as chile colorado and dried California chile; has a mild, crisp heat and earthy flavor with tones of dried cherry.

Pasilla Also known as chile negro; has a deep complex flavor including berry, tobacco, and licorice tones.

Pasilla de Oaxaca A smoked chile; fruity and smoky with a sharp heat.

Ancho A dried poblano with a sweet fruity flavor and mild to medium heat.

beef and black bean chili with chipotle and avocado

SERVES 4

- **3 15-oz. cans black beans, rinsed and drained**
- **1 14½-oz. can diced tomatoes**
- **1 medium chipotle chile plus 2 Tbs. adobo sauce (from a can of chipotles in adobo sauce)**
- **2 Tbs. extra-virgin olive oil**
- **1 lb. ground beef (85% lean)**
- **Kosher salt**
- **1 large red onion, finely diced**
- **1½ Tbs. chili powder**
- **2 tsp. ground cumin**
- **1 lime, juiced**
- **½ cup chopped fresh cilantro**
- **Freshly ground black pepper**
- **1 ripe avocado, cut into medium dice**

Coarsely crumble about 3 handfuls of tortilla chips in a zip-top bag and sprinkle them on the chili as an additional topping.

1. Put one-third of the beans into the bowl of a food processor, along with the tomatoes and their juices, chipotle, and adobo sauce. Process until smooth and set aside.

2. Heat the oil in a 5- to 6-quart Dutch oven or similar heavy-duty pot over medium-high heat until it's shimmering hot, about 2 minutes. Add the beef, season with ½ tsp. salt, and cook, using a wooden spoon to break up the meat, until it loses its raw color, about 3 minutes. Transfer the beef to a large plate using a slotted spoon. Add half of the onion and ¼ tsp. salt and cook, stirring, until it begins to brown and soften, about 3 minutes. Reduce the heat to medium. Add the chili powder and cumin and cook for 20 seconds. Add the remaining black beans, the puréed bean mixture, and the beef to the pot and simmer for 10 minutes, stirring frequently. Add half of the lime juice, half of the cilantro, and salt and pepper to taste. If the chili is thicker than you like, it may be thinned with water.

3. Meanwhile, in a small bowl, mix the remaining lime juice and onion with the avocado. Season generously with salt and pepper. Serve the chili topped with the avocado mixture and remaining cilantro. —*Tony Rosenfeld*

PER SERVING: 670 CALORIES | 42G PROTEIN | 64G CARB | 29G TOTAL FAT | 7G SAT FAT | 16G MONO FAT | 2.5G POLY FAT | 85MG CHOL | 1,070MG SODIUM | 18G FIBER

classic new orleans seafood gumbo

YIELDS ABOUT 3 QUARTS;
SERVES 6 TO 8

1½ lb. medium shrimp (41 to 50 or 51 to 60 per lb.) or 2 lb. if using head-on shrimp

2 cups chopped white onion (about 1 large onion; reserve the skin)

1 cup chopped celery (about 2 medium stalks; reserve the trimmings)

¼ cup plus 6 Tbs. vegetable oil

1 lb. fresh or thawed frozen okra, sliced ¼ inch thick (about 4 cups)

½ cup unbleached all-purpose flour

1 cup chopped green bell pepper (about 1 medium pepper)

1 cup canned crushed tomatoes

½ lb. fresh or pasteurized lump crabmeat (about 1½ cups), picked over for shells, or 4 to 6 frozen gumbo crabs (about 1 lb. total), thawed

1 Tbs. dried thyme

1 bay leaf

Kosher salt and freshly ground black pepper

1 cup fresh shucked oysters (halved if large)

½ cup thinly sliced scallions (about 8; white and green parts)

Louisiana-style hot sauce

¼ cup hot cooked white rice per serving

If you can, buy fresh shrimp with the shells and heads intact. If not, just the shells can be used to make the stock.

MAKE THE SHRIMP STOCK
Remove the shrimp heads, if necessary. Peel and devein the shrimp and refrigerate the shrimp until needed. Combine the shrimp peels and heads and the reserved onion skin and celery trimmings in a 6- to 8-quart pot. Cover with 9 cups of cold water and bring to a boil over high heat. Reduce the heat to a vigorous simmer and cook, uncovered, for 10 minutes. Strain and reserve. You should have about 2 quarts.

PREPARE THE OKRA
In a 10-inch straight-sided sauté pan, heat ¼ cup of the vegetable oil over medium-high heat until hot. Fry the okra in two batches until it becomes lightly browned on the edges, 3 to 5 minutes per batch (fry undisturbed for the first minute or two until browning begins and then stir once or twice to flip most pieces and brown evenly). With a slotted spoon, transfer each batch of okra to a plate or platter lined with paper towels.

MAKE THE ROUX
Heat the remaining 6 Tbs. oil over medium-high heat in a 6-quart Dutch oven. Once it's hot, add the flour and stir constantly with a wooden spoon or heatproof spatula until the roux reaches the color of caramel, about 5 minutes. Add the onion and stir until the roux deepens to a chocolate brown, 1 to 3 minutes. Add the celery and bell pepper and cook, stirring frequently, until slightly softened, about 5 minutes. Add the shrimp stock, okra, tomatoes, gumbo crabs (if using), thyme, bay leaf, 2 tsp. salt, and 1 tsp. pepper. Adjust the heat to medium low or low and simmer uncovered, stirring occasionally, for 45 minutes.

SERVE THE GUMBO
Five minutes before serving, add the shrimp, fresh or pasteurized lump crabmeat (if using), oysters, and scallions. Add hot sauce, salt, and pepper to taste; discard the bay leaf. Serve in large soup bowls over ¼ cup cooked rice per serving. Pass additional hot sauce at the table. —*Poppy Tooker*

PER SERVING: 370 CALORIES | 24G PROTEIN | 32 G CARB | 17G TOTAL FAT | 2G SAT FAT | 7G MONO FAT | 7G POLY FAT | 150MG CHOL | 600MG SODIUM | 4G FIBER

Gumbo crabs are small blue crabs that have been cleaned and halved or quartered. They're served in the shell, and you pick out the meat as you eat the gumbo. Fresh or pasteurized lump crabmeat is a reasonable alternative. Don't use shredded or imitation crabmeat.

Rigatoni with Brisket and Porcini Ragù
(recipe on p. 90)

pasta & grains

baked macaroni and cheese

Kosher salt

6 Tbs. unsalted butter

1 medium onion, finely diced

6 Tbs. unbleached all-purpose flour

1 Tbs. Dijon mustard

1 quart whole milk, heated

1 large sprig fresh thyme, plus 1 tsp. chopped thyme leaves

1 bay leaf

8 oz. (2 packed cups) grated extra-sharp white Cheddar (the sharpest you can find; I like Cabot® Seriously Sharp Hunter's Cheddar)

4 oz. (1 packed cup) grated Monterey Jack

½ tsp. Worcestershire sauce

½ tsp. Tabasco sauce

Freshly ground black pepper

1 lb. elbow macaroni or other small pasta, such as pipette or small shells

2 Tbs. extra-virgin olive oil; more for the baking dish

2 cups fresh breadcrumbs

1½ oz. (½ lightly packed cup) freshly grated Parmigiano-Reggiano

This is great on its own, but if you want to try something different, use one of the add-ins below.

1. Position a rack in the center of the oven and heat to 400°F. Put a large pot of well-salted water on to boil over high heat.

2. Meanwhile, in a 5- to 6-quart Dutch oven or other heavy-duty pot, melt the butter over medium heat. Add the onion and ½ tsp. salt and cook, stirring occasionally with a wooden spoon, until softened, 4 to 5 minutes. Add the flour and cook, stirring, until slightly darker, 1 to 2 minutes. Stir in the mustard. Switch to a whisk and gradually add the milk, whisking constantly.

3. When all the milk is in, switch back to the spoon and stir in the thyme sprig, bay leaf, and ½ tsp. salt. Let come to a bare simmer, and cook, stirring frequently, for 15 minutes to meld the flavors (reduce the heat to medium low or low as needed to maintain the bare simmer).

4. Discard the thyme sprig and bay leaf. Add the Cheddar and Jack cheeses, stirring until melted, and then add the Worcestershire and Tabasco. Season to taste with salt and pepper. Keep warm, stirring occasionally.

5. Cook the pasta in the boiling water until al dente. Pour into a colander and shake it a few times to drain really well. Add the pasta to the cheese sauce and stir until well combined. Generously season to taste with salt and pepper. Lightly oil a 9x13-inch baking dish and spread the pasta in the dish.

6. In a medium bowl, toss the breadcrumbs, Parmigiano, olive oil, chopped thyme, ½ tsp. salt, and ¼ tsp. pepper. Scatter the crumbs evenly over the pasta.

7. Bake until the crumb topping is golden, about 15 minutes. Let rest for 5 to 10 minutes before serving. *—Jennifer Armentrout*

PER SERVING: 630 CALORIES | 25G PROTEIN | 60G CARB | 32G TOTAL FAT | 18G SAT FAT | 10G MONO FAT | 2G POLY FAT | 80MG CHOL | 830G SODIUM | 3G FIBER

Mac and Cheese Add-Ins

Pancetta or bacon Sauté ¼ lb. pancetta or bacon (finely chopped if using pancetta) until crisp and golden. Drain on paper towels, leaving the fat in the pan. Crumble the bacon, if using. Substitute the fat for part of the butter so that you have about 6 Tbs. total, and proceed with the recipe. Add the pancetta or bacon to the sauce along with the pasta.

Ham Brown 2 cups of small-diced smoked ham in the butter over medium-high heat. Drain on paper towels and proceed with the recipe, reducing the heat to medium to cook the onion. Add the ham to the sauce along with the pasta.

Hot chiles Cook 2 Tbs. minced fresh serrano chiles along with the onions. Or add ¼ to ½ tsp. crushed red pepper flakes with the mustard.

Make Single Servings

To bake the macaroni and cheese in individual servings, choose small baking dishes that hold 1½ to 2 cups each. You can fill them to within about ½ inch of the rim.

The number of servings will, of course, depend on the volume of your baking dishes. Without any of the add-ins, this recipe yields about 9 cups.

pulled-pork macaroni and cheese with caramelized onions and four cheeses

- **1** 4-lb. smoked pork shoulder
- **12** oz. dried ridged pasta, preferably radiatore
- Kosher salt
- **4** Tbs. (2 oz.) unsalted butter
- **2** small yellow onions, chopped (1½ cups)
- **1⅛** oz. (¼ cup) unbleached all-purpose flour
- **3½** cups whole milk
- **1½** cups dry white wine
- **2** Tbs. finely chopped fresh sage leaves
- Freshly ground black pepper
- **4** oz. grated Gruyère (1½ cups)
- **4** oz. grated Emmentaler (1½ cups)
- **4** oz. grated fontina (1½ cups)
- **⅔** cup panko
- **2** oz. (2 cups) finely grated Parmigiano-Reggiano
- **2** Tbs. extra-virgin olive oil
- **2** Tbs. thinly sliced fresh chives

If you're looking for an over-the-top indulgence, you won't soon forget this version of mac and cheese.

1. Position a rack in the center of the oven and heat the oven to 325°F.

2. Put the pork in a large heavy-duty roasting pan, cover with foil, and roast until the meat is falling off the bone, 5 to 6 hours. Cool until warm enough to handle, about 1 hour.

3. Meanwhile, cook the pasta in a large pot of well-salted water according to package directions until just barely al dente. Drain and set aside.

4. Shred the pork by hand, pulling it into 2-inch-long pieces. Discard the bone and any excess fat. Set aside 1 lb. of the pulled pork (about 4 cups) and save the rest for another use.

5. Raise the oven temperature to 350°F. Melt the butter in a large 8-quart saucepan over medium heat. Add the onions, reduce the heat to low, and cook, stirring frequently, until golden and very soft, about 20 minutes.

6. Whisk in the flour and cook for 30 seconds. Whisk in the milk in a slow, steady stream. Raise the heat to medium high and whisk constantly until the mixture begins to thicken and bubble, 3 to 5 minutes.

7. Whisk in the white wine, sage, and ½ tsp. each salt and pepper. Bring the mixture to a low simmer, whisking constantly.

8. Reduce the heat to low and use a wooden spoon to stir in the Gruyère, Emmentaler, and fontina. Stir in the reserved pork and pasta until well coated. Pour the mixture into a 12-inch cast-iron skillet.

9. In a small bowl, mix the panko, Parmigiano, and olive oil. Sprinkle evenly over the mixture in the skillet.

10. Bake until the topping is browned and the cheese sauce is bubbling through the topping and around the edges of the skillet, 40 to 45 minutes. (If the topping begins to brown too deeply, tent loosely with foil.) Let the macaroni and cheese rest for at least 15 minutes. Sprinkle with the chives and serve. —*Bruce Weinstein and Mark Scarbrough*

PER SERVING: 920 CALORIES I 51G PROTEIN I 63G CARB I 46G TOTAL FAT I 23G SAT FAT I 16G MONO FAT I 3G POLY FAT I 170MG CHOL I 690MG SODIUM I 3G FIBER

tex-mex macaroni and cheese with green chiles

SERVES 8 TO 10 AS A SIDE DISH, 4 TO 6 AS A MAIN DISH

Softened butter for the baking dish

1 lb. poblano chiles (4 to 6)

Olive oil for the chiles

6 white corn tortillas (5½ inches in diameter)

1 cup fresh cilantro leaves

2 cups half-and-half

3 large eggs

Kosher salt and freshly ground black pepper

½ lb. dried elbow macaroni

½ lb. Monterey Jack, grated

½ lb. sharp Cheddar, grated

The poblanos' heat plays well off the creaminess of the cheese and the savory custard. Poblanos can vary in heat level; smaller, darker ones can sometimes be spicier. If your nose stings or if the raw chile tastes wildly spicy when you bite into it, go easy. As a side dish, serve with barbecued ribs or chicken or with a seared skirt or flank steak.

1. Put a pot of water on to boil. Butter a shallow 2- to 3-quart baking dish.

2. Heat the broiler on high. Rub the poblanos lightly with olive oil and broil them as close to the element as possible on a baking sheet lined with foil, turning as needed, until the skins are blackened all over. Transfer to a bowl, cover the bowl with plastic, and let cool to room temperature. Turn off the broiler and heat the oven to 350°F. Remove and discard the charred poblano skins, the stems, and the seeds. Chop the chiles roughly and put them in a food processor.

3. In a hot, dry skillet over medium-high heat, lightly toast the tortillas until they're just softened and give off a toasted corn aroma, 30 to 60 seconds per side (don't let them become crisp). Roughly chop the tortillas and add them to the chiles in the food processor, along with the cilantro leaves. Pulse until finely chopped but not puréed. In a large bowl, whisk the half-and-half, eggs, ¼ tsp. salt, and a few grinds of pepper until well combined. Stir in the chopped chile mixture.

4. When the water boils, salt it well and boil the macaroni until al dente, following the package directions. Drain well. Add the pasta to the egg mixture, along with two-thirds of the grated cheeses; stir to combine. Pour the mixture into the buttered baking dish. Scatter the remaining cheese evenly over the macaroni. (If baking in a 2-quart dish, set it on a baking sheet to catch any drippings.) Bake until browned and bubbling, about 40 minutes. If you want to brown the center more, flash it briefly under the broiler. Let rest for 10 minutes before serving. —*Robert Del Grande*

PER SERVING: 400 CALORIES | 19G PROTEIN | 30G CARB | 23G TOTAL FAT | 13G SAT FAT | 7G MONO FAT | 1G POLY FAT | 125MG CHOL | 570 MG SODIUM | 2G FIBER

quick skillet mac and cheese

Kosher salt

12 oz. **dried spiral pasta, such as cavatappi, rotini, or double elbows**

3 Tbs. **unsalted butter**

3 Tbs. **unbleached all-purpose flour**

2 cups **low-fat (2%) milk**

4 oz. **(1¼ cups) grated Emmentaler**

4 oz. **(1¼ cups) grated Gruyère**

1 Tbs. **Dijon mustard**

1 Tbs. **Worcestershire sauce**

½ tsp. **dried thyme**

Freshly ground black pepper

3 oz. **(3 cups) finely grated Parmigiano-Reggiano**

Who says you can't have indulgent comfort food on a weeknight? Be sure to use a broiler-safe skillet, such as cast iron.

1. Position a rack about 4 inches from the broiler and heat the broiler on high.

2. Bring a large pot of well-salted water to a boil over high heat. Add the pasta and cook according to package directions until just tender. Drain well and set aside.

3. Meanwhile, melt the butter in a 12-inch ovenproof skillet (preferably cast iron) over medium heat. Whisk in the flour and continue whisking until well combined, about 15 seconds. Whisk in the milk and continue to cook, whisking constantly, until the mixture thickens, 1 to 2 minutes.

4. Add the Emmentaler, Gruyère, mustard, Worcestershire sauce, and thyme and whisk until the cheese is melted and the mixture is smooth, 2 minutes. Stir in the pasta to coat with the sauce. Move off the heat, and season to taste with salt and pepper. Sprinkle the Parmigiano-Reggiano evenly over the pasta.

5. Broil until the top is browned, 3 to 4 minutes, and serve.
—*Bruce Weinstein and Mark Scarbrough*

PER SERVING: 750 CALORIES I 36G PROTEIN I 77G CARB I 32G TOTAL FAT I 19G SAT FAT I 8G MONO FAT I 2G POLY FAT I 95MG CHOL I 930MG SODIUM I 4G FIBER

shells with gorgonzola

Kosher salt

8 oz. medium pasta shells

½ cup heavy cream

1 Tbs. dry sherry (optional)

6 oz. Gorgonzola, crumbled;
1 oz. reserved

Freshly ground black pepper

1 slice stale bread, chopped
coarsely

¼ cup chopped toasted walnuts

This makes a great side dish to a beef filet, but if you want to serve it as a main course, you can easily double the recipe.

Bring a large pot of salted water to a boil, add the pasta, and cook until just tender following the package directions. Meanwhile, combine the cream, sherry (if using), and 5 oz. of the Gorgonzola in a medium saucepan and stir constantly over low heat until the cheese is almost melted, about 5 minutes. Drain the pasta when done, return it to its pot, and add the cheese sauce. Stir over medium-low heat until the sauce thickens slightly, about 2 minutes. Add pepper to taste. Pour the mixture into a shallow baking dish. Combine the breadcrumbs and nuts and sprinkle the topping over the pasta. Dot with the remaining 1 oz. Gorgonzola. If you like, brown the casserole under a broiler very close to the flame until crunchy and browned, about 2 minutes.
—*Mary Pult and Rebecca Fasten*

PER SERVING: 540 CALORIES | 20G PROTEIN | 47G CARB | 30G TOTAL FAT | 16G SAT FAT | 8G MONO FAT | 5G POLY FAT | 80 MG CHOL | 820MG SODIUM | 2G FIBER

What Is Gorgonzola?

A cow's milk blue cheese from Italy, Gorgonzola comes in two varieties. **Gorgonzola Dolce** (sweet) is mild with a rich, creamy interior that makes it an excellent choice for cooking. It has an ivory-colored interior that can be lightly or thickly streaked with bluish-green veins in layers.
Mountain Gorgonzola (also called naturale) has a crumbly, dry texture and a potent blue flavor that's best if left unheated and served with fruits like pears and apples or with nuts and sweet wine to offset its intensity. If you don't have Gorgonzola you can substitute Maytag, Roquefort, Stilton, or any other crumbly blue.

When aged more than 6 months, the flavor and aroma of Gorgonzola can be quite strong— sometimes downright stinky because of its brine-washed rind. Because of this tendency, pay particular attention to the quality of any Gorgonzola you buy (an interior that's more yellow than ivory is another sign of excessive aging).

Trim away the rind before slicing or crumbling, and store well wrapped in the refrigerator.

rigatoni with sun-dried tomato and fennel sauce

SERVES 4

Kosher salt

2 Tbs. extra-virgin olive oil

1 cup chopped fennel (about ½ medium bulb)

2 medium cloves garlic, very coarsely chopped

1 cup heavy cream

1 cup lower-salt chicken broth

⅓ cup drained oil-packed sun-dried tomatoes, very coarsely chopped

¼ tsp. crushed red pepper flakes

1 Tbs. Pernod (optional)

1 lb. rigatoni

The sauce in this pasta dish is enhanced by the subtle lico-rice flavor of Pernod®, but any pastis or anise-flavored liqueur could work. Add sliced, cooked sweet Italian sausage for a more substantial meal (its flavors work well with the sauce).

1. Bring a large pot of well-salted water to a boil. Meanwhile, heat the olive oil in a 10- to 11-inch straight-sided sauté pan over medium heat. Add the fennel and garlic and cook, stirring occasionally, until the fennel starts to soften and brown, about 5 minutes. Stir in 1 cup water, the cream, chicken broth, sun-dried tomatoes, red pepper flakes, and 1 tsp. salt. Bring to a boil, reduce the heat, and simmer briskly, uncovered, until the tomatoes are plump and soft, about 15 minutes.

2. Remove from the heat and stir in the Pernod, if using. Let cool slightly and then purée in a blender until smooth. Wipe out the skillet, return the sauce to the skillet, season to taste with salt, and keep hot.

3. Cook the rigatoni until just barely al dente, 1 to 2 minutes less than the package instructions. Drain well and return to the pot. Add the sauce and toss over medium-low heat for a minute or two so the pasta finishes cooking and absorbs some of the sauce. —*Tony Rosenfeld*

Storing Sun-Dried Tomatoes

After opening, refrigerate oil-packed sun-dried tomatoes. They will keep for up to a month. Store dried sun-dried tomatoes (those not packed in oil) in a zip-top bag in the refrigerator for up to a year.

cavatappi with artichokes and three cheeses

SERVES 4

Kosher salt

1 lemon

1 Tbs. unsalted butter

1 Tbs. olive oil

½ cup chopped shallot

1 9-oz. package frozen artichoke hearts, cut into ¼-inch slices while frozen

¼ tsp. crushed red pepper flakes

Coarsely ground black pepper

⅓ cup thinly sliced fresh chives

2 Tbs. thinly sliced fresh mint leaves

12 oz. cavatappi

½ cup (4 oz.) mascarpone

½ cup (3 oz.) mild goat cheese

½ cup finely grated pecorino-romano; more for serving

Cavatappi resemble elongated elbow macaroni and are the perfect shape for this rich and creamy dish—the herbs, cheeses, and sliced artichoke hearts cling to the spirals. By using a combination of frozen artichoke hearts and fresh chives and mint, you can produce a fast and flavorful vegetarian meal in no time.

1. Bring a large pot of well-salted water to a boil over high heat. From the lemon, grate 1½ tsp. of zest and squeeze 1 Tbs. of juice; set aside. Heat the butter and oil in a 12-inch skillet over medium heat until the butter has melted. Add the shallot and cook until just softened, about 3 minutes. Increase the heat to high and add the frozen artichokes, red pepper flakes, ½ tsp. salt, and ¼ tsp. pepper. Cook until the artichokes are golden-brown, 3 to 4 minutes. Remove from the heat and stir in 3 Tbs. of the chives, the mint, and the lemon zest.

2. Meanwhile, cook the cavatappi according to package directions until al dente. Drain, reserving ½ cup of the water. Return the pasta to the pot and stir in the mascarpone, goat cheese, pecorino, lemon juice, and ¼ cup of the water until smooth. Gently stir in the artichoke mixture and add more water if necessary to moisten the pasta. Season to taste with salt and pepper. Serve sprinkled with the remaining chives and additional cheese.

—*Samantha Seneviratne*

PER SERVING: 650 CALORIES | 22G PROTEIN | 74G CARB | 30G TOTAL FAT | 15G SAT FAT | 8G MONO FAT | 1.5G POLY FAT | 65MG CHOL | 730MG SODIUM | 8G FIBER

turkey bolognese

YIELDS 5½ CUPS

- ½ lb. pancetta, finely diced
- ¼ cup finely chopped carrot
- ¼ cup finely chopped yellow onion
- ¼ cup finely chopped celery
- 4 medium cloves garlic, minced
- 1½ tsp. fennel seed, lightly crushed
- ¼ to ½ tsp. crushed red pepper flakes
- 1 28-oz. can diced tomatoes with juice
- 1 cup dry white wine
- 1 cup homemade turkey broth or lower-salt canned chicken broth
- 1 cup whole milk
- ½ cup packed fresh flat-leaf parsley
- 2 dried bay leaves
- Kosher salt
- 4 cups medium-diced roast turkey

For a spin on the classic, we've replaced the customary ground meat with diced roast turkey, making this a great recipe for leftover bird. There's enough of this flavorful sauce to coat 1 lb. of your favorite pasta. Try it with a sturdy shape like rigatoni or penne. For a smoky flavor, substitute bacon for the pancetta.

1. Heat a wide, heavy-duty 6- to 8-quart pot over medium heat. Add the pancetta and cook until its fat begins to render, 2 to 3 minutes. Add the carrot, onion, celery, and garlic and cook until the vegetables begin to brown, 4 to 6 minutes. Stir in the fennel seed and red pepper flakes.

2. Add the tomatoes and white wine. Boil for 2 to 3 minutes, then add the broth, milk, parsley, and bay leaves. Stir well, return to a boil, and season with a little salt. (Underseason, as the sauce will reduce and concentrate the salt.) Lower the heat to medium low and simmer until reduced by about one-third, 30 to 40 minutes.

3. Add the turkey, raise the heat to medium, and bring to a boil. Reduce the heat to medium low and simmer until the flavors are fully developed and the sauce is thick and rich, 10 to 15 minutes. Discard the bay leaves and season to taste with salt. —*Maria Helm Sinskey*

PER 1 CUP: 420 CALORIES | 32G PROTEIN | 12G CARB | 23G TOTAL FAT | 8G SAT FAT | 9G MONO FAT | 3.5G POLY FAT | 100MG CHOL | 1,980MG SODIUM | 1G FIBER

wild mushroom risotto

SERVES 3 OR 4

- **3** cups homemade or lower-salt chicken broth; more if needed
- **1** oz. dried porcini mushrooms, soaked and chopped as directed below
- **4** Tbs. unsalted butter
- **¾** cup arborio rice
- **2** cups (about ½ lb.) mixed fresh mushrooms (preferably some wild), cleaned, trimmed, and coarsely chopped
- **⅔** cup dry white wine

  Kosher salt
- **¼** cup chopped fresh flat-leaf parsley
- **2** Tbs. freshly grated Parmigiano-Reggiano

soaking dried mushrooms

Put the dried mushrooms in a medium heatproof bowl and pour in 2 cups of boiling water. Use a small plate to weight the mushrooms so they stay submerged. (If you're using smaller or larger amounts of mushrooms, just use enough water to completely submerge them.) Soak until the mushrooms are plumped and softened, about 20 minutes (some varieties might take longer).

Use a slotted spoon to transfer the mushrooms to a cutting board, squeezing any excess liquid from the mushrooms back into the soaking liquid. Remove and discard any tough stems and coarsely chop the mushrooms. Strain the soaking liquid through a coffee filter (or a paper towel set in a strainer). Set aside the mushroom "broth" for the dish you're making or freeze it to use in another recipe.

Intensely flavored mushroom risotto is best in small portions; serve it with lemon chicken and a crisp green salad to balance its deep earthiness.

1. In a medium saucepan, heat the chicken broth along with 1 cup of the reserved strained porcini soaking liquid. Keep at a simmer.

2. In another medium, heavy-based saucepan, melt 2 Tbs. of the butter over medium-high heat. Stir in the rice, toasting just until it starts to sizzle and pop, about 1 minute. It should not color. Stir the porcini and the fresh mushrooms into the rice. Stir in the wine. When almost all the liquid has disappeared, after about 2 minutes, add just enough hot broth to cover the rice. Lower the heat to maintain a vigorous simmer; stir occasionally. When the broth is almost gone, add more just to cover the rice, along with a pinch of salt.

3. Check on the risotto every 3 or 4 minutes, giving it an occasional stir to make sure it isn't sticking to the bottom of the pan and adding just enough broth to cover the rice when the liquid has almost disappeared. Continue this way until the rice is just al dente, about 20 minutes total cooking time. Bite into a grain; you should see a white pin-dot in the center.

4. Take the risotto off the heat. Add the remaining 2 Tbs. butter; stir vigorously for a few seconds. Add the parsley, cheese, and more salt, if needed. The risotto should be moist and creamy, not runny. Stir in more broth to loosen the risotto, if you like. Serve immediately. —*Alan Tardi*

PER SERVING: 620 CALORIES | 15G PROTEIN | 75G CARB | 27G TOTAL FAT | 16G SAT FAT | 8G MONO FAT | 1G POLY FAT | 65MG CHOL | 1,010MG SODIUM | 4G FIBER

Buying and Storing Dried Mushrooms

The quality of dried mushrooms can vary greatly. Your best bet is to buy them from a trusted source. If possible, take a peek inside the package before buying; you want to see nicely sized and shaped mushrooms. Avoid buying overly shriveled or very broken mushrooms.

For long-term storage, seal dried mushrooms in doubled-up zip-top freezer bags and freeze; they'll keep indefinitely that way. For storage of a month or less, seal mushrooms in an airtight container or zip-top bag and store in a cool, dark place.

parsnip risotto with pancetta and sage

SERVES 4 TO 6

Kosher salt

1½ lb. medium parsnips, peeled, cored, and cut into medium dice (2½ cups)

¼ cup extra-virgin olive oil

Freshly ground black pepper

3 oz. thinly sliced pancetta, cut into ½-inch-wide strips (about 1 cup)

3 Tbs. roughly chopped fresh sage

3 medium cloves garlic, roughly chopped

1 medium yellow onion, cut into small dice

2 cups arborio rice

Pinch of crumbled saffron (optional)

6 cups lower-salt chicken broth

½ cup dry white wine

2 Tbs. unsalted butter

2 oz. freshly grated Parmigiano-Reggiano; more for serving

A parsnip looks like an overgrown white carrot, but its flavor is more complex. This root vegetable is sweet, with a perfumed nuttiness, a touch of chestnut, and a hint of winter squash, combined with a starchy texture.

1. Bring a large pot of lightly salted water to a boil. Add the parsnips and boil until firm-tender, 3 to 5 minutes. Drain and spread on a rimmed baking sheet to cool to room temperature.

2. Heat 2 Tbs. of the olive oil in a large cast-iron skillet over medium-high heat. Add the parsnips, a pinch of salt, and a few grinds of pepper and cook, stirring occasionally, until softened and lightly browned, about 4 minutes. Add the pancetta and cook until sizzling and crisp, about 2 minutes. Add the sage and garlic and cook, stirring frequently, until the garlic is fragrant and the sage is starting to crisp, about 2 minutes more. Set aside.

3. Heat the remaining 2 Tbs. olive oil in an 11- to 12-inch straight-sided sauté pan over medium-high heat. Add the onion, a small pinch of salt, and a few grinds of pepper and cook, stirring occasionally, until beginning to soften, about 5 minutes.

4. Add the rice, 2 tsp. salt, and the saffron (if using), stirring well to coat. Add 2 cups of the broth and the wine; simmer, stirring, until the liquid is completely absorbed, 3 to 4 minutes. Continue adding the broth in 1-cup increments, stirring and adjusting the heat to maintain a brisk simmer and letting each addition be almost absorbed before adding the next. The risotto is done when the rice is nearly but not fully tender (al dente) and still a little soupy (this usually takes 14 to 16 minutes after the first addition of liquid). You may not use all the broth, but you should use at least 4 cups.

5. Fold the parsnip mixture into the risotto. Add the butter and Parmigiano and stir gently to incorporate. Season to taste with salt and pepper. Serve sprinkled with more grated Parmigiano. —*David Tanis*

PER SERVING: 590 CALORIES | 17G PROTEIN | 81G CARB | 22G TOTAL FAT | 7G SAT FAT | 11G MONO FAT | 2.5G POLY FAT | 25MG CHOL | 990MG SODIUM | 6G FIBER

how to core a parsnip

Running down the center of a parsnip is a tough woody core that should be removed before cooking. Here's how.
    After trimming the ends and peeling the parsnip, quarter it lengthwise. Hold a sharp paring knife parallel to the cutting board and slowly run the knife between the core and the tender outer part of the parsnip. The core curves with the shape of the parsnip, so you won't be able to get it all, but that's fine—just remove as much as you can without sacrificing too much of the tender part.

Selecting and Storing Parsnips

Grown in cold climates, parsnips are usually harvested in the fall and, like carrots, stored in cool root cellars. However, frost will convert their starches to sugar, concentrating their sweet flavor, so many home gardeners and small growers keep their parsnips in the ground and dig them as needed through winter and early spring. That's why you're likely to find the sweetest parsnips at a farmstand or farmers' market.

While there are several varieties of parsnips, most markets don't usually indicate which they're selling, mainly because the differences in flavor, texture, and appearance are minimal. Your best bet is to choose what looks freshest.

Here are some tips:

- When shopping, look for parsnips that are firm and of uniform color; blemishes can be a sign of decay. Opt for medium parsnips, as very large ones can be woody and bitter.
- Wrap unwashed parsnips in paper towels or newspaper and store them in a loosely closed plastic bag in the crisper drawer of the refrigerator for up to 2 weeks.

cavatappi with roasted peppers, capocollo & ricotta

Olive oil

5 medium red bell peppers

1 large onion, thinly sliced

Kosher salt and freshly ground black pepper

5 plum tomatoes, seeded and chopped (or one 14.5-oz. can diced tomatoes, drained)

⅓ lb. very thinly sliced capocollo, chopped

A few large sprigs fresh thyme, leaves chopped

1½ cups ricotta

1½ cups heavy cream, preferably not ultrapasteurized

1 to 2 tsp. finely grated orange zest

Pinch of nutmeg, preferably freshly grated

1 lb. cavatappi (or fusilli or penne)

¼ cup freshly grated pecorino romano

⅓ cup coarse fresh breadcrumbs

Capocollo is a lightly aged pork sausage usually flavored with white wine and nutmeg. If you can't find it, an excellent substitute is prosciutto di Parma.

1. Bring a large pot of salted water to a boil. Lightly coat a large shallow baking dish with olive oil.

2. Roast the peppers by turning them over the flames of a gas burner until the skins are charred or by putting them under a broiler, turning until all sides are well blistered. When they're cool enough to handle, peel off the skins, core and seed the peppers, and cut the flesh into thin strips.

3. Heat the oven to 425°F. In a large skillet, heat about 3 Tbs. of olive oil over medium heat. Add the onion and cook, stirring occasionally, until it begins to soften. Add the peppers, season with salt and pepper, and sauté until soft and fragrant, about 5 minutes. Add the tomatoes and cook for another 5 minutes. Turn off the heat and add the capocollo and thyme. Mix and set aside.

4. In a medium bowl, combine the ricotta, cream, orange zest, and nutmeg. Season with salt and pepper and whisk until smooth (you can do this in a food processor if you like).

5. Cook the cavatappi in the boiling water until al dente. Meanwhile, in a small bowl, toss the pecorino with the breadcrumbs. Season with salt and pepper and add a drizzle of olive oil. Mix well.

6. Drain the pasta well and return it to the pot. Add the pepper mixture and toss. Add the ricotta mixture, toss again, and taste for seasoning.

7. Pour the pasta into the baking dish. Top with an even coating of the breadcrumb mixture and a drizzle of olive oil. Bake uncovered until browned and bubbling, 15 to 20 minutes. Serve right away. —*Erica DeMane*

PER SERVING: 1,080 CALORIES I 35G PROTEIN I 106G CARB I 57G TOTAL FAT I 32G SAT FAT I 18G MONO FAT I 3G POLY FAT I 190MG CHOL I 780MG SODIUM I 9G FIBER

double-cheese penne with sausage and hot cherry peppers

SERVES 4 TO 6

Kosher salt

2 Tbs. plus 1 tsp. extra-virgin
   olive oil

¾ lb. dried penne or ziti

1 lb. sweet Italian sausage
   (4 or 5 links), casings removed

2 large cloves garlic, minced
   (about 2 tsp.)

1 28-oz. can whole peeled
   tomatoes

2 or 3 pickled Italian hot cherry
   peppers (from the jar), cored,
   seeded, and diced (about
   1½ Tbs.)

⅔ cup freshly grated Parmigiano-
   Reggiano (about 2½ oz.); more
   for sprinkling (optional)

   Freshly ground black pepper

8 oz. shredded low-moisture
   part-skim mozzarella (about
   2 cups)

Mild-tasting mozzarella is available as fresh or low-moisture. This recipe calls for the low-moisture because of its shreddable texture and meltability. You'll find it in the supermarket in a plastic-wrapped brick or ball.

1. In a large covered pot, bring 4 quarts salted water to a boil. Lightly grease an 8x11-inch baking dish or 6 individual (1½-cup) gratin dishes with 1 tsp. of the olive oil.

2. Add the penne or ziti to the boiling water and cook until it's just tender but still firm to the tooth, about 11 minutes. Drain the pasta well and return it to its cooking pot.

3. Meanwhile, heat the remaining 2 Tbs. oil in a large straight-sided skillet over medium-high heat. When the oil is hot, add the sausage, let it sit for a minute, and then start stirring and breaking it into bite-size pieces with the side of a slotted metal spoon. Cook until lightly browned, another 2 to 3 minutes. Transfer to a plate using the slotted spoon.

4. Add the garlic to the pan, season with salt, and cook, stirring constantly, until it colors slightly, about 30 seconds. Add the tomatoes and their juices and cook at a rapid simmer, stirring occasionally and breaking up the tomatoes with the spoon, for 5 minutes so the sauce thickens slightly.

5. Meanwhile, position an oven rack about 6 inches from the broiler element and heat the broiler on high. Stir the sausage and its juices, the diced peppers, and ⅓ cup of the Parmigiano into the sauce. Cook, stirring, until the sausage is cooked through, 3 to 5 minutes. Taste for salt and pepper. Pour the sauce over the cooked pasta in the pot and stir well. Spread the pasta and sauce evenly in the baking dish or gratin dishes. Sprinkle with the mozzarella and the remaining ⅓ cup Parmigiano. Put the baking dish or gratin dishes on a baking sheet and broil until the cheese melts and browns in places, 2 to 4 minutes (check often to be sure the cheese doesn't burn). Serve immediately with more Parmigiano, if you like.   —Fine Cooking *editors*

PER SERVING: 610 CALORIES | 40G PROTEIN | 49G CARB | 28G TOTAL FAT | 11G SAT FAT | 13G MONO FAT | 3G POLY FAT | 65MG CHOL | 1,270MG SODIUM | 4G FIBER

rigatoni with brisket and porcini ragù

SERVES 6

- **1** oz. dried porcini mushrooms (1 cup)
- **3** Tbs. extra-virgin olive oil
- **4** oz. pancetta, chopped (1 cup)
- **1** large stalk celery, chopped
- **1** large carrot, chopped
- **1** large yellow onion, chopped

  Kosher salt
- **3** large cloves garlic, minced
- **4** cups coarsely chopped Red-Wine–Braised Brisket (about 1 lb.; recipe p. 119), plus 2 cups leftover brisket juices
- **2** cups dry red wine; more as needed
- **2** tsp. chopped fresh thyme

  Freshly ground black pepper
- **1** lb. dried rigatoni

  Freshly grated Parmigiano-Reggiano, for serving

Though this recipe calls for dried pasta, you can also use any shape of fresh pasta. Once you've drained it, just toss it with a few tablespoons of butter to prevent it from sticking together.

1. Soak the porcini in 1 cup hot water for 30 minutes. Drain, straining and reserving the soaking liquid. Chop the porcini and set aside.

2. Heat the oil in an 11- to 12-inch straight-sided sauté pan over medium heat. Add the pancetta, celery, carrot, onion, and 1 tsp. salt; cook, stirring often, until the vegetables are soft and lightly golden, about 15 minutes. Add the garlic and cook, stirring, for 1 minute. Add the brisket and its juices, wine, thyme, and the porcini and their soaking liquid. Bring to a simmer, reduce the heat to low, and cook until the sauce is very thick, about 30 minutes. Season to taste with salt and pepper.

3. Meanwhile, bring a large pot of well-salted water to a boil. Cook the pasta in the boiling water until al dente. Drain and toss with most of the meat sauce. Top with the remaining sauce and pass the Parmigiano at the table.
—Joyce Goldstein

PER SERVING: 700 CALORIES I 39G PROTEIN I 68G CARB I 22G TOTAL FAT I 5G SAT FAT I 11G MONO FAT I 3.5G POLY FAT I 55MG CHOL I 1,040MG SODIUM I 6G FIBER

What Is Parmigiano-Reggiano?

Genuine Parmigiano-Reggiano is made only in the Emilia-Romagna region of northern Italy, following stringent guidelines. The milk used to make the cheese comes from cows that spend most of their days grazing in grassy meadows. The farmers pay special attention to their animals, knowing that their reward will be a truly unique cheese, with an unrivaled texture and nutty taste. Each wheel is aged for at least 12 months before the Parmigiano-Reggiano stamp is imprinted on its rind and it's ready for the market.

Purchase a chunk of Parmigiano-Reggiano and grate it freshly yourself, rather than buying it already grated. When you buy pregrated cheese, you have no way of knowing how long ago it was grated, and as the cheese sits, it loses moisture and flavor.

turkey noodle casserole

SERVES 6 TO 8

- 2 oz. (4 Tbs.) unsalted butter; more for the baking dish

  Kosher salt

- ¾ cup coarse dry breadcrumbs

- 2 Tbs. extra-virgin olive oil

- 1 Tbs. freshly grated Parmigiano-Reggiano

- 1 Tbs. finely chopped fresh sage

  Freshly ground black pepper

- 1 lb. assorted fresh mushrooms, cleaned and sliced ⅛ to ¼ inch thick

- 3 Tbs. minced shallots

- 2 medium cloves garlic, minced

- 2¼ oz. (½ cup) unbleached all-purpose flour

- 6 cups low-fat milk

- 3½ oz. (1½ cups) grated sharp white Cheddar

- 3 Tbs. finely chopped fresh flat-leaf parsley

- 8 oz. egg pappardelle pasta

- 3 cups shredded or diced roast turkey

Turkey is combined with earthy mushrooms, a creamy cheese sauce, and a crunchy, sage-scented crumb topping to make this tasty, comforting dish. You can substitute wide egg noodles for the pappardelle.

1. Position a rack in the center of the oven and heat the oven to 350°F.

2. Butter a 3-quart baking dish. Bring a large pot of well-salted water to a boil over high heat.

3. Mix the breadcrumbs, 1 Tbs. of the olive oil, Parmigiano, and sage in a small bowl. Season to taste with salt and pepper. Set aside.

4. Heat a large (12-inch) skillet over medium heat. Add the remaining 1 Tbs. olive oil to the pan and then add the mushrooms; cook, stirring frequently, until softened and golden on the edges, about 10 minutes. Reduce the heat to medium low and add the shallots and garlic; cook, stirring until softened, about 2 minutes. Season to taste with salt and pepper and set aside.

5. Melt the butter in a 4-quart saucepan over medium heat. Add the flour and whisk constantly until it colors slightly, 2 to 3 minutes. Remove the pan from the heat and gradually whisk in enough of the milk to form a thick, smooth paste. Set the pan back over the heat and whisk in the remaining milk in a steady stream. Add 1 tsp. of salt. Bring to a boil over medium-high heat, whisking constantly. Reduce the heat to medium low and simmer for 3 minutes, whisking constantly. Turn off the heat and stir in the Cheddar and parsley. Season to taste with more salt and pepper. Set aside.

6. Cook the pasta in the boiling water until al dente, about 1 minute less than package timing. Drain and spread the pasta in an even layer on the bottom of the prepared baking dish. Sprinkle the turkey and mushrooms over the pasta. Pour the sauce on top and use a fork to distribute it evenly.

7. Sprinkle the breadcrumbs over the entire casserole. Set on a baking sheet to catch drips and bake until golden-brown and bubbling, 50 to 60 minutes. Let rest for 20 to 30 minutes before serving. —*Maria Helm Sinskey*

PER SERVING: 500 CALORIES I 28G PROTEIN I 43G CARB I 24G TOTAL FAT I 11G SAT FAT I 9G MONO FAT I 2.5G POLY FAT I 100MG CHOL I 760MG SODIUM I 2G FIBER

pasta puttanesca

SERVES 4

Kosher salt

3 **Tbs. extra-virgin olive oil**

4 **large cloves garlic, minced**

3 **oil-packed anchovy fillets, finely chopped (scant 1 Tbs.)**

¼ **tsp. crushed red pepper flakes**

1 **28-oz. can crushed tomatoes**

1 **lb. dried spaghetti**

½ **cup pitted brine-cured black olives, such as Kalamata, coarsely chopped**

2 **Tbs. nonpareil capers, rinsed and drained**

1 **Tbs. chopped fresh oregano or marjoram**

Freshly ground black pepper

Many of the ingredients for this classic flavor-packed pasta may already be in your pantry, making this a perfect weeknight meal.

1. Bring a large pot of well-salted water to a boil over high heat.

2. Meanwhile, heat 1 Tbs. of the olive oil with the garlic in a 3-quart saucepan over medium heat. Cook, stirring frequently, until the garlic is sizzling, about 2 minutes. Add the anchovies and red pepper flakes and cook, stirring frequently, until the garlic is very pale golden, 1 to 2 minutes more. Stir in the tomatoes. Increase the heat to medium high, bring to a boil, and then reduce the heat to medium low and simmer, stirring occasionally, until the sauce is slightly thickened, 8 to 10 minutes.

3. After adding the tomatoes to the pan, add the pasta to the boiling water and cook according to the package directions until al dente.

4. When the tomato sauce is ready, add the olives, capers, and oregano and stir. Simmer until just heated through, about 2 minutes. Stir in the remaining 2 Tbs. olive oil and season the sauce to taste with salt and pepper.

5. When the pasta is ready, reserve ½ cup of the cooking water and drain well. Return the pasta to the pot, set it over medium-low heat, pour in the sauce, and toss, adding cooking water as needed for the sauce to coat the pasta. Serve immediately. *—Dawn Yanagihara*

PER SERVING: 720 CALORIES | 30G PROTEIN | 103G CARB | 22G TOTAL FAT | 3.5G SAT FAT | 13G MONO FAT | 3.5G POLY FAT | 30MG CHOL | 2,590MG SODIUM | 10G FIBER

What Are Capers?

The distinctive zing in puttanesca sauce comes from capers, which pack big flavor in a tiny package. These little spheres are the flower buds of a prickly shrub that grows all over the Mediterranean. Some caper shrubs are cultivated, but most grow wild, and the harvest is done by hand. Eaten raw, capers are unpalatably bitter, but once cured in a vinegar brine or salt, they develop an intense flavor that is all at once salty, sour, herbal, and slightly medicinal. If the buds are allowed to go to seed, they become caper berries, which are also packed in brine and can be added to salads or eaten out of hand like olives.

pork ragoût with soft polenta

SERVES 4

- 2 cups whole milk; more as needed

  Kosher salt

- 1 cup stone-ground yellow cornmeal

- ¼ cup freshly grated Parmigiano-Reggiano; more for sprinkling

- 1½ Tbs. unsalted butter

- 2 Tbs. extra-virgin olive oil

- 2 medium carrots, cut into small dice

- 2 medium stalks celery, cut into small dice

- 1 medium yellow onion, cut into small dice

  Pinch of crushed red pepper flakes

- 3 canned tomatoes, drained and cut into medium dice

- 3 cloves garlic, finely chopped

- 3 cups leftover shredded Slow-Roasted Pork Shoulder (recipe p. 138)

- 3 cups lower-salt chicken broth

  Freshly ground black pepper

- 2 Tbs. chopped fresh flat-leaf parsley

Comfort on a plate, this dish is a great way to use leftover roast pork.

1. Combine the milk with 2 cups water in a medium heavy-duty saucepan and bring to a boil over medium-high heat (watch carefully to prevent a boilover). Add 1½ tsp. salt and whisk in the cornmeal in a fine stream. Continue to whisk until the polenta begins to thicken, 1 to 3 minutes. Reduce the heat so that the polenta slowly bubbles and cook, uncovered, stirring frequently, until tender and no longer gritty, 20 to 40 minutes depending on the cornmeal. If the polenta becomes too thick in the process, add milk, a little at a time, to maintain a soft consistency. When the polenta is done, stir in the Parmigiano and ½ Tbs. of the butter and season to taste with salt. Keep warm until serving. (The polenta will thicken as it sits. If necessary, add a splash of milk to thin it just before serving.)

2. Heat the oil in a 10-inch straight-sided sauté pan over medium heat. Add the carrots, celery, onion, red pepper flakes, and a generous pinch of salt and cook, stirring often, until tender and starting to brown, 8 to 10 minutes. Add the tomatoes and garlic and cook, stirring, for another minute. Add the pork and chicken broth. Bring to a boil and then lower the heat to maintain a simmer. Cook until the broth has reduced by half, about 10 minutes. Stir in the remaining 1 Tbs. butter. Season to taste with salt and pepper.

3. Spoon the polenta into shallow bowls and then spoon the ragoût on the top and to one side, with the broth pooling around the polenta. (Make sure each portion gets a fair share of broth.) Sprinkle each portion with parsley and Parmigiano-Reggiano and serve immediately. —*Tasha DeSerio*

PER SERVING: 550 CALORIES | 35G PROTEIN | 44G CARB | 27G TOTAL FAT | 10G SAT FAT | 12G MONO FAT | 3G POLY FAT | 95MG CHOL | 1,090MG SODIUM | 5G FIBER

linguine with lemon-garlic shrimp

SERVES 3

Kosher salt

½ **lb. dried thin linguine**

1 **lemon**

1 **lb. extra-large (26 to 30 per lb.) shrimp, peeled and deveined**

Freshly ground black pepper

2 **Tbs. unsalted butter**

3 **medium cloves garlic, thinly sliced (1 Tbs.)**

⅛ **to ¼ tsp. crushed red pepper flakes**

¼ **cup dry white wine, such as Pinot Grigio**

½ **cup mascarpone**

2 **Tbs. thinly sliced chives**

This easy pasta gets its luxurious creaminess from mascarpone, an Italian cream cheese.

1. Bring a large pot of well-salted water to a boil over high heat. Cook the linguine in the boiling water according to package directions until al dente. Reserve about ¾ cup of the cooking water and then drain the pasta.

2. Meanwhile, finely grate 1¼ tsp. of zest from the lemon and squeeze 2 Tbs. of juice. Toss the shrimp with ½ tsp. of the zest and ¼ tsp. each salt and pepper.

3. In a 12-inch skillet, melt the butter over medium-high heat until the foam subsides. Add the garlic and red pepper flakes and cook until the garlic just begins to brown, about 1 minute. Add the shrimp and cook until just opaque, about 3 minutes. Add the wine and lemon juice, bring to a boil, and cook until slightly reduced, 1 minute.

4. Add the drained pasta, mascarpone, and ½ cup of the cooking water. Toss well, adding more cooking water as needed, until the pasta and shrimp are coated and the sauce looks creamy. Remove from the heat. Toss in the remaining ¾ tsp. lemon zest and the chives. Season to taste with salt and pepper and serve. *—Melissa Gaman*

PER SERVING: 830 CALORIES I 40G PROTEIN I 62G CARB I 45G TOTAL FAT I 24G SAT FAT I 12G MONO FAT I 2.5G POLY FAT I 340MG CHOL I 640MG SODIUM I 4G FIBER

linguine with clam sauce

SERVES 2 OR 3

24 littleneck clams

6 Tbs. extra-virgin olive oil

½ tsp. crushed red pepper flakes

⅓ cup dry white wine

5 Tbs. finely chopped fresh flat-leaf parsley, plus a few whole leaves for garnish

3 large cloves garlic, minced

Kosher salt

8 oz. linguine or spaghettini (I like De Cecco®, Due Pastori, and Rustichella d'Abruzzo brands)

Freshly ground black pepper

Linguine with clam sauce should be packed with flavor: nicely garlicky and a little spicy. Most of all it should taste of fresh, delicious clams with the unmistakable tang of the sea. Fresh, in-the-shell clams are the key to getting this true clam flavor, and tiny littlenecks are the tenderest.

1. Scrub the clams under cold water and set aside. In a heavy 3-quart saucepan, heat 3 Tbs. of the oil over medium heat. Add the red pepper flakes and cook briefly to infuse the oil, about 20 seconds. Immediately add the wine, 2 Tbs. of the chopped parsley, and half of the minced garlic. Cook for 20 seconds and add the clams.

2. Cover and cook over medium-high heat, checking every 2 minutes and removing each clam as it opens. It will take 5 to 6 minutes total for all the clams to open. Transfer the clams to a cutting board and reserve the broth. Remove the clams from the shells and cut them in half, or quarters if they're large. Return the clams to the broth. Discard the shells.

3. Bring a large pot of well-salted water to a boil over high heat. Add the pasta and cook until it's almost al dente, 6 to 9 minutes. Don't overcook.

4. While the pasta is cooking, heat the remaining 3 Tbs. olive oil in a 10- or 12-inch skillet over medium heat. Add the remaining 3 Tbs. chopped parsley and the rest of the garlic and cook until the garlic is just soft, about 1 minute. Set the skillet aside.

5. When the pasta is done, reserve about ¼ cup of the pasta cooking water and then drain the pasta. Add the pasta, the clams, and the broth the clams were cooked in to the skillet. Return to low heat, toss the pasta in the sauce, and simmer for another minute to finish cooking it, adding a little of the pasta water if you prefer a wetter dish.

6. Taste for salt and add a generous grind of black pepper. Serve immediately, garnished with the parsley leaves. *—Perla Meyers*

PER SERVING: 670 CALORIES | 31G PROTEIN | 63G CARB | 30G TOTAL FAT | 4G SAT FAT | 20G MONO FAT | 4G POLY FAT | 50MG CHOL | 330MG SODIUM | 4G FIBER

Buying Clams

When shopping for clams, you'll want to head for a market with rapid turnover. Since clams are such an important part of this dish, it'll be worth the extra time it takes to get to a good seafood market.

Look for intact, tightly closed (or just slightly gaping) shells and a sea-like smell. Clams are sold alive, so don't store them in plastic or they'll suffocate. As soon as you get home, put them in a bowl, cover with a wet towel, and refrigerate.

Just before cooking, look for any shellfish that are open and tap them on the counter. If they don't close, discard them. Also discard any clams that remain closed after cooking.

If you are not preparing your dish the day you buy the clams, it's smart to wash and cook them in the wine and herb broth, remove them from their shells, and refrigerate; they will keep for 2 or 3 days.

classic meat lasagne

YIELDS 3 LASAGNES OF
4 AMPLE SERVINGS EACH

2   Tbs. plus ⅓ cup olive oil

2   lb. mild (sweet) Italian
    sausage, casing removed
    and broken into pieces

8   cloves garlic, peeled and
    slightly crushed

2   large onions, finely chopped

1½ cups dry red wine
    (such as Chianti)

4   28-oz. cans (or three 35-oz.
    cans) crushed tomatoes
    (about 14 cups total)

2   Tbs. dried oregano

2   tsp. dried thyme

1   Tbs. chopped fresh rosemary
    (you can substitute 2 tsp.
    dried, but I prefer fresh)

1   tsp. fennel seeds, crushed

1½ tsp. salt

½   tsp. freshly ground black
    pepper

1   Tbs. sugar

3   large eggs

1½ cups freshly grated Parmesan,
    preferably Parmigiano-Reggiano

32 oz. ricotta

    A large handful of fresh
    basil leaves, washed well
    and chopped

2½ lb. fresh mozzarella cheese,
    sliced as thinly as possible

1   lb. instant (no-boil) lasagne
    noodles

Pop the mozzarella in the freezer for a few minutes before slicing; the firmer cheese will be easier to slice thinly.

1. In a heavy-based pot, heat the 2 Tbs. olive oil over medium-high heat. Add the sausage and brown it all over, breaking it up into small pieces with a wooden spoon and stirring, 10 to 12 minutes. Remove the sausage with a slotted spoon and reserve. Pour off most of the fat, but leave some behind for flavor.

2. To the pot, add the ⅓ cup of olive oil and the garlic and heat over medium-high heat until the garlic just begins to turn light brown, about 5 minutes. Remove and discard the garlic immediately, leaving the oil in the pot. Add the onions to the pot and cook, stirring frequently, until translucent, 5 to 6 minutes. Return the sausage to the pot. Add the red wine and cook until it has reduced by at least half, about 10 minutes.

3. Add the crushed tomatoes and stir in the oregano, thyme, rosemary, fennel seeds, salt, pepper, and sugar. Reduce the heat to medium low and cook to blend and develop the flavors, about 30 minutes. Taste for seasoning. You should have about 16 cups of sauce.

4. Meanwhile, in a large bowl, beat the eggs and add the Parmesan. Beat in the ricotta. Season with salt and pepper and fold in the chopped basil.

5. Heat the oven to 400°F. To make three lasagne of four layers each, begin by lightly oiling three 9x9x2- or 8x8x2-inch metal or ceramic pans (disposable pans are also fine). Cover the bottom of each pan lightly with some of the sauce. Lay down a layer of pasta in each of the three pans. Spread enough of the ricotta cheese mixture on top of the pasta to cover, about ½ cup. Top the ricotta with enough sauce to cover it completely, about ½ cup. Cover with another layer of pasta and ladle more sauce over that, followed by enough mozzarella cheese to cover, enough ricotta cheese to cover, and some more sauce. Continue with two more layers in that order: pasta, sauce, mozzarella, ricotta, and sauce. Finish with a layer of pasta, some sauce, some mozzarella cheese, and a final light layer of sauce. You should be able to easily get four layers into each pan; if you have extra components, go ahead and add another layer to one or more of the lasagne. Don't worry if the height of the lasagne exceeds the pan; it settles as it bakes. Save any remaining sauce to serve with the lasagne.

6. Seal the pans with aluminum foil, tented so it doesn't stick to the cheese. Bake until the edges are bubbling and a knife inserted into the center of each lasagne comes out very hot, 40 to 50 minutes. Let sit for 15 minutes before serving or cool completely on a rack before freezing. Defrost frozen lasagne overnight in the refrigerator and then bake at 400°F for about 1 hour.
—*Clifford A. Wright*

PER SERVING: 920 CALORIES | 63G PROTEIN | 57G CARB | 51G TOTAL FAT | 24G SAT FAT | 20G MONO FAT | 5G POLY FAT | 170MG CHOL | 1,480MG SODIUM | 7G FIBER

fresh pasta with sausage and mushrooms

Kosher salt

2 Tbs. extra-virgin olive oil

¾ lb. sweet Italian chicken sausage, cut into 1-inch pieces

½ lb. mixed sliced fresh mushrooms (like oyster, shiitake, and cremini)

4 medium scallions (white and green parts), trimmed and thinly sliced

2 tsp. chopped fresh rosemary

⅛ tsp. crushed red pepper flakes

Freshly ground black pepper

1 cup drained canned diced tomatoes

1 cup lower-salt chicken broth

1 12-oz. package fresh linguine or fettuccine

¾ cup freshly grated Parmigiano-Reggiano

You can find fresh pasta in the refrigerated section of your supermarket. For a spicier dish, use hot Italian chicken sausage.

1. Bring a medium pot of salted water to a boil. Meanwhile, heat the oil in a large, heavy skillet over medium-high heat until shimmering hot. Add the sausage and cook, stirring occasionally, until browned, about 3 minutes. Add the mushrooms, scallions, rosemary, red pepper flakes, ¾ tsp. salt, and ½ tsp. pepper and cook, stirring often, until the mushrooms soften and start to brown, about 3 minutes. Add the tomatoes and chicken broth, bring to a boil, and then cover and reduce to a gentle simmer. Cook until the sausage is heated through and the flavors are melded, about 5 minutes.

2. Meanwhile, cook the pasta according to the package directions until it's just al dente. Drain well and add to the sauce along with half of the Parmigiano. Cook over medium heat, tossing for 1 minute. Serve sprinkled with the remaining Parmigiano and some black pepper. —*Tony Rosenfeld*

PER SERVING: 490 CALORIES | 30G PROTEIN | 55G CARB | 17G TOTAL FAT | 4.5G SAT FAT | 5G MONO FAT | 1.5G POLY FAT | 115MG CHOL | 1,280MG SODIUM | 5G FIBER

beef and pork ragù lasagne

SERVES 8 TO 10

FOR THE RAGÙ

- **3 oz. (6 Tbs.) unsalted butter**
- **¼ cup extra-virgin olive oil**
- **2 medium stalks celery, finely chopped (1⅓ cups)**
- **2 medium carrots, peeled and finely chopped (⅔ cup)**
- **2 small yellow onions, finely chopped (1⅓ cups)**
- **1 lb. boneless beef brisket or chuck, finely diced or ground (2 cups)**
- **1 lb. boneless pork shoulder, finely diced or ground (1½ cups)**
- **8 oz. pancetta, finely diced (1¼ cups)**
- **2 cups dry red wine**
- **½ cup canned tomato purée**
- **¼ cup tomato paste diluted in ½ cup water**
- **2 cups homemade or lower-salt canned beef or chicken broth; more as needed**
- **1 cup whole milk**
- **Kosher salt and freshly ground black pepper**

TO ASSEMBLE

- **½ oz. (1 Tbs.) unsalted butter, cut into small cubes; more for the pan**
- **¾ lb. fresh or dried lasagne noodles, cooked according to package instructions**
- **Double recipe of Basic Cream Sauce (recipe facing page)**
- **1 cup freshly grated Parmigiano-Reggiano**

Prepare the ragù up to 4 days ahead and refrigerate it, or freeze it for up to 1 month. Reheat gently until the sauce is warm enough to spread for assembling the lasagne.

MAKE THE RAGÙ

In a 5- to 6-quart Dutch oven, melt the 6 Tbs. butter with the olive oil over medium heat. Add the celery, carrots, and onion and cook, stirring occasionally, until softened and lightly golden, about 15 minutes. Add the beef, pork, and pancetta and cook, breaking up the meats with a spoon and stirring often, until the meats lose their redness, 5 to 8 minutes. Stir in the wine, tomato purée, and tomato paste and simmer vigorously until the liquid is almost evaporated, 15 to 20 minutes. Add the beef or chicken broth and the milk, cover with the lid ajar, reduce the heat to low, and simmer gently until you have a rich, concentrated sauce, about 2½ hours. Check every 30 minutes to see if more liquid is needed, adding more broth if necessary to prevent scorching. Season to taste with salt and pepper, if needed. Let cool. Skim off the fat from the top, if desired. You should have about 6 cups.

ASSEMBLE THE LASAGNE

1. Position a rack in the center of the oven and heat the oven to 350°F. Choose a baking dish that's about 9x12 inches and 3 inches deep, or about 10x14 inches and 2 inches deep. Butter the baking dish. Spread ½ cup of ragù in a sparse layer on the bottom of the dish. Then cover with a slightly overlapping layer of cooked noodles, cutting them as needed to fill the gaps. Spread one-third of the remaining ragù (about 1½ cups) over the first layer of noodles. Drizzle on one-third of the cream sauce (about 1 cup) and spread it with a spatula or the back of a spoon. Sprinkle with ⅓ cup Parmigiano. Add a new layer of noodles, overlapping them slightly.

2. Repeat the layers as instructed above, until all of the filling ingredients are used, to make a total of three layers (you may not need all the pasta). Dot the top with the butter cubes.

3. Put the baking dish on a baking sheet and bake until heated through and bubbling at the edges, 45 to 50 minutes. Remove from the oven and let rest for 10 to 15 minutes before serving. —*Joyce Goldstein*

PER SERVING: 620 CALORIES | 30G PROTEIN | 29G CARB | 39G TOTAL FAT | 17G SAT FAT | 15G MONO FAT | 3G POLY FAT | 170MG CHOL | 1,140MG SODIUM | 2G FIBER

basic cream sauce

YIELDS ABOUT 1½ CUPS

1½ oz. (3 Tbs.) unsalted butter

3 Tbs. unbleached all-purpose flour

1¾ cups whole milk, heated

½ tsp. kosher salt

⅛ tsp. freshly ground black pepper

Small pinch of freshly grated nutmeg

Double this recipe, using a 3-quart saucepan, to make enough sauce for the ragù lasagne.

In a 2-quart saucepan, melt the butter over medium-low heat. Add the flour and cook, whisking constantly for 2 to 3 minutes. Do not let the mixture brown. Slowly whisk in the hot milk and bring just to a simmer, whisking frequently. Reduce the heat to low and cook, whisking often, until the sauce has thickened to a creamy, gravy-like consistency and no longer tastes of raw flour, 6 to 8 minutes for a single batch, 10 to 12 minutes for a double batch. Remove from the heat and whisk in the salt, pepper, and nutmeg. If not using right away, transfer to a bowl and press a piece of plastic wrap directly on the surface of the sauce to keep a skin from forming. Plan to use the sauce within 30 minutes because it thickens if it's left to sit for too long. Should that happen, add a little warm milk and whisk well to thin it.

Beef Stew with Red Wine and Carrots
(recipe on p. 137)

one-pot meals, casseroles & more

best-ever roast chicken

SERVES 4

1 4-lb. roasting chicken, giblets removed

Kosher salt and freshly ground black pepper

1 Tbs. extra-virgin olive oil

To get the most accurate temperature reading, insert the instant-read thermometer in the thickest part of the thigh, toward the interior rather than the exterior of the bird. Make sure you don't touch the bone with the tip of the thermometer, or you'll get a higher reading.

This classic dish should be part of every cook's arsenal—and it's surprisingly simple. Roast two birds if want to be sure you have leftovers, which are perfect for quick weeknight soups, stews, and casseroles.

1. Position a rack in the center of the oven and heat the oven to 450°F.

2. Put the chicken breast side up on a roasting rack in a medium (9x13-inch or similar) flameproof baking dish or roasting pan. Tuck the wing tips behind the neck and loosely tie the legs together with a piece of kitchen twine. Season the breast all over with ½ tsp. each salt and pepper. Turn the chicken over. Season the back all over with ½ tsp. each salt and pepper. Drizzle the oil evenly over the back of the chicken.

3. Roast the chicken breast side down for 30 minutes. Turn it over by inserting sturdy tongs into the cavity and flipping it. Continue roasting until an instant-read thermometer inserted into the thigh reads 165° to 170°F, an additional 30 to 35 minutes.

4. Transfer the chicken to a cutting board, loosely tent it with foil, and let it rest for 15 minutes. Snip the twine from the chicken's legs, carve the chicken, and serve. *—Susie Middleton*

PER SERVING: 560 CALORIES I 56G PROTEIN I 0G CARB I 35G TOTAL FAT I 9G SAT FAT I 15G MONO FAT I 7G POLY FAT I 180MG CHOL I 450MG SODIUM I 0G FIBER

five essential tips to roasting a perfect chicken

- **Use high-quality chicken.** Starting with the best bird is the first step to tasty results.

- **Start breast side down.** Positioning the chicken breast side down allows all the juices to gather in the breast meat during the first half of cooking. When you flip the bird, those juices slowly redistribute but leave plenty of moisture behind to keep that white meat ultra juicy.

- **Use high heat.** Heat is roast chicken's best friend. A 450°F oven browns the skin quickly and keeps it nice and crisp.

- **Don't overcook.** An overcooked chicken is a dry chicken. To prevent overcooking, use an instant-read thermometer as your most reliable indicator of doneness (see the tip above for how to use it). It should read 165° to 170°F.

- **Let it rest.** Don't be tempted to cut into the chicken as soon as it's out of the oven. Resting for at least 15 minutes on the cutting board allows the juices to redistribute into the meat, making it moist and tender.

chicken with vinegar and onions

SERVES 4 TO 6

- 3   Tbs. unsalted butter
- 2   small-medium yellow onions, thinly sliced (about 2½ cups)
-     Kosher salt and freshly ground black pepper
- 3   Tbs. Champagne vinegar
- 1   4-lb. chicken, cut into 8 pieces (or 2 bone-in, skin-on breasts and 4 bone-in, skin-on thighs)
- ½   cup unbleached all-purpose flour
- 2   Tbs. extra-virgin olive oil
- ½   cup dry white wine, such as Sauvignon Blanc or Pinot Gris
- 2   tsp. chopped fresh tarragon leaves
- 2   Tbs. crème fraîche (or heavy cream)

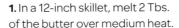

Make Ahead

This dish can be made a day or two ahead, but don't add the last teaspoon of tarragon. Reheat gently in a covered baking dish in a 325°F oven for about 30 minutes, adding a few tablespoons of water or chicken broth if the chicken appears dry. Sprinkle with the tarragon and serve.

Leave the lid of the skillet slightly ajar to let some steam escape during cooking. This concentrates the liquid for a more intense sauce, and it also ensures that the liquid doesn't boil or simmer too hard, which would overcook the chicken.

1. In a 12-inch skillet, melt 2 Tbs. of the butter over medium heat. Add the onion, sprinkle with a couple of big pinches of salt and a few grinds of pepper, and stir to coat the onions. Cover, reduce the heat to medium low, and continue to cook, stirring occasionally, until the onion is tender and lightly browned, about 20 minutes. Scrape into a small bowl and set the skillet over medium-high heat. Add 1 Tbs. of the vinegar and stir with a wooden spoon to dissolve any browned bits on the bottom of the pan. Pour the vinegar into the onion and set the skillet aside.

2. If using chicken parts, cut each breast crosswise into two equal-size portions and trim any excess fat or skin from the thighs. Rinse and pat dry.

3. Spread the flour in a pie plate, and season the chicken pieces with salt and pepper. Set the skillet over medium-high heat and add the olive oil and the remaining 1 Tbs. butter. While the butter melts, dredge half of the seasoned chicken pieces in the flour, shaking off the excess. Set them skin side down in the skillet. Brown, turning once, until the skin is crisp and the chicken is evenly browned, 6 to 8 minutes total. Lower the heat if the chicken or the drippings threaten to burn. Transfer the chicken pieces to a pan or platter and repeat with the remaining chicken.

4. When all the chicken is browned, pour off all of the fat. Return the skillet to medium-high heat, add the wine, and scrape the bottom of the pan with a wooden spoon to dissolve the drippings. Add the remaining 2 Tbs. of vinegar, the sautéed onion, and 1 tsp. of the tarragon. Return the chicken pieces, skin side up, to the skillet, arranging them in a single snug layer. Partially cover, leaving a small gap for the steam to escape, and lower the heat to maintain a low simmer. Continue to simmer gently, turning every 10 minutes, until the chicken is tender and cooked through, about 30 minutes total.

5. Transfer the chicken to a platter. Increase the heat to a more rapid simmer, and stir in the crème fraîche (or cream); the sauce may appear broken at first, but it will come together. Taste for salt and pepper. Add the remaining 1 tsp. tarragon and spoon over the chicken to serve.   *—Molly Stevens*

PER SERVING: 500 CALORIES I 40G PROTEIN I 9G CARB I 32G TOTAL FAT I 11G SAT FAT I 13G MONO FAT I 5G POLY FAT I 145MG CHOL I 400MG SODIUM I 1G FIBER

chicken tikka masala

SERVES 6 TO 8

- **1** 2-inch-long fresh hot green chile (preferably serrano), stemmed but not seeded, chopped
- **1** 1-inch piece fresh ginger, peeled and chopped
- **1** 28-oz. can whole tomatoes
- **8** Tbs. unsalted butter
- **1** recipe Roasted Tandoori Chicken (recipe facing page), meat removed from bones in large pieces; try not to shred (about 5 cups)
- **2** tsp. sweet paprika
- **2** Tbs. cumin seeds, toasted and ground in a spice grinder
- **1** cup heavy cream
- Kosher salt
- **2** tsp. garam masala
- **¾** cup coarsely chopped fresh cilantro

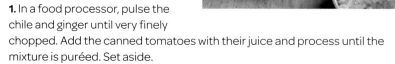

This popular dish appears on most Indian restaurant menus; it originated in Delhi, India, and in India, the dish is known as chicken makhanwalla ("makhan" in Hindi means butter), but in Britain, this dish was renamed chicken tikka masala ("tikka" means "boneless," and "masala" means "spices").

1. In a food processor, pulse the chile and ginger until very finely chopped. Add the canned tomatoes with their juice and process until the mixture is puréed. Set aside.

2. Melt 6 Tbs. of the butter in a 6- to 8-quart Dutch oven over medium heat. When the foam subsides, add about a third of the chicken pieces and cook, stirring frequently, until the chicken absorbs some of the butter and begins to brown, 3 to 4 minutes. With a slotted spoon, transfer the chicken to a plate. Repeat with the remaining two batches of chicken.

3. Add the remaining 2 Tbs. butter to the pan. When it's melted, add the paprika and 4 tsp. of the cumin and stir until the spices just begin to darken, 10 to 15 seconds.

4. Immediately add the tomato mixture. Simmer vigorously, uncovered, stirring frequently, until the sauce has thickened slightly, 6 to 8 minutes. Add the cream and 1 tsp. salt and stir well.

5. Add the chicken and stir gently to mix. Reduce the heat to medium low and simmer, uncovered, stirring occasionally, for 10 minutes. Stir in the garam masala and remaining cumin. Remove from the heat, cover, and allow to rest for 15 minutes. Taste and add more salt if necessary.

6. Transfer to a serving bowl, garnish with cilantro, and serve. —*Suneeta Vaswani*

PER SERVING: 410 CALORIES I 23G PROTEIN I 9G CARB I 32G TOTAL FAT I 16G SAT FAT I 10G MONO FAT I 3G POLY FAT I 145MG CHOL I 410MG SODIUM I 2G FIBER

Toasting and Grinding Spices

Spices generally taste better when they're toasted. The heat opens up their complex flavors, making them full and smooth instead of harsh and raw.

To toast whole or ground spices, put them in a dry skillet over medium-low heat and stir frequently just until they become very fragrant and darken slightly (or pop, in the case of mustard seeds). It shouldn't take more than a few minutes; watch carefully so they don't burn. Immediately transfer to a dish to cool (if left in the hot pan, they could burn).

To grind the spices to a coarse or fine powder, use an electric coffee grinder or a mortar and pestle.

roasted tandoori chicken

SERVES 6

12 bone-in chicken thighs

 1 cup plain nonfat yogurt

 ⅓ cup freshly squeezed lemon
    juice (from about 2 medium
    lemons)

 1 Tbs. peeled and finely
    chopped fresh ginger

 1 Tbs. finely chopped garlic

 2 tsp. ground coriander

 2 tsp. ground cumin

 2 tsp. garam masala

1½ tsp. kosher salt

 ½ tsp. cayenne

    Few drops of red and yellow
    food coloring (optional)

 1 lemon, cut in half

Restaurants use food coloring to give this chicken its traditional red color, but this ingredient is optional.

MARINATE THE CHICKEN

1. Remove the skin and trim excess fat from the chicken. With a sharp chef's knife, cut three or four long, diagonal slits on each thigh against the grain, almost to the bone.

2. In a large, shallow bowl, mix together the yogurt, lemon juice, ginger, garlic, coriander, cumin, garam masala, kosher salt, and cayenne. Stir in the food coloring, if using. Add the chicken, turning to coat and making sure that the marinade gets into all of the slits in the chicken. Cover and marinate in the refrigerator for at least 2 hours and up to 12 hours.

ROAST THE CHICKEN

1. Position a rack in the center of the oven and heat the oven to 375°F. Line a large rimmed baking sheet with foil.

2. Transfer the chicken from the marinade to the baking sheet, spacing the thighs evenly. Discard any remaining marinade. Roast until the juices run clear when the chicken is pierced and an instant-read thermometer in a meaty party of a thigh registers 170°F, about 45 minutes.

3. Squeeze the lemon halves over the chicken. Let it cool before using in the Chicken Tikka Masala. Refrigerate if making ahead.

PER SERVING: 230 CALORIES | 28G PROTEIN | 2G CARB | 11G TOTAL FAT | 3G SAT FAT | 4.5G MONO FAT | 2.5G POLY FAT | 100MG CHOL | 170MG SODIUM | 0G FIBER

What Is Garam Masala?

Garam masala, which means "hot spice," is the Indian equivalent of the French herbes de Provence or the Chinese five-spice powder. The recipe changes from region to region in northern India, with each household adding its own touch. As a rule, garam masala is added at the last step of cooking, almost like a fresh herb. If cooked too long, it tends to become bitter.

Garam masala is available in some grocery stores as well as in Indian markets, but for the best flavor, toast and grind your own. It's most authentic when made with whole spices, but ground spices are fine. You'll find a recipe for garam masala on p. 109.

classic fried chicken

SERVES 4 OR 5

1½ cups buttermilk

Fine sea salt and freshly ground black pepper

1 whole small (3- to 3¼-lb.) chicken, cut into 10 pieces

9 oz. (2 cups) unbleached all-purpose flour

1 Tbs. sweet paprika

2 to 3 cups vegetable oil

This Southern staple should be part of every cook's recipe collection. It's cheaper to buy a whole chicken and cut it up yourself than it is to buy one sold in parts.

1. In a large bowl, mix the buttermilk with 2 tsp. salt and ½ tsp. pepper. Add the chicken and toss to coat. Cover and refrigerate for at least 4 and up to 24 hours, turning occasionally.

2. When you're ready to fry the chicken, put the flour, paprika, 2 tsp. salt, and ½ tsp. pepper in a large doubled brown paper bag, and shake to combine. Working in 2 batches, drop the chicken pieces into the flour mixture, fold the top of the bag closed, and shake to coat completely. Arrange the coated chicken on a large wire rack set over a large rimmed baking sheet. Discard the remaining flour mixture.

3. Pour enough oil into a deep heavy-duty 12-inch skillet (preferably cast iron) to reach a depth of ½ inch. Heat the oil over medium-high heat until a deep fat/candy thermometer clipped to the side of the skillet without touching the bottom registers 350°F.

4. Carefully arrange the chicken skin side down in the hot oil—it's fine if the pan is very crowded. The temperature will drop to about 300°F. Partially cover the skillet with a lid or a baking sheet, leaving the thermometer visible, and fry until golden-brown, about 5 minutes, adjusting the heat as needed to maintain 300° to 325°F. If necessary, move the pieces around for even browning. Turn the chicken over and fry, uncovered, until browned all over and an instant-read thermometer registers 165°F when inserted into the thickest part of each piece, 5 to 7 minutes more.

5. Meanwhile, wash and dry the wire rack and baking sheet and set the rack over the sheet near the skillet. Using tongs, transfer the chicken to the rack to drain briefly. Serve warm or at room temperature. —*Pam Anderson*

PER SERVING: 350 CALORIES | 36G PROTEIN | 5G CARB | 19G TOTAL FAT | 5G SAT FAT | 8G MONO FAT | 4.5G POLY FAT | 140MG CHOL | 390MG SODIUM | 0G FIBER

Don't toss out the frying oil. Instead, cool and strain out any crumbs and then refrigerate the oil in a large glass jar for up to 6 months. You can use it two or three more times.

quick chicken parmesan

SERVES 4

Nonstick cooking spray

2¼ oz. (½ cup) unbleached
all-purpose flour

Freshly ground black pepper

2 large eggs

1½ cups panko breadcrumbs

4 thin-sliced boneless, skinless
chicken breast cutlets (about
14 oz.)

Kosher salt

5 Tbs. olive oil

¼ cup freshly grated Parmigiano-
Reggiano (use the small holes
on a box grater)

4 oz. fresh mozzarella,
thinly sliced

1 small yellow onion, chopped

2 medium cloves garlic, finely
chopped

1 14.5-oz. can crushed tomatoes
(preferably Muir Glen® fire-
roasted crushed tomatoes)

¼ cup packed fresh basil,
chopped (½ oz.)

*Crisp chicken cutlets are topped
with two cheeses and a super-
fast tomato sauce in this easy
take on an Italian restaurant
favorite.*

1. Position a rack in the center of
the oven and heat the oven to
425°F. Line a large rimmed baking
sheet with foil and lightly coat the
foil with nonstick cooking spray.

2. Mix the flour and ¼ tsp. pepper
in a wide, shallow dish. In a second wide, shallow dish, lightly beat the eggs with
1 Tbs. water. Put the panko in a third wide, shallow dish. Season the chicken
with salt and coat each piece in the flour, tapping off the excess, then the egg,
and then the panko, pressing the panko to help it adhere.

3. Heat 2 Tbs. of the oil in a 12-inch nonstick skillet over medium-high heat.
Working in two batches, cook the chicken, flipping once, until the crumbs are
golden and the chicken is almost cooked through, 1 to 2 minutes per side, adding 2 Tbs. more oil for the second batch. Transfer the chicken to the prepared
baking sheet. Sprinkle the chicken with the Parmigiano and then top evenly
with the mozzarella. Bake until the cheese is melted and the chicken is cooked
through, 5 to 7 minutes.

4. Meanwhile, wipe the skillet clean and set over medium heat. Pour in the
remaining 1 Tbs. oil and then add the onion and garlic. Cook, stirring often, until
the onion is tender and lightly browned, 3 to 4 minutes. Stir in the tomatoes
and ¼ tsp. salt. Simmer, stirring occasionally, until thickened, 4 to 5 minutes.
Remove from the heat and stir in the basil. Season to taste with salt and pepper. Serve the sauce over the chicken. *—Melissa Gaman*

PER SERVING: 480 CALORIES I 33G PROTEIN I 24G CARB I 28G TOTAL FAT I 8G SAT FAT I
16G MONO FAT I 3G POLY FAT I 160MG CHOL I 610MG SODIUM I 3G FIBER

yogurt-marinated roast chicken

SERVES 4

1　4-lb. chicken

2　cups plain full-fat or low-fat yogurt

3　medium cloves garlic, chopped

1　large shallot, chopped

⅓　cup chopped fresh flat-leaf parsley

¼　cup chopped fresh dill

1　Tbs. cracked black peppercorns

1　tsp. finely grated lemon zest

　　Kosher salt and freshly ground black pepper

Yogurt is mildly acidic, so it's a great tenderizer. Marinate chicken in it overnight for moist and flavorful meat.

1. Put the chicken on a cutting board breast side down. Use poultry shears to cut along both sides of the backbone; remove and discard the backbone. Flip the chicken over and press down gently to break the breastbone and flatten the breast slightly.

2. In a gallon-size zip-top plastic bag, combine the yogurt, garlic, shallot, parsley, dill, cracked peppercorns, lemon zest, and 2 tsp. salt. Add the chicken to the bag and turn to coat well. Set in a bowl and refrigerate overnight.

3. Position a rack in the center of the oven and heat the oven to 450°F. Remove the chicken from the marinade and put it skin side up on a broiler pan or on a rack set inside a rimmed baking sheet. Season both sides well with salt and pepper. Roast the chicken, uncovered, until an instant-read thermometer inserted in the thigh reads 170°F, 45 to 50 minutes. Transfer the chicken to a carving board and loosely tent it with foil; let rest for 10 minutes before carving. —*Samantha Seneviratne*

PER SERVING: 530 CALORIES | 59G PROTEIN | 1G CARB | 30G TOTAL FAT | 8G SAT FAT | 12G MONO FAT | 6G POLY FAT | 190MG CHOL | 520MG SODIUM | 0G FIBER

All about Plain Yogurt

With its natural creaminess and distinctive tang, plain yogurt is a key ingredient for many soups, sauces, and drinks. In India, cooks rely on yogurt for its marvelous ability to marinate meats, keep foods moist during lengthy cooking, make curries creamy, and deliver tangy flavor.

Made from milk that's been fermented and coagulated (thanks to the introduction of good-for-you bacteria), plain yogurt contains no additional sugar or flavorings (though it may contain starch and pectin for texture). It ranges from full-fat to non-fat. Because low-fat yogurts tend to be more acidic than whole-milk, the two can't necessarily be substituted for each other.

How to choose　There are many varieties of plain yogurt available, from those made by giant companies to artisanal ones made in small batches to the super thick and rich Greek yogurts.

Their tanginess ranges, as does their texture (from rich, thick and billowy to soupy and thin), so sample different brands to see which you prefer.

How to prep　It's often a good idea to stir yogurt before using it. Most yogurt will curdle over high heat, so gentle heating is your best bet. Greek yogurt, which is strained, has more fat, so it's your best bet when cooking yogurt with high heat. You can also strain plain yogurt in a sieve lined with cheesecloth, a coffee filter, or a plain white paper towel set over a bowl. Refrigerate and allow the liquid to drain off for 2 hours. One cup of regular yogurt yields about ½ cup of thick, Greek-style yogurt.

How to store　Keep yogurt refrigerated and use by the date stamped on the package.

north indian chicken curry

SERVES 5 OR 6

- **2 Tbs. canola or peanut oil**
- **2 cups finely chopped onions (from 2 medium onions)**
- **1 cup plain nonfat yogurt, at room temperature**
- **1 tsp. cornstarch**
- **1 Tbs. minced fresh ginger**
- **1 Tbs. minced garlic**
- **1 to 2 fresh hot green chiles (preferably serranos), minced**
- **4 lb. bone-in chicken thighs (10 to 12), skin and excess fat removed**
- **1 Tbs. ground coriander**
- **1½ tsp. ground cumin**
- **¾ tsp. ground turmeric**
- **¾ tsp. cayenne**
- **1 28-oz. can whole peeled tomatoes, chopped, with their juices**
- **½ cup chopped fresh cilantro leaves; more for garnish**
- **Kosher salt**
- **1½ tsp. garam masala (look for it in the supermarket spice aisle or make your own using the recipe below)**

Thick gravies and a moderate spice level characterize curries from northern India.

1. Heat the oil in a Dutch oven or a deep, wide saucepan over medium-high heat. Add the onion and stir to coat with the oil. Spread in an even layer and cook for 2 minutes. Stir well, rearrange in an even layer again, and cook for 2 minutes; the onion should have begun to brown at the edges. Reduce the heat to medium and cook, stirring occasionally, until the onion is a rich brown, another 10 to 12 minutes. Lower the heat if necessary so the onion caramelizes but doesn't burn.

2. Meanwhile, put the yogurt in a small bowl, stirring until it's creamy. Add the cornstarch and mix well.

3. Add the ginger, garlic, and chiles to the onion. Cook over medium heat, stirring frequently, for 2 minutes so they meld with the onion. Add all the chicken thighs and cook, stirring occasionally, until they lose their raw color and begin to brown, 5 to 6 minutes. Lower the heat to medium low and add the coriander, cumin, turmeric, and cayenne. Cook for 2 minutes, stirring frequently and scraping the bottom of the pan.

4. Add the tomatoes and their juices, the yogurt mixture, the chopped cilantro, and 2 tsp. salt. Stir well, cover with a tight-fitting lid, and bring to a boil. Lower the heat and simmer until the chicken is cooked through, 20 to 25 minutes. Remove from the heat and taste for salt.

5. To serve, sprinkle on the garam masala, transfer to a serving dish, and garnish with cilantro. *—Suneeta Vaswani*

PER SERVING: 280 CALORIES | 32G PROTEIN | 15G CARB | 11G TOTAL FAT | 2G SAT FAT | 5G MONO FAT | 3G POLY FAT | 115MG CHOL | 990MG SODIUM | 3G FIBER

garam masala

YIELDS 1 TBS.

- **¾ tsp. coriander seeds (or ¾ tsp. ground)**
- **½ tsp. cumin seeds (or ¾ tsp. ground)**
- **10 black peppercorns (or ⅛ tsp. finely ground)**
- **1 1-inch cinnamon stick (or ½ tsp. ground)**
- **4 or 5 green cardamom pods (or ¼ tsp. ground)**
- **4 whole cloves (or ⅛ tsp. ground)**

This recipe makes enough for a few chicken curry recipes; stored in an airtight container, it will keep for up to 4 months.

In a dry skillet, toast the coriander and cumin until aromatic. Put them in a spice grinder or a coffee mill, add all the remaining ingredients, and grind to a powder.

braised mediterranean chicken

1 cup dried Black Mission figs (about 15)

2 3-lb. chickens, rinsed and patted dry

Kosher salt and freshly ground black pepper

¼ cup olive oil

2 medium onions, finely diced (about 2½ cups)

6 cloves garlic, peeled and smashed

1 tsp. ground cumin

¼ tsp. saffron threads, crumbled

2 3-inch cinnamon sticks

14 oz. (1¾ cups) homemade or lower-salt canned chicken broth

2 medium tomatoes (about 1¼ pounds total), cored, seeded, and cut into ½-inch cubes (about 3 cups)

1 cup coarsely chopped fresh flat-leaf parsley; plus another ¼ cup for garnish

1 cup coarsely chopped fresh cilantro

1 Tbs. freshly squeezed lemon juice; more if needed

1 butternut squash (about 1½ pounds), peeled and cut into ¾-inch dice

6 drops Tabasco or other hot sauce

Couscous with Chickpeas and Pistachios (recipe on p. 205)

½ cup pomegranate seeds (from about ½ pomegranate)

Savory Lemon Garnish (recipe facing page)

For this braise, use whole chickens cut into pieces to get the perfect mix of white and dark meat to please all of your guests. If you prefer either all dark or all white meat, you can instead buy about 5 pounds of the chicken parts you like.

1. Soak the dried figs in ½ cup boiling water for 30 minutes.

2. Cut each chicken into 6 or 8 pieces, reserving the backs for a soup or stock. Season the chicken parts with salt and pepper. In a Dutch oven or a large, heavy pot, heat the olive oil over medium-high heat and sauté as many chicken pieces as will fit into the pan without crowding (about a third to a half) on both sides until golden brown. Transfer to a plate and repeat with the remaining chicken; set aside.

3. Put the onion, garlic, cumin, saffron, and cinnamon sticks into the pot and stir, scraping up the browned bits clinging to the bottom. Sauté, stirring often, until the onion is soft and translucent, about 5 minutes. If the mixture begins to dry out or burn, add some of the fig soaking liquid.

4. Add the chicken broth, the figs and their soaking liquid, the tomatoes, 1 cup of the parsley, the cilantro, and the lemon juice, and return the reserved chicken pieces and any accumulated juices to the pot. Bring to a boil and then reduce the heat to low. Partially cover the pot and simmer, skimming any fat or froth as necessary. After 20 minutes, add the squash and nestle it into the stew so that it's completely submerged. Cook until the chicken is cooked through and tender and the squash has softened, about another 20 minutes.

5. Remove the chicken and squash from the broth and set aside. Discard the cinnamon sticks. Increase the heat to medium high and, stirring, reduce the broth by half or until it attains a saucy consistency, 10 to 15 minutes. Return the chicken only to the pot. At this point, you can cool and refrigerate the braise.

6. Before serving, gently reheat the braise over low heat. If the broth is too thick, thin it with a bit of water. When the chicken is hot, stir in the squash and toss gently until warmed through. Add the Tabasco and adjust the salt, pepper, and lemon juice to taste. Mound the couscous on a platter and surround it with the chicken. Drizzle with the sauce. Arrange the squash on top of the couscous. Garnish with the pomegranate seeds, lemon garnish, and the remaining ¼ cup parsley. —*Arlene Jacobs*

PER SERVING: 820 CALORIES I 52G PROTEIN I 70G CARB I 38G TOTAL FAT I 8G SAT FAT I 20G MONO FAT I 7G POLY FAT I 130MG CHOL I 990MG SODIUM I 13G FIBER

savory lemon garnish

2 lemons, scrubbed

1 Tbs. kosher salt

1 Tbs. freshly squeezed
 lemon juice

1. With a vegetable peeler, remove the zest from both lemons in wide strips, taking care not to include any of the white pith. Cut the strips of zest into thinner strips, about ¼ inch wide.

2. Put the zest in a small saucepan of boiling water and boil for 3 minutes. Drain in a strainer and rinse with cold water. Repeat this procedure of boiling (with fresh water) and draining two more times. The zest will be somewhat soft and most of the bitterness will be gone.

3. Drain well and put the zest in a ramekin with the salt and lemon juice. Cover and let the flavors develop overnight in the refrigerator. Rinse gently with water before using.

pan-seared chicken thighs with beer and grainy mustard sauce

SERVES 4

- 8 small bone-in, skin-on chicken thighs (4 to 5 oz. each), trimmed of excess skin and fat

  Kosher salt and freshly ground black pepper

- 2 tsp. vegetable oil

- 2 medium shallots, minced

- 1½ tsp. unbleached all-purpose flour

- 1 cup amber lager, such as Dos Equis Amber

- ½ cup lower-salt chicken broth

- 1½ Tbs. pure maple syrup

- ½ tsp. chopped fresh thyme; more for garnish

- 1 Tbs. whole-grain mustard

- 1 oz. (2 Tbs.) unsalted butter

Maple syrup adds a hint of sweetness that rounds out the mustard's bite in this quick pan sauce. Not in the mood for chicken? Try it with pork chops instead.

1. Position a rack in the lower third of the oven, set a large rimmed baking sheet on the rack, and heat the oven to 475°F. Season the chicken thighs all over with salt and pepper.

2. Heat the oil in a heavy-duty ovenproof 12-inch skillet over medium-high heat until shimmering hot. Swirl to coat the pan bottom. Arrange the chicken in the pan skin side down in a single layer (it will likely be a snug fit), cover with an ovenproof splatter screen (if you have one), and cook until the skin is deep golden-brown, about 7 minutes. Turn the thighs and transfer the skillet and splatter screen, if using, to the oven. Roast until an instant-read thermometer inserted into the thickest part of a thigh registers 170°F, 5 to 8 minutes. Transfer to a plate.

3. Pour off all but 1 Tbs. fat from the skillet. Add the shallot and sauté over medium heat until softened, about 2 minutes. Stir in the flour until combined. Stir in the beer, chicken broth, maple syrup, and thyme. Increase the heat to high and bring to a boil, scraping up any browned bits from the skillet with a wooden spoon. Simmer vigorously until reduced to about 1 cup, about 3 minutes. Remove from the heat and whisk in the mustard, then the butter. Season the sauce to taste with salt and pepper.

4. To serve, dip each chicken thigh in the sauce and turn to coat. Arrange 2 thighs on each of 4 plates, spoon additional sauce over them, and garnish with the thyme. Serve immediately. —*Dawn Yanagihara*

PER SERVING: 420 CALORIES | 32G PROTEIN | 9G CARB | 27G TOTAL FAT | 9G SAT FAT | 10G MONO FAT | 5G POLY FAT | 125MG CHOL | 480MG SODIUM | 1G FIBER

chicken cacciatore with sautéed mushrooms and zucchini

SERVES 4 TO 6

- **6** bone-in, skinless chicken thighs (about 2¼ lb.), large pieces of fat trimmed

  Kosher salt and freshly ground black pepper

- **¼** cup extra-virgin olive oil

- **1** large red onion, finely diced

- **½** red bell pepper, cored, seeded, and diced

- **2** cloves garlic, smashed

- **⅓** cup dry red wine (like Chianti)

- **1** 28-oz. can whole peeled tomatoes

- **2** sprigs fresh thyme, plus 1 tsp. chopped

- **2** small sprigs fresh rosemary

  Pinch of crushed red pepper flakes

- **1** medium zucchini, quartered lengthwise and sliced into ¼-inch pieces

- **½** lb. fresh white mushrooms, cleaned and thinly sliced

- **⅓** cup pitted mixed green and black olives, quartered

- **3** Tbs. chopped fresh flat-leaf parsley; more for garnish

Canned tomatoes give this stew a chunky, full texture, so don't purée the vegetables. Serve the stew over white rice, if you like.

1. Season the chicken well with salt and pepper. Heat 2 Tbs. of the oil in a large Dutch oven or heavy soup pot over medium-high heat. When the oil is hot, add half the thighs and brown them well, 2 to 3 minutes per side. Transfer to a large plate. Brown the remaining thighs and reserve with the rest.

2. Reduce the heat to medium and add the onion, red pepper, and garlic. Season generously with salt and cook, stirring often with a wooden spoon and scraping up any browned bits, until the onion softens and browns, about 12 minutes. Turn the heat to high, add the wine, and cook until it's almost completely reduced, about 2 minutes. Reduce the heat to medium and add the tomatoes and their juices, the thyme sprigs, rosemary, and red pepper flakes. Nestle the chicken into the sauce and add any accumulated juices. Cook, stirring and breaking up the tomatoes with a wooden spoon, for 10 minutes. Adjust the heat to maintain a gentle simmer, cover the pot with the lid slightly ajar, and stew the chicken, turning it occasionally, until it's cooked through (check by slicing through the bottom of one of the thighs to the bone), another 25 to 30 minutes. If you like, discard the thyme sprigs, rosemary, and garlic.

3. When the stew is almost done, heat 1 Tbs. of the oil in a large skillet over high heat. When hot, add the zucchini. Season well with salt and pepper; sauté until the zucchini is tender and lightly browned, 3 to 4 minutes. Transfer to a bowl. Heat the remaining 1 Tbs. oil in the skillet and add the mushrooms. Season with salt and pepper. Cook, tossing occasionally, until soft and lightly browned, 3 to 4 minutes. Add the olives and chopped thyme, return the zucchini to the pan, and toss. Fold the zucchini mixture and the parsley into the stew. Taste for salt and pepper. Serve immediately with a sprinkling of parsley.

—Tony Rosenfeld

PER SERVING: 240 CALORIES | 17G PROTEIN | 14G CARB | 13G TOTAL FAT | 2G SAT FAT | 8G MONO FAT | 2G POLY FAT | 55MG CHOL | 460MG SODIUM | 4G FIBER

classic chicken pot pie

SERVES 6

FOR THE CRUST

- **9** oz. (2 cups) unbleached all-purpose flour
- **¾** tsp. table salt
- **6** oz. (12 Tbs.) cold unsalted butter, cut into 10 pieces

FOR THE FILLING

- **5** Tbs. olive oil
- **2½** lb. boneless, skinless chicken thighs or breasts

  Kosher salt and freshly ground black pepper
- **½** lb. medium fresh cremini mushrooms, quartered (2 cups)
- **1½** cups frozen pearl onions, thawed and patted dry
- **4** medium carrots, peeled and sliced ½ inch thick (1½ cups)
- **3** medium cloves garlic, minced
- **2** oz. (4 Tbs.) unsalted butter, cut into 3 pieces
- **2¼** oz. (½ cup) unbleached all-purpose flour
- **3** cups lower-salt chicken broth
- **1** cup half-and-half or heavy cream
- **1¾** lb. red potatoes, cut into ½-inch dice (5 cups)
- **1** cup frozen petite peas, thawed
- **¼** cup dry sherry
- **¼** cup chopped fresh flat-leaf parsley
- **2** Tbs. chopped fresh thyme
- **1½** Tbs. Dijon mustard

You can assemble the pot pies and refrigerate them, covered, for up to 1 day before baking and serving.

MAKE THE CRUST

1. Put the flour and salt in a food processor and pulse to blend. Add the butter and pulse until the butter pieces are the size of peas, 10 to 12 pulses. Drizzle 3 Tbs. cold water over the mixture. Pulse until the dough forms moist crumbs that are just beginning to clump together, 8 or 9 pulses more.

2. Turn the crumbs onto a large piece of plastic wrap and gather into a pile. With the heel of your hand, gently smear the dough away from you until the crumbs come together (two or three smears should do it). Shape the dough into a 4-inch square, wrap tightly in the plastic, and refrigerate until firm, at least 2 hours or up to 2 days. (The dough can also be frozen for up to 1 month. Thaw in the refrigerator overnight or at room temperature for about 1 hour before rolling.)

MAKE THE FILLING

1. Heat 2 Tbs. of the oil in a 7- to 8-quart Dutch oven over medium-high heat until very hot. Generously season the chicken with salt and pepper. Working in two batches, brown the chicken well on both sides, 4 to 5 minutes per side, adding 1 Tbs. oil with the second batch. Transfer the chicken to a cutting board and cut into ¾- to 1-inch pieces (it's fine if the chicken isn't fully cooked; it will finish cooking later). Put the chicken in a large bowl.

2. Add 1 Tbs. oil to the pot and heat over medium-high heat until hot. Add the mushrooms. Cook without stirring for 1 minute. Continue cooking, stirring occasionally, until well browned, 3 to 4 minutes. Transfer the mushrooms to the bowl of chicken.

3. Reduce the heat to medium and add the remaining 1 Tbs. oil and then the onions and carrots to the pot. Cook, stirring occasionally, until the edges are browned, 8 to 9 minutes. Add the garlic and stir constantly until fragrant, about 30 seconds more. Scrape the vegetables into the bowl of chicken and mushrooms.

4. Melt the butter in the same pot over low heat. Add the flour and cook, whisking constantly, until the texture, which will be clumpy at first, loosens and smooths out, about 4 minutes. Slowly whisk in the chicken broth and half-and-half. Bring to a boil over medium-high heat, whisking to scrape up any browned bits from the bottom of the pan. Reduce the heat to low and add the potatoes, chicken, and vegetables (and any accumulated juice), and a generous pinch each of salt and pepper. Partially cover the pot and simmer gently (adjusting the heat as necessary), stirring occasionally, until the potatoes and carrots are just tender, 15 to 18 minutes. Stir in the peas, sherry, parsley, thyme, and mustard. Season to taste with salt and pepper. (At this point, the filling can be cooled and refrigerated for up to 8 hours.)

ASSEMBLE THE POT PIES

1. Distribute the filling evenly among 6 ovenproof bowls or ramekins that are 2 to 3 inches deep and hold at least 2 cups.

2. Let the dough soften slightly at room temperature, about 20 minutes. On a lightly floured surface, roll the dough into a ⅛-inch-thick rectangle. With a round cookie cutter (or using a plate as a guide), cut 6 dough circles that are slightly wider than the inner diameter of the bowls (reroll the scraps if necessary). Cut one small X in the center of each circle.

3. Top each bowl of stew with a dough round. With your fingertips, gently press the dough down into the edge of the stew, so that it flares up the sides of the bowl.

BAKE THE POT PIES
Position a rack in the center of the oven and heat the oven to 425°F. Put the pot pies on a foil-lined rimmed baking sheet. Bake until the filling is bubbling and the crust is deep golden-brown, about 45 minutes. Cool on a rack for 20 to 30 minutes before serving. *—Abigail Johnson Dodge*

PER SERVING: 860 CALORIES | 45G PROTEIN | 64G CARB | 47G TOTAL FAT | 20G SAT FAT | 19G MONO FAT | 4.5G POLY FAT | 195MG CHOL | 770MG SODIUM | 7G FIBER

roasted turkey breast, porchetta style

SERVES 7 TO 9

- **1 tsp. coriander seeds**
- **1 tsp. fennel seeds**
- **1 Tbs. chopped fresh rosemary**
- **2 tsp. chopped fresh sage**
- **3 medium cloves garlic**
- **Kosher salt and freshly ground black pepper**
- **3 Tbs. olive oil**
- **1 whole skin-on turkey breast (5 to 7 lb.), boned, or 2 boneless, skin-on turkey breast halves (2 to 3 lb. each)**
- **8 pancetta slices, ⅛ in. thick, unrolled into strips, or 8 strips thick-cut bacon**

This centerpiece dish starts with a boned breast (do this yourself or ask the butcher to do it for you) or two boneless breast halves. It's rubbed with a spice paste and topped with pancetta for a clever take on porchetta, a traditional Italian preparation.

1. In a large mortar, pound the coriander and fennel seeds with a pestle to form a coarse powder. Add the rosemary and sage and pound to crush and bruise the herbs. Add the garlic and 1 Tbs. salt and pound until a paste begins to form. Stir in 2 tsp. pepper and 2 Tbs. of the olive oil and set aside.

2. Pat the turkey breast dry with a paper towel and lay it skin side down on a work surface. Rub half the spice paste over the meat. Turn the turkey over and carefully separate the skin from the meat without tearing the skin. Rub the remaining spice paste under the skin. Re-form the breast and tie with 4 to 6 loops of butcher's twine to make a roll. (If you're using boneless halves, season them, lay them on top of each other skin side out, and tie them together.) Wrap in plastic and refrigerate for at least 2 hours and up to 24 hours.

3. Position a rack in the center of the oven and heat the oven to 350°F.

4. Heat the remaining 1 Tbs. oil in a 12-inch skillet over medium heat. Add the turkey breast and cook until golden-brown on all sides, about 5 minutes total. Transfer the breast seam side down to a roasting pan fitted with a rack. Crisscross the pancetta over the top of the breast. Roast until the internal temperature reaches 165°F on an instant-read thermometer, 1¼ to 1½ hours. Let the turkey breast rest for 15 to 20 minutes.

5. Remove the pancetta and chop or crumble it. Remove the strings from the turkey, slice into ¼-inch slices, and serve, sprinkled with the pancetta.
—*Bruce Aidells*

PER SERVING: 480 CALORIES | 56G PROTEIN | 1G CARB | 26G TOTAL FAT | 7G SAT FAT | 11G MONO FAT | 4.5G POLY FAT | 155MG CHOL | 960MG SODIUM | 0G FIBER

What Is Porchetta?

Porchetta (pronounced por-KETT-ah) refers to an Italian preparation of a crisp-skinned whole roasted pig. The pig is boned, rubbed with herbs and spices, filled with strips of pork loin, and roasted. A simplified version is often made by wrapping a skin-on pork belly around herb-rubbed pork loin.

turkey thighs stuffed with porcini, sausage & artichoke hearts

SERVES 6

FOR THE STUFFING

- ¾ oz. dried porcini mushrooms (about ½ cup)
- 1 Tbs. olive oil
- ¼ lb. sweet Italian sausage, casings removed (1 link)
- 1 cup finely chopped yellow onion
- 2 tsp. minced garlic
- ½ cup coarsely chopped frozen artichoke hearts (no need to thaw)
- ½ tsp. chopped fresh thyme
- ½ tsp. chopped fresh rosemary
- ½ cup coarse breadcrumbs, made from day-old bread
- ¼ cup freshly grated Parmigiano-Reggiano
- Kosher salt and freshly ground black pepper
- 1 large egg, lightly beaten

FOR THE THIGHS

- 3 turkey thighs (14 to 18 oz. each), boned
- Kosher salt and freshly ground black pepper
- 2 Tbs. extra-virgin olive oil

Buy skin-on, bone-in thighs at the grocery store and remove the bones yourself—it's as easy as boning chicken thighs.

MAKE THE STUFFING

1. Put the porcini in a bowl and cover with boiling water. Soak until soft, about 30 minutes. With a slotted spoon, remove the mushrooms from the liquid and chop finely. Save the liquid for another use or discard.

2. Heat the olive oil in a heavy-duty 10-inch skillet over medium heat. Add the sausage and cook, using the side of a metal spoon or fork to break the meat into small pieces, until browned, about 5 minutes. Add the onion and garlic and cook, stirring, until the vegetables are soft and translucent, about 3 minutes. Stir in the chopped porcini, artichokes, thyme, and rosemary and cook for 2 minutes more. Transfer the sausage mixture to a large bowl and stir in the breadcrumbs and the Parmigiano. Season to taste with salt and pepper, and then stir in the egg. Spread the mixture on a plate and chill in the freezer for 15 to 20 minutes.

STUFF AND BAKE THE TURKEY THIGHS

1. Position a rack in the center of the oven and heat the oven to 350°F.

2. Lightly season the boned thighs with salt and pepper. Spoon ½ to ⅔ cup of the stuffing into the empty cavity of one of the turkey thighs and spread the stuffing with the back of a spoon to fill the cavity completely. Repeat with the other thighs. Roll each thigh into a roughly cylindrical shape.

3. Tie each stuffed thigh with 2 to 4 loops of twine to secure. (It's OK if some of the stuffing pokes out at the ends, because the egg holds the stuffing together.) Brush the skin side of the thighs with the olive oil. Lay the thighs seam side down in a small roasting pan or heavy-duty rimmed baking sheet and roast for 30 minutes. Brush the thighs with the pan drippings and continue to roast until the internal temperature reaches 165°F, 15 to 30 minutes more. Remove the strings and transfer the thighs to a warm platter. Let rest for 10 minutes and then cut into ½-inch-thick slices and serve. *—Bruce Aidells*

PER SERVING: 270 CALORIES | 19G PROTEIN | 8G CARB | 17G TOTAL FAT | 4G SAT FAT | 8G MONO FAT | 2.5G POLY FAT | 105MG CHOL | 640MG SODIUM | 2G FIBER

braised duck legs with figs, star anise & winter squash

SERVES 6

- 6   12- to 16-oz. fresh duck legs, trimmed of excess fat

  Kosher salt and freshly ground black pepper

- 1   Tbs. canola oil

- 4   medium carrots, cut into 1½-inch pieces

- 2   medium stalks celery, cut into 1½-inch pieces

- 1   medium yellow onion, cut into 1½-inch pieces

- 6   medium cloves garlic, minced

- 1   lb. dried figs, stemmed and thinly sliced (about 3 cups)

- 4   sprigs fresh thyme

- 2   star anise

- 1   2½- to 3-lb. winter squash (such as red kuri, buttercup, or kabocha), peeled, seeded, and cut into 1½-inch cubes

- 6   to 8 cups lower-salt chicken broth

- 1   Tbs. Champagne vinegar

- 2   Tbs. finely chopped fresh flat-leaf parsley

The duck becomes meltingly tender as it braises, soaking up all of the rich flavors of the sauce. Steamed brown jasmine rice is the perfect accompaniment. Save any leftover duck fat to make roasted potatoes or French fries.

1. Season the duck legs with 1 Tbs. salt and 1½ tsp. pepper. Heat the oil in an 8-quart Dutch oven or other heavy-duty pot over medium-high heat for 2 minutes. Working in 2 batches, put the duck legs in the pot skin side down and cook until the skin is very well browned and crisp, about 10 minutes (reduce the heat to medium if they brown too fast). Use tongs to transfer them to a large plate. Drain off all but 2 Tbs. of the fat from the pot (save the fat for another use).

2. Add the carrots, celery, onion, and garlic to the pot and cook over medium heat, stirring often, until the garlic is just starting to turn golden-brown, 3 to 4 minutes. Stir in the figs, thyme, and star anise, and then stir in the squash. Arrange the duck legs skin side up on top of the vegetables and add enough chicken broth to cover the duck by about ½ inch, up to 8 cups—it's fine if a few of the legs on top aren't completely submerged. Increase the heat to high and bring the liquid to a boil. Add 1 tsp. salt and ½ tsp. pepper, reduce the heat to low, cover the pot, and cook until fork-tender, 1½ to 2 hours. Turn off the heat and let the duck rest in the juice for 15 to 30 minutes; then skim off and discard the fat from the surface of the sauce.

3. With a slotted spoon, distribute the vegetables among 6 plates or mound them on a platter. Top with the duck legs. Stir the vinegar into the sauce in the pot, and then drizzle the sauce over each serving, or serve the sauce on the side (you won't need it all). Garnish with chopped parsley and serve.
—*Koren Grieveson*

PER SERVING: 660 CALORIES | 48G PROTEIN | 75G CARB | 21G TOTAL FAT | 5G SAT FAT | 10G MONO FAT | 4G POLY FAT | 165MG CHOL | 1,030MG SODIUM | 12G FIBER

red-wine-braised brisket with cremini, carrots & thyme

SERVES 12 (OR 4 TO 6 WITH LEFTOVERS)

2 Tbs. sweet paprika

Kosher salt and freshly ground black pepper

8½ to 9 lb. beef brisket (whole brisket or flat and/or point halves), untrimmed of fat

5 Tbs. vegetable oil

6 large yellow onions, diced (about 12 cups)

3 or 4 cloves garlic, thinly sliced

1 15-oz. can tomato purée

1 cup dry red wine

4 large sprigs fresh thyme

8 large carrots, cut into 2-inch pieces

10 oz. fresh cremini or white mushrooms, quartered if large, halved if small (3 cups)

To get a jump-start on this recipe, you can season the brisket up to 1 day ahead.

1. In a small bowl, combine the paprika, 1 Tbs. salt, and 1 Tbs. pepper. Rub the mixture all over the brisket. Let rest at room temperature for 2 hours or cover and refrigerate overnight (bring the meat to room temperature before cooking).

2. Position a rack in the center of the oven and heat the oven to 350°F.

3. Meanwhile, heat the oil in a large pot over medium heat. Add the onion and garlic and cook, stirring occasionally, until very soft and pale gold, 15 to 20 minutes. Transfer the onion to a large heavy-duty roasting pan and spread in an even layer. Set the brisket fat side up on the onion (it's OK if the pieces overlap), cover tightly with heavy-duty foil (or a double layer of regular foil), and braise in the oven for 1 hour. As the brisket cooks, it will give off quite a bit of liquid.

4. Pour the tomato purée and wine around the brisket and add the thyme sprigs. Cover and continue to braise the meat for another 2½ hours.

5. Add the carrots and mushrooms and continue to braise, covered, until the meat is fork-tender, about 1 hour more.

6. Transfer the meat to a cutting board and trim the fat. If using a whole brisket or a point half, separate the two layers of meat and trim the fat. With a slotted spoon, transfer the vegetables to a serving bowl.

7. Skim the excess fat from the pan juices, strain 2 cups of the juices, and bring to a boil in a small saucepan over medium-high heat. Boil until reduced to about 1 cup; the sauce should be rich and flavorful. Season to taste with salt and pepper.

8. Slice as much brisket across the grain as you need for the meal and serve with the vegetables and reduced sauce. Wrap the leftover brisket, vegetables, and juices separately. Leftovers will keep in the fridge for 3 to 4 days, or in the freezer for up to 2 months. —*Joyce Goldstein*

PER SERVING: 440 CALORIES | 53G PROTEIN | 17G CARB | 15G TOTAL FAT | 4G SAT FAT | 6G MONO FAT | 3G POLY FAT | 90MG CHOL | 540MG SODIUM | 4G FIBER

braised beef short ribs with salsa verde and feta

SERVES 6

FOR THE SHORT RIBS

- **6** large beef short ribs (14 to 16 oz. each)
- **1** Tbs. fresh thyme leaves, plus 4 whole sprigs
- Freshly ground black pepper
- Kosher salt
- **3** Tbs. extra-virgin olive oil
- **1** medium yellow onion, finely chopped
- **1** medium carrot, finely chopped
- **1** medium stalk celery, finely chopped
- **2** dried bay leaves
- **1½** cups ruby port
- **2** Tbs. balsamic vinegar
- **2½** cups hearty red wine (like Zinfandel or Côtes du Rhône)
- **6** cups homemade or lower-salt canned beef broth
- **4** sprigs fresh flat-leaf parsley

FOR THE SALSA VERDE

- **1** cup coarsely chopped fresh flat-leaf parsley
- **¼** cup coarsely chopped fresh mint
- **1** tsp. finely chopped fresh marjoram or oregano
- **1** small clove garlic, chopped
- **1** anchovy fillet (preferably salt-packed), rinsed
- **¾** cup extra-virgin olive oil
- **1** Tbs. capers, drained and rinsed
- Kosher salt and freshly ground black pepper
- **3** oz. feta (preferably French), crumbled (½ cup)

This recipe for braised short ribs features a surprisingly delicious twist—a fresh, feta-spiked salsa verde as topping. Round out the meal with a simple arugula salad and warm bread.

SEASON THE RIBS

1. Put the short ribs in a large mixing bowl and rub them with the thyme leaves and 1 Tbs. black pepper. Cover the bowl with plastic wrap and refrigerate overnight.

2. Remove the ribs from the refrigerator and let sit at room temperature for 30 minutes. Rub 1 Tbs. salt all over the ribs and set them aside for another 30 minutes.

BRAISE THE RIBS

1. Position a rack in the center of the oven and heat the oven to 325°F.

2. Heat an 8-quart Dutch oven or other heavy-duty pot over high heat for 3 minutes. Pour in the olive oil, and when it just begins to smoke (after about 1 minute), add as many short ribs as will fit in the pan in a single layer. Sear on the three meaty sides until browned, about 3 minutes per side. Transfer the browned short ribs bone side up to a large bowl. Repeat with the remaining short ribs, reducing the heat to medium high if necessary.

3. Reduce the heat to medium, add the onion, carrot, celery, bay leaves, and thyme sprigs to the pan and cook, stirring to scrape up the browned bits from the bottom of the pan, until the vegetables begin to brown around the edges, 6 to 8 minutes. Add the port and balsamic vinegar and then the red wine. Increase the heat to high and bring to a boil. Reduce the heat to medium high and simmer until the liquid is reduced by half, about 10 minutes.

4. Add the beef broth and return to a boil. Return the short ribs and any accumulated juice to the pot, making sure the vegetables are in the broth and not on the short ribs (the short ribs should be nearly submerged). Tuck the parsley sprigs in around the meat, seal the top of the pot with aluminum foil, and cover with the lid. Put the pot in the oven and braise until the meat falls away from the bone when poked with a paring knife, about 3 hours. Remove the short ribs from the oven and set aside for 30 minutes.

MAKE THE SALSA VERDE

1. While the short ribs are resting, combine the parsley, mint, and marjoram or oregano in a medium bowl and toss. Transfer about half of the herbs to a food processor, add the garlic, and pulse until very finely chopped, about five 1-second pulses. Add the remaining herbs and the anchovy and pulse about 3 more times to combine. While pulsing, pour about half of the olive oil into the food processor.

2. Put the capers in a medium bowl and use a fork to mash them. Using a rubber spatula, scrape the sauce from the food processor over the capers. Whisk in the remaining olive oil, 1 tsp. salt, and ¼ tsp. pepper, and then add the feta. Season to taste with salt and pepper.

FINISH AND SERVE

1. Use tongs to transfer the short ribs from the pot to a large platter. Cover the platter with foil. Strain the braising liquid through a fine sieve into a large bowl, pressing on the vegetables with the back of a ladle to extract as much liquid as possible. Skim the fat off the top and pour the liquid back into the braising pot. Bring to a simmer over medium-high heat and cook until the broth is reduced slightly, 10 to 15 minutes.

2. Divide the short ribs among 6 bowls. Moisten with some braising liquid, drizzle with the feta salsa verde, and serve. —*Suzanne Goin*

PER SERVING: 940 CALORIES | 49G PROTEIN | 18G CARB | 59G TOTAL FAT | 16G SAT FAT | 35G MONO FAT | 5G POLY FAT | 115MG CHOL | 1,390MG SODIUM | 2G FIBER

All about Beef Short Ribs

Short ribs are the meaty ends of the beef ribs from the hardworking chest and front shoulders of cattle. Short ribs are best cooked using slow, moist-heat methods like braising. What makes this often-overlooked cut so remarkable is its dense, well-marbled meat and its connective tissue, which softens as it cooks to help create a velvety, deeply flavored sauce.

The meatiest short ribs with the best ratio of fat and bone come from the chuck—the labels might say beef chuck short ribs or arm short ribs. Look for well-marbled, meaty ribs, firmly attached to the bone and without a huge amount of surface fat. You may find short ribs cut two ways: English style, which are 2- to 4-inch segments with one section of rib bone, or flanken style, which are 1½- to 2-inch strips containing multiple bone segments. For most recipes, they can be used interchangeably, though English style offers thicker, meatier bites. Avoid boneless short ribs; meat cooked on the bone will provide the best flavor.

pecan-crusted skirt steak

SERVES 4

- 1½ tsp. olive oil
- 1½ lb. skirt steak, trimmed
- Kosher salt and freshly ground black pepper
- ¾ cup pecan pieces
- 2 Tbs. cold butter, cut into small pieces
- 2 tsp. honey
- 1½ tsp. roughly chopped fresh rosemary

A blend of chopped pecans, honey, butter, and rosemary give broiled skirt steak a crunchy, toasty crust.

1. Position an oven rack about 6 inches from the broiler and heat the broiler on high.

2. Line a large rimmed baking sheet with foil and grease the foil with the oil. If necessary, cut the steak crosswise into pieces 8 to 10 inches long. Arrange the steak on the baking sheet in a single layer and season with 1 tsp. salt and ¼ tsp. pepper. Put the pecans, butter, honey, rosemary, 1 tsp. salt, and ¼ tsp. pepper in a food processor and pulse until well combined and the pecans are finely chopped.

3. Broil the steak until lightly browned, 3 to 4 minutes. Flip it and broil until it's cooked nearly to your liking, about 3 minutes more for medium rare. Spread the pecan mixture over the steak, patting the mixture with the back of a spoon to help it adhere. Continue broiling until the pecan coating is toasted and fragrant, 1 to 2 minutes. Set the steak aside to rest for 5 minutes.

4. Thinly slice the steak against the grain and transfer to plates. If the pecan coating falls off the steak as you're slicing it, spoon it over the top.

—Liz Pearson

PER SERVING: 510 CALORIES | 36G PROTEIN | 6G CARB | 39G TOTAL FAT | 11G SAT FAT | 20G MONO FAT | 6G POLY FAT | 100MG CHOL | 680MG SODIUM | 2G FIBER

bacon-wrapped meatloaf

SERVES 8

The bacon wrapped around the meatloaf increases both flavor and moisture.

- **4** oz. fresh cremini (baby bella) or white mushrooms, cleaned and finely chopped (1⅓ cups)
- **½** cup minced yellow onion
- **3** Tbs. dry sherry
- **1** Tbs. minced garlic

  Kosher salt and freshly ground black pepper
- **2** oz. day-old rustic or dense white bread, torn into about ½-inch pieces (1½ cups)
- **¼** cup whole milk
- **1** large egg, lightly beaten
- **1** lb. ground beef (85% lean)
- **½** lb. ground veal
- **½** lb. ground pork
- **2** Tbs. light or dark brown sugar
- **1** Tbs. Worcestershire sauce
- **8** slices center-cut bacon

  Mushroom Gravy (recipe below)

1. Position a rack in the center of the oven and heat the oven to 350°F.

2. In a medium bowl, toss the mushrooms with the onion, sherry, garlic, 1½ tsp. salt, and ½ tsp. pepper.

3. In a large mixing bowl, combine the bread, milk, and egg. Stir well, lightly mashing the bread until most of the liquid is absorbed. Add the beef, veal, pork, brown sugar, Worcestershire, and the onion-mushroom mixture. Using a large, sturdy wooden spoon or your hands, gently mix just until all the ingredients are blended; you may need to push the meat against the side of the bowl to get the pieces to break up.

4. Put the meat mixture in a 9x13-inch metal baking pan. Shape the mixture into a rectangular loaf about 10x4 inches. Wrap the strips of bacon around the loaf crosswise, overlapping them slightly and tucking the ends securely under the loaf. Pat the loaf back into shape if necessary. You can form the meatloaf up to 8 hours ahead and refrigerate until ready to bake.

5. Bake until an instant-read thermometer inserted into the center of the loaf reads 160°F, 60 to 70 minutes. Take the meatloaf out of the oven and position the oven rack about 6 inches from the broiling element. Heat the broiler to high. Broil the meatloaf until the bacon is brown and crisp, about 3 minutes. Let the loaf rest at room temperature for at least 10 minutes.

6. Use two flat spatulas to transfer the meatloaf to a serving platter. Slice and serve with the mushroom gravy. —*Jessica Bard*

PER SERVING: 340 CALORIES | 26G PROTEIN | 15G CARB | 19G TOTAL FAT | 6G SAT FAT | 9G MONO FAT | 1.5G POLY FAT | 105MG CHOL | 610MG SODIUM | 1G FIBER

mushroom gravy

SERVES 8

This gravy can be made up to 1 day ahead and reheated over medium-low heat.

- **1** cup lower-salt beef or chicken broth; more as needed
- **2** Tbs. extra-virgin olive oil
- **2** slices center-cut bacon, minced
- **6** oz. fresh cremini (baby bella) or white mushrooms, cleaned and sliced about ⅛ inch thick (2 packed cups)
- **½** cup minced yellow onion

  Kosher salt and freshly ground black pepper
- **3** Tbs. dry sherry
- **3** Tbs. unbleached all-purpose flour

1. Combine the broth with 1 cup of hot water. Heat the oil in a 12-inch skillet over medium-high heat. Add the bacon and cook, stirring to break apart the pieces, until just starting to crisp, 1 to 2 minutes. Add the mushrooms, onion, ½ tsp. salt, and ½ tsp. pepper. Cook, stirring often, until the mushrooms have cooked through and start to brown the bottom of the pan, 5 to 8 minutes.

2. Add the sherry and stir to release the browned bits from the bottom of the pan, about 1 minute. Sprinkle in the flour and stir constantly until the mixture has browned and is slightly dry and crumbly, about 30 seconds.

3. Whisk in half of the broth mixture and continue whisking until the liquid is absorbed into the flour, about 30 seconds. Whisk in the remaining broth mixture and bring the gravy to a boil. Reduce the heat and simmer, stirring occasionally, until thickened, 5 to 10 minutes.

4. Season to taste with salt and pepper and thin with water or broth if necessary. Transfer to a small saucepan, cover, and keep warm. Reheat the gravy if necessary before serving.

meatloaf with fresh scallions and herbs

SERVES 8

- 1 Tbs. plus 1 tsp. vegetable oil; more as needed
- 1 cup finely chopped yellow onion
- ¾ lb. ground beef (80% lean)
- ½ lb. ground veal
- ½ lb. ground pork
- 1 tsp. sweet paprika, preferably Hungarian

  Kosher salt and freshly ground black pepper
- 3 large eggs, lightly beaten; 1 more if needed
- 1½ cups homemade dry bread-crumbs or panko bread-crumbs; more if needed
- 1 cup thinly sliced scallions (green and white parts)
- 1 cup sour cream
- ¾ cup chopped fresh flat-leaf parsley
- ⅔ cup ketchup
- ⅓ cup chopped fresh tarragon
- 1 tsp. lightly chopped fresh thyme
- 2 cloves garlic, finely chopped

You can shape the raw meatloaf up to 1 day ahead. Refrigerate it overnight to meld the flavors for a tastier meatloaf the next day.

1. Position a rack in the center of the oven and heat the oven to 350°F.

2. Heat 1 Tbs. of the oil in a 10-inch skillet over medium heat. When hot, add the onion and cook, stirring frequently, until softened, 3 to 5 minutes. Transfer to a plate to cool.

3. Put the ground beef, veal, and pork in a large bowl and gently knead them with your hands until just combined. Add the cooled onion, paprika, 2 tsp. salt, and 1 tsp. pepper and gently knead to blend. Add the remaining ingredients (except for the remaining vegetable oil) and gently knead with your hands or stir with a large spoon until just incorporated.

4. Wipe out the skillet and heat the remaining 1 tsp. oil over medium heat. When the oil is hot, add a quarter-size piece of the meat and cook, turning halfway through cooking, until the meat is cooked through, about 1 minute on each side. Cool briefly and taste. If it's too moist to hold together, add up to ½ cup more breadcrumbs to the meat mixture; if it's too dry, add an extra egg. If necessary, add salt and pepper. Repeat cooking quarter-size pieces of the meat until you're satisfied with the flavor and consistency.

5. On a parchment-lined rimmed baking sheet, mold the meat mixture into a 9x5-inch loaf. Bake until the meat is firm to the touch and has an internal temperature of 160°F, about 1 hour. Allow the meatloaf to rest for 15 to 20 minutes before serving —*Alexandra Guarnaschelli*

PER SERVING: 390 CALORIES | 24G PROTEIN | 25G CARB | 22G TOTAL FAT | 9G SAT FAT | 8G MONO FAT | 2.5G POLY FAT | 155MG CHOL | 750MG SODIUM | 2G FIBER

glazed meatloaf with peppers and warm spices

YIELDS 2 MEATLOAVES, EACH SERVING 8

FOR THE MEATLOAVES

- 3 Tbs. unsalted butter
- ½ cup fresh breadcrumbs
- 1 large red onion, thinly sliced (about 2 cups)
- 3 Tbs. canola oil
- Kosher salt
- 1 piece (1 inch) fresh ginger, peeled and minced
- 1 small green bell pepper, finely diced
- 4 cloves garlic, minced
- 1 Tbs. ground coriander
- 1 tsp. ground cumin
- 1 tsp. cracked black pepper
- 1 lb. fresh white mushrooms, finely diced or finely chopped in a food processor
- ½ tsp. cayenne
- 1 tsp. garam masala
- 2 lb. ground beef (80% lean)
- 1 lb. ground pork
- 1 lb. ground turkey
- 1 red bell pepper, finely chopped
- ¼ cup fresh cilantro, finely chopped
- 3 large eggs
- ½ cup ketchup
- 2 oz. (1½ cups) finely grated Parmigiano-Reggiano
- ½ tsp. sweet or hot paprika, preferably Hungarian

FOR THE GLAZE

- 1 cup ketchup
- 1 tsp. Worcestershire sauce
- 2 tsp. ground coriander
- 1 tsp. ground cumin
- 1 tsp. cracked black pepper
- ½ tsp. cayenne

If you plan to freeze one of the meatloaves from this recipe, you'll need to make only a half-recipe of the glaze. To freeze, shape a loaf on its own parchment-lined rimmed baking sheet. Cover loosely with plastic and freeze until firm. Wrap in the parchment and then wrap tightly in foil. It will keep for 1 month. To bake, unwrap the frozen loaf, transfer to a rimmed baking sheet lined with fresh parchment, and thaw completely overnight in the refrigerator. Bake as directed.

MAKE THE MEATLOAVES

1. Melt the butter in a 12-inch skillet over medium-high heat. Add the breadcrumbs and toast, stirring constantly, until deeply browned, about 3 minutes. Transfer to a large bowl to cool. Wipe the skillet clean.

2. In the skillet, combine the onion, oil, and 2 tsp. salt. Cook over medium heat, stirring frequently with a wooden spoon, until the onion is soft and just starting to brown, 4 to 5 minutes. Stir in the ginger and cook, stirring constantly, until fragrant, about 30 seconds. Add the green bell pepper and garlic and cook until the garlic is fragrant, about 1 minute. Stir in the coriander, cumin, and cracked pepper and cook, stirring and scraping the bottom of the skillet for 1 minute to diffuse the spices.

3. Add the mushrooms and cook, stirring often, until they release their liquid and the liquid has evaporated, 6 to 8 minutes. Stir in the cayenne and cook for 30 seconds. Stir in the garam masala, turn off the heat, and set aside to cool.

4. Position a rack in the center of the oven and heat the oven to 300°F. Add the beef, pork, turkey, red bell pepper, cilantro, eggs, ketchup, Parmigiano, and paprika to the bowl with the breadcrumbs and knead gently until everything is incorporated. Add the cooled mushroom mixture and knead gently until combined. Divide the mixture in half. On a parchment-lined rimmed baking sheet, mold the meat into two 9x5-inch loaves and bake for 1 hour.

MAKE THE GLAZE

While the meatloaves bake, whisk the glaze ingredients in a small bowl. After 1 hour of baking, remove the meatloaves from the oven. Evenly brush the glaze over each meatloaf and continue to bake until an instant-read thermometer reads 165°F when inserted into the center of a meatloaf, 30 to 40 minutes more. Let the meatloaves cool for 15 minutes before moving to a platter or cutting board with a large spatula (leave the juices and fat behind). Slice and serve. *—Suvir Saran*

PER SERVING: 300 CALORIES | 24G PROTEIN | 10G CARB | 19G TOTAL FAT | 7G SAT FAT | 7G MONO FAT | 1.5G POLY FAT | 115MG CHOL | 490MG SODIUM | 1G FIBER

slow-cooker osso buco

SERVES 4

- ½ cup unbleached all-purpose flour
- 4 1½- to 2-inch-thick veal shanks (about 2½ lb.)
- Kosher salt and freshly ground black pepper
- 2 Tbs. unsalted butter
- 1 cup dry white wine
- 1 14½-oz. can diced tomatoes
- ¾ cup lower-salt chicken broth
- 1 small red onion, chopped (1½ cups)
- 1 medium carrot, peeled and cut into ¼-inch-thick rounds (½ cup)
- 1 stalk celery, chopped (½ cup)
- 5 sprigs fresh thyme
- 3 Tbs. finely chopped fresh flat-leaf parsley
- 1 Tbs. finely grated lemon zest
- 1 large clove garlic, minced (1 tsp.)

There are two tricks to this recipe: browning the veal shanks before they go into the slow cooker and reducing the sauce before serving. The result is an osso buco you'd be hard-pressed to distinguish from the labor-intensive classic.

1. Put the flour in a wide, shallow dish. Season the veal shanks all over with salt and pepper and dredge in the flour; shake off the excess flour.

2. Heat a 12-inch skillet over medium heat. Add the butter, and when it foams, add the shanks to the skillet. Cook until golden, turning once, about 10 minutes. Transfer the shanks to a slow cooker.

3. Add the wine to the skillet. Scrape up any browned bits from the bottom of the skillet and pour the contents of the skillet into the slow cooker. Add the tomatoes and their juices, chicken broth, onion, carrot, celery, and thyme. Cover and cook on low heat for 6 to 8 hours—the meat will be very tender and almost falling off the bone.

4. Transfer the shanks to a platter and cover with foil to keep warm. Pour the sauce from the slow cooker into a large skillet. Simmer over medium heat until reduced to about 2 cups, 10 to 15 minutes. Season to taste with salt and pepper.

5. Meanwhile, in a small bowl, combine the parsley, lemon zest, and garlic to make a gremolata. Serve the veal shanks topped with the sauce and the gremolata. —*Allison Fishman*

PER SERVING: 460 CALORIES | 46G PROTEIN | 15G CARB | 19G TOTAL FAT | 9G SAT FAT | 7G MONO FAT | 1G POLY FAT | 205MG CHOL | 710MG SODIUM | 1G FIBER

beef ragù chiantigiana

YIELDS ABOUT 8 CUPS, ENOUGH
FOR ABOUT 1 LB. OF PASTA;
SERVES 8

- **4** lb. beef chuck or 4 lb. packaged ground chuck
- **2** to 3 Tbs. olive oil; more as needed
- **1** tsp. salt
  Freshly ground black pepper
- **1** large carrot, finely chopped
- **2** stalks celery, finely chopped
- **1** large yellow onion, finely chopped
- **1** Tbs. minced garlic
- **2** tsp. chopped fresh rosemary
- **2** Tbs. chopped fresh sage
- **2** tsp. dried marjoram
- **2** cups Chianti or other light-bodied dry red wine
- **2** cups canned puréed tomatoes
- **2** cups homemade or lower-salt canned beef stock
  Unsalted butter, ½ Tbs. per serving
- **1** lb. pasta, cooked al dente
  Freshly grated Parmesan (optional)

This recipe is easily halved, but even if you're cooking for fewer people, you might as well make a whole batch and freeze the leftover sauce.

1. If using beef chuck, cut it into 1-inch chunks, leaving on some of the fat. In a food processor, pulse the chunks in batches, about five times for a few seconds each time; set aside.

2. Heat the olive oil in a large, heavy-based pot. When the oil is hot, add just enough of the meat to make one layer. If using packaged ground meat, don't crumble it; instead, break it into pieces (about 1 inch) to brown. Season with salt and pepper. Brown the meat all over, stirring occasionally, 3 to 5 minutes. Transfer the first batch of meat to a bowl and sear the remaining meat in batches, if necessary, adding more olive oil as needed. In the same pot, sauté the carrot, celery, and onion until soft and lightly browned, about 10 minutes.

3. Return all the seared meat to the pot. Add the garlic, rosemary, sage, and marjoram and sauté briefly until fragrant. Add 1¾ cups of the wine and stir, scraping the bottom of the pot to loosen any browned bits. Let the wine reduce until it's almost gone, about 5 minutes. Reduce the heat to low. Add the tomato purée and simmer the ragù, uncovered, for 1½ to 2 hours. As it cooks, juices will evaporate; add ½ cup beef stock periodically (to total about 2 cups), letting it reduce after each addition. After 1½ to 2 hours, the meat should be tender and the flavors melded. Add the remaining wine to taste toward the end of cooking to enhance the ragù's wine flavor, but allow some simmering time for the wine to cook off. Taste and adjust the seasonings.

4. Immediately before serving, whisk ½ Tbs. butter per serving into the sauce; toss with the pasta. Serve sprinkled with Parmesan, if you like.
—*Suzette Gresham-Tognetti*

PER SERVING: 690 CALORIES | 61G PROTEIN | 52G CARB | 22G TOTAL FAT | 10G SAT FAT | 10G MONO FAT | 1G POLY FAT | 175MG CHOL | 670MG SODIUM | 4G FIBER

marinated braised short ribs with mashed potatoes

- **2 large cloves garlic, smashed and peeled**
- **2 large sprigs fresh thyme**
- **2 strips orange zest (about 1 inch wide and 3 to 4 inches long)**
- **2 bay leaves**
- **¼ tsp. allspice berries, coarsely crushed in a mortar or with the side of a chef's knife**
- **¼ tsp. black peppercorns**
- **4 whole cloves**
- **1 750 ml bottle hearty, dry red wine, such as Zinfandel**
- **4 to 5 lb. meaty bone-in beef short ribs**
- **1½ tsp. kosher salt; more as needed**
- **3 Tbs. extra-virgin olive oil**
- **1 medium to large yellow onion, coarsely chopped**
- **1 medium stalk celery, coarsely chopped**
- **1 medium carrot, peeled and coarsely chopped**
- **Freshly ground black pepper**
- **2 Tbs. tomato paste**
- **2 cups homemade or lower-salt beef or chicken broth**
- **2 Tbs. red-wine vinegar; more if needed**
- **Traditional Mashed Potatoes (recipe facing page)**

Mashed potatoes make a perfect bed for tender short ribs. Marinating the ribs overnight deeply infuses them with the flavors of the wine and spice.

MARINATE THE RIBS

1. Make a sachet by wrapping the garlic, thyme, orange zest, bay leaves, allspice, peppercorns, and cloves in a 6-inch square of cheesecloth, pouch style. Tie the sachet closed with kitchen twine.

2. Pour the wine into a medium saucepan, add the sachet, and bring to a boil over high heat. Reduce the heat and simmer gently for 10 minutes. Set the marinade aside to cool.

3. Meanwhile, trim away any excess fat from the top of each rib down to the first layer of meat, but don't remove the silverskin or tough-looking tissue that holds the ribs together or onto the bone. Put the ribs in a container wide enough to fit them in a snug single layer (a 9x13-inch dish works well), season with 1½ tsp. salt, and pour over the cooled marinade and sachet. Cover with plastic wrap and refrigerate for 12 to 24 hours, turning the ribs once or twice.

COOK THE RIBS

1. Position a rack in the lower third of the oven and heat the oven to 300°F. Remove the ribs from the marinade, reserving the marinade and the sachet. Pat the ribs dry thoroughly with paper towels.

2. Heat 2 Tbs. of the oil in a 5- to 6-quart Dutch oven (or other heavy pot with a lid) over medium heat until hot. Add only as many ribs as will fit without touching and brown them, turning with tongs, until nicely browned on all sides, 3 to 4 minutes per side. Transfer to a platter and continue until all the ribs are browned.

3. Pour off and discard most of the fat from the pot. Add the remaining 1 Tbs. oil and return the pot to medium heat. Add the onion, celery, and carrot, season with salt and pepper, and cook, stirring occasionally, until browned in spots, about 8 minutes. Stir in the tomato paste and cook for 2 minutes, stirring. Add half of the reserved wine marinade, increase the heat to high, stir to scrape up any browned bits, and bring to a boil. Continue to boil until the liquid is reduced by half, 2 to 4 minutes. Add the remaining marinade and reduce again by about half, another 3 to 5 minutes. Add the broth and vinegar and boil for 3 minutes.

4. Return the ribs to the pot, preferably in a single layer, along with any accumulated juices and the sachet. Crumple a large sheet of parchment and smooth it out again. Arrange it over the pot, pressing it down so it nearly touches the ribs, allowing any overhang to extend up and over the edges of the pot. Set the lid in place, and transfer to the oven. Braise, turning the ribs with tongs every 45 minutes, until the meat is fork-tender and pulling away from the bone, about 2½ hours. Use tongs or a slotted spoon to carefully transfer the ribs to a serving dish. Don't worry if some bones slip out. Cover loosely with foil to keep warm.

MAKE THE SAUCE

Strain the braising liquid through a fine sieve into a 4-cup measuring cup, pressing gently on the solids and sachet to extract the liquid. When the fat has risen to the top, tilt the measuring cup so that you can spoon off and discard as much of the fat as you can. You should have about 1 cup of sauce that's the consistency of a vinaigrette. If the sauce seems thin and the flavor weak, heat it in a small saucepan over high heat until reduced to an intensity and consistency you like. Taste and season with salt and pepper. If the sauce needs more punch, add a splash of vinegar. Spoon the sauce over the ribs and serve with the mashed potatoes. *—Molly Stevens*

PER SERVING: 410 CALORIES | 26G PROTEIN | 7G CARB | 21G TOTAL FAT | 7G SAT FAT | 11G MONO FAT | 1G POLY FAT | 75MG CHOL | 410MG SODIUM | 1G FIBER

Don't begin to make the mashed potatoes until the ribs are completely cooked and fork-tender. The meat will hold better than the potatoes, and will only taste better for being made ahead.

traditional mashed potatoes

SERVES 4

2½ **lb. medium-starch potatoes (such as Yukon Gold or Yellow Finn), peeled and cut into 2-inch chunks**

2 **tsp. kosher salt**

⅔ **cup light cream**

6 **Tbs. unsalted butter**

Freshly ground black pepper

Consider this recipe your template and add more butter and cream to tailor the potatoes to your taste.

Put the potatoes in a large pot, cover with water, and add the salt. Bring the water to a boil and cook until the potatoes are very soft and starting to fall apart, 20 to 30 minutes. Drain the potatoes well, return them to the pot, and mash with a potato masher, a fork, or a sturdy whisk (or use a food mill), adding the cream and butter a little at a time as you mash. Make the potatoes as lumpy or as smooth as you like, but don't keep mashing once they're smooth or they may become gluey. Season to taste with salt and pepper.

marinated beef pot roast

SERVES 4 TO 6

2½ to 3 lb. rump, chuck, eye of
       round, or shoulder roast

3 cloves garlic, slivered

1 cup balsamic vinegar

2 Tbs. chopped fresh rosemary

3 medium onions, peeled and
     thinly sliced

    Salt and freshly ground
    black pepper

1 14½-oz. can whole tomatoes,
     chopped, all juices reserved

*An overnight soak makes the
meat especially tasty.*

1. Poke the meat all over with a
thin-bladed knife and insert the
garlic slivers into the holes.

2. In a large ceramic dish or bowl,
or in a zip-top bag, combine the
vinegar and rosemary. Add the
meat and turn to coat completely. Cover and refrigerate
overnight.

3. Heat the oven to 350°F. Spread the sliced onions in a large casserole or
small roasting pan. Nestle the meat into the onions and pour in the remaining
marinade.

4. Season the meat with salt and pepper. Add the tomatoes and juice. Cover
the pot or pan tightly with a lid or aluminum foil. Cook the beef until it is easily
pierced with a fork and its juices run clear, 3 to 3½ hours.

5. Remove the roast from the oven and allow it to rest in the pan for 5 to
10 minutes before carving. Serve the sliced meat with the onions, tomatoes,
and pan juices (degreased if necessary). *—Beth Dooley and Lucia Watson*

PER SERVING: 310 CALORIES | 41G PROTEIN | 15G CARB | 9G TOTAL FAT | 3G SAT FAT |
4G MONO FAT | 0G POLY FAT | 120MG CHOL | 540MG SODIUM | 2G FIBER

Degrease Pan Juices for a Better Tasting Sauce

When making a sauce for pot roast, it's important
to remove any fat from the cooking liquid. While
the roast is resting, you can degrease the juices in
a few different ways.

• Gently tilt the pan and spoon the fat away, being
careful not to stir it into the juices.

• Pour the juices into a saucepan and set half of
the pan over a high flame. The fat will travel to
the coolest part of the pot, where it can be more
easily spooned off.

• If there's a lot of liquid, skim the fat off the
surface by dipping a soup ladle under the layer
of fat so that it swirls into the ladle's bowl.

• Strain the juices into a degreasing cup (its spout
starts at the bottom of the cup). The fat will rise
to the top, and the juices can be poured from
the spout.

• If you're making the pot roast ahead of time,
put the strained juices in the refrigerator and let
the fat solidify on the surface. To remove the
fat, slide the edge of a metal spoon under the fat
and lift it out. To reheat the roast, return the
meat to the pan, add the degreased juices,
cover the roast tightly, and warm it in a low oven.

moroccan-spiced roasted hanger steak with carrots and warm lentil salad

SERVES 4

FOR THE LENTIL SALAD

	Generous pinch of saffron threads
1½	cups French green lentils, picked through, rinsed, and drained
2	Tbs. extra-virgin olive oil
1	medium red onion, finely chopped
1	medium clove garlic, minced
1	tsp. cumin seeds, toasted and ground
½	tsp. coriander seeds, toasted and ground
	Kosher salt
¼	cup chopped fresh cilantro
¼	cup chopped fresh flat-leaf parsley
2	to 3 Tbs. freshly squeezed lemon juice
2	tsp. finely grated lemon zest
¼	to ½ tsp. crushed red pepper flakes
	Freshly ground black pepper

FOR THE STEAK AND CARROTS

2	Tbs. extra-virgin olive oil
½	tsp. coriander seeds, toasted and ground
½	tsp. ground cinnamon
½	tsp. ground ginger
2	medium cloves garlic, mashed into a paste
	Kosher salt and freshly ground black pepper
1½	lb. beef hanger steak, trimmed
8	medium carrots (about 1½ lb.), halved crosswise, thicker ends halved or quartered lengthwise, cut into uniform 1-inch pieces
2	tsp. granulated sugar

Toasting and grinding coriander and cumin seeds makes them more fragrant and flavorful than preground versions. A clean spice grinder, coffee grinder, or mortar and pestle does the job beautifully.

Position a rack in the center of the oven and heat the oven to 450°F.

MAKE THE LENTIL SALAD

1. Toast the saffron in a 4-quart saucepan set over medium-low heat until fragrant, 30 to 60 seconds. Off the heat, use the back of a spoon to crush the saffron as finely as possible. Add 6 cups water and the lentils and bring to a boil. Reduce the heat to medium low, cover, and simmer until tender, about 35 minutes. Reserve ⅓ cup of the cooking liquid and then drain well. Transfer the lentils to a large bowl and set aside. Return the pan to the stove.

2. Heat 1 Tbs. of the oil in the pan over medium-high heat. Add the onion, garlic, cumin, coriander, and 1 tsp. salt and cook until softened and golden-brown, 5 to 6 minutes. Add the reserved cooking liquid and cook until most of it is absorbed, scraping up any browned bits, about 2 minutes. Transfer the onion mixture to the bowl with the lentils. Add the cilantro, parsley, lemon juice, lemon zest, red pepper flakes, and the remaining 1 Tbs. oil; fold together to combine. Season to taste with salt and pepper and keep warm.

ROAST THE STEAK AND CARROTS

1. While the lentils cook, combine 1 Tbs. of the oil with the coriander, cinnamon, ginger, garlic paste, 1 tsp. salt, and ¼ tsp. pepper in a small bowl. Rub the mixture all over the steak, transfer to a plate, and set aside.

2. In a large bowl, toss the carrots with the remaining 1 Tbs. oil, the sugar, ¾ tsp. salt, and ⅛ tsp. pepper and spread on a rimmed baking sheet. Roast, stirring halfway through, until the carrots are just becoming tender, about 20 minutes. Push the carrots to one side of the baking sheet and arrange the steak on the other side. Roast until the carrots are very tender and golden-brown and the steak is medium rare (an instant-read thermometer inserted in the thickest part of the steak should read 130° to 135°F), 15 to 18 minutes. Transfer the steak to a plate, tent with foil, and let rest for 10 minutes; keep the carrots warm.

3. Thinly slice the steak against the grain and serve on top of the lentils, drizzled with any accumulated meat juices. Arrange the roasted carrots on the side. *—Liz Pearson*

PER SERVING: 660 CALORIES | 47G PROTEIN | 60G CARB | 27G TOTAL FAT | 6G SAT FAT | 16G MONO FAT | 2G POLY FAT | 80MG CHOL | 960MG SODIUM | 15G FIBER

smoky rib-eye steaks with loaded mashed potatoes

SERVES 4

- 2 lb. Yukon Gold potatoes, scrubbed and cut into 1-inch chunks
- 4 slices thick-cut bacon
- 2 boneless beef rib-eye steaks (about 2 lb. total)
- 1½ tsp. smoked sweet paprika
- Kosher salt and freshly ground black pepper
- ½ cup whole milk
- 2 Tbs. unsalted butter
- 3 oz. grated sharp Cheddar (¾ cup)
- ½ cup sour cream
- 2 medium scallions, thinly sliced

All the ingredients in a loaded baked potato—bacon, scallions, cheese, and sour cream—are added to mashed potatoes in this hearty meal.

1. Arrange a steamer basket in a large pot with 1 inch of water in the bottom. Spread the potatoes in the basket in an even layer, cover, and bring to a boil. Reduce the heat to medium low and steam until the potatoes are tender, about 15 minutes.

2. Meanwhile, cook the bacon in a large cast-iron skillet over medium heat, turning once, until crisp, 7 to 8 minutes total. Transfer the bacon to a paper-towel-lined plate; discard all but 1 Tbs. of the fat from the skillet.

3. Season the steaks all over with the paprika, 1½ tsp. salt, and ½ tsp. pepper. Heat the skillet with the reserved bacon fat over medium-high heat. Arrange the steaks in the skillet in a single layer. Cook, flipping once, until deep golden-brown outside and medium rare inside, 10 to 12 minutes total. Transfer the steaks to a cutting board and let rest for 5 minutes.

4. Meanwhile, transfer the hot potatoes to a large bowl. Stir in the milk and butter and mash with a potato masher until just combined. Stir in the cheese, sour cream, scallions, and salt and pepper to taste.

5. Slice the steaks across the grain and transfer to dinner plates. Serve the potatoes on the side with the bacon crumbled on top. *—Liz Pearson*

PER SERVING: 870 CALORIES | 59G PROTEIN | 41G CARB | 52G TOTAL FAT | 25G SAT FAT | 19G MONO FAT | 2G POLY FAT | 170MG CHOL | 910MG SODIUM | 4G FIBER

country-style curry with beef, shiitake & edamame

SERVES 4

1   lb. flank steak

5   oz. fresh shiitake mushrooms

2   Tbs. vegetable oil

3   Tbs. jarred or homemade
    red curry paste

2¾ cups homemade or lower-salt
    chicken broth

5   wild lime leaves, torn or cut
    into quarters (optional)

1½ cups frozen shelled edamame
    (soybeans), thawed

3   Tbs. fish sauce

1   Tbs. palm sugar or light brown
    sugar

    Kosher salt

    A handful of fresh Thai or
    Italian basil leaves

    Hot cooked rice or rice
    noodles, for serving

1   long, slender fresh red chile
    (such as red jalapeño or
    serrano), thinly sliced on the
    diagonal (optional)

Country-style curry usually has no coconut milk. Red curry pastes vary in hotness; be sure to taste and adjust to your likeness.

1. Slice the beef across the grain ¼ inch thick, then cut the slices into 1½- to 2-inch pieces.

2. Trim and discard the stems from the shiitake; slice the caps ¼ inch thick (you should have 1½ to 2 cups).

3. Heat the oil in a 2- to 3-quart saucepan over medium heat until a bit of curry paste just sizzles when added to the pan. Add all the curry paste and cook, pressing and stirring with a wooden spoon or heatproof spatula to soften the paste and mix it in with the oil, until fragrant, about 2 minutes.

4. Increase the heat to medium high, and add the beef. Spread it in an even single layer and cook undisturbed until it just begins to lose its pink color, about 1 minute. Turn the beef and continue cooking, stirring occasionally to coat it with the curry paste, until most of the beef no longer looks raw, 1 to 2 minutes.

5. Stir the shiitake into the beef. Add the chicken broth and stir again. Add half of the lime leaves (if using) and bring to a simmer. Simmer gently, stirring occasionally, until the shiitake are tender and the beef is cooked through, about 5 minutes.

6. Add the edamame, stir well, and cook for about 1 minute, just to blanch them. Add the fish sauce, sugar, and ¼ tsp. salt and stir to combine. Remove the pan from the heat. Tear the basil leaves in half (or quarters if they're large) and stir them into the curry, along with the remaining lime leaves (if using). Let the curry rest for 5 minutes to allow the flavors to develop. Season to taste with salt.

7. Serve hot or warm with rice or noodles, garnished with the chile slices, if you like. *—Nancie McDermott*

PER SERVING: 350 CALORIES | 33G PROTEIN | 15G CARB | 18G TOTAL FAT | 4.5G SAT FAT | 7G MONO FAT | 3.5G POLY FAT | 45MG CHOL | 1,370MG SODIUM | 3G FIBER

spice-rubbed prime rib

- **3** cloves garlic, minced
- **1** Tbs. kosher salt
- **2** tsp. coarsely ground black pepper
- **2** tsp. chopped fresh thyme (or rosemary)
- **2** tsp. crushed fennel seeds
- **1½** Tbs. olive oil
- **1** 3-bone standing rib roast (6 to 7 lb.), chine bones removed

For the easiest carving, have your butcher remove the chine, or feather, bones, which make up part of the spinal column. For a larger crowd, cook a five-bone (10- to 12-pound) rib roast and double the dry rub. For more intense flavor, season the roast a day ahead, cover it loosely with plastic, and refrigerate it overnight.

1. Crush the garlic with the salt in a mortar and pestle or mix it well in a small bowl. Mix in the pepper, thyme or rosemary, fennel seeds, and olive oil. Rub all over the roast, especially in any spaces between the meat and bones. Let the rub sit on the roast for at least 30 minutes and up to 24 hours, refrigerated and loosely covered. (After being refrigerated, let the meat come to room temperature for 1 hour before roasting.)

2. Heat the oven to 450°F. Lay the roast, bone side down, in a large shallow roasting pan and roast for 15 minutes. Turn the oven down to 350°F without opening the door. After about 45 minutes (or after 1 hour for a 5-bone roast), check the temperature of the roast by inserting the instant-read meat thermometer in the direct center of the roast. If it isn't 115°F, continue roasting, checking every 15 minutes or so, until it reaches 115°F. This temperature will give you a mostly rare roast, except for the end cuts, which will be medium-rare to medium. You can roast it to 120° to 125°F if you want medium-rare meat, but be careful not to overcook it. Remove from the oven and cover loosely with foil. Let the roast rest for at least 15 and up to 45 minutes. During this time, the temperature will rise another 5° to 10°F and the juices within the roast will be redistributed. Carve and serve. *—Bruce Aidells*

PER SERVING: 720 CALORIES I 44G PROTEIN I 0G CARB I 59G TOTAL FAT I 23G SAT FAT I 26G MONO FAT I 2G POLY FAT I 165MG CHOL I 760MG SODIUM I 0G FIBER

how to carve a standing rib roast

Tilt the roast onto its spinal side (the rounded, meaty side facing downward). Stab the meat with a large fork and run your knife parallel to the ribs, separating the rib bones from the large chunk of meat.

Set the deboned roast on its rib side and cut into slices of whatever thickness you want.

beef picadillo

SERVES 4 TO 6

- 3 Tbs. extra-virgin olive oil
- 1½ lb. lean ground beef
- ⅓ cup dry red wine
- 1 small yellow onion, minced
- 3 cloves garlic, minced
- 1 cup canned crushed tomatoes
- ½ cup golden raisins

  Kosher salt and freshly ground black pepper
- 2 large hard-cooked eggs, finely chopped
- 6 Tbs. chopped pimiento-stuffed green olives
- ¼ cup minced fresh cilantro
- 1 small head Boston lettuce, cored and leaves separated

A Latin American and Caribbean favorite, picadillo is a savory-sweet ground beef filling that's delicious wrapped in lettuce leaves. It's also good in tacos, quesadillas, and omelets.

1. Heat the oil in a large skillet over medium heat. Add the ground beef and cook, stirring occasionally and breaking up the meat with the edge of a spoon, until done, about 5 minutes. Add the wine, onion, and garlic and cook, stirring occasionally, until the wine is almost evaporated, about 5 minutes.

2. Add the tomatoes and raisins and simmer, stirring occasionally, until the liquid has almost evaporated, 2 to 3 minutes. Season with 1½ tsp. salt and a few grinds of pepper.

3. Remove the skillet from the heat and stir in the chopped eggs, olives, and cilantro. Serve hot with the lettuce leaves for wrapping.

—*Bruce Weinstein and Mark Scarbrough*

PER SERVING: 420 CALORIES | 34G PROTEIN | 17G CARB | 23G TOTAL FAT | 7G SAT FAT | 12G MONO FAT | 1.5G POLY FAT | 165MG CHOL | 610MG SODIUM | 2G FIBER

slow-cooker steak and guinness pie

SERVES 4

- 1⅛ oz. (¼ cup) unbleached all-purpose flour; more for rolling

  Kosher salt and freshly ground black pepper

- 2 lb. boneless beef chuck, trimmed of excess fat, cut into 1-inch pieces

- 2 large carrots, cut into ¼-inch-thick rounds

- 1 large yellow onion, coarsely chopped

- 3 large cloves garlic, minced

- 2 sprigs fresh thyme

- 1 12-oz. bottle Guinness (or other stout)

- 1 cup lower-salt beef broth

- 2 large russet potatoes (about 1½ lb.), washed and cut into 1-inch cubes

  Nonstick cooking spray

- 1 sheet frozen puff pastry (about 9 oz.), thawed overnight in the refrigerator

This simple version of the classic Irish dish has the distinctive bitter flavor of Guinness® stout. Although it's slow-cooked, the hearty beef stew requires minimal prep time. When it's ready, the puff pastry "tops" are baked separately and served alongside.

1. In a large bowl, combine the flour, 2 tsp. salt, and 1 tsp. pepper. Toss the beef in the flour mixture to coat. Transfer the mixture (including excess flour) to a 6-quart slow cooker and then add the carrots, onion, garlic, and thyme. Slowly pour in the Guinness and then stir in the beef broth. Cover and cook on low for 6 to 7 hours or on high for 4 to 5 hours. Add the potatoes and continue cooking until the meat and the potatoes are fork-tender, about 1 hour more.

2. Position a rack in the center of the oven and heat the oven to 375°F. Coat a large rimmed baking sheet with the cooking spray. On a lightly floured surface, roll the puff pastry sheet into a 10x14-inch rectangle. Put it on the prepared baking sheet and bake until golden-brown, 15 to 18 minutes. Remove from the oven, let cool slightly on a rack, and cut into quarters.

3. To serve, lay the puff pastry quarters in 4 wide, shallow bowls and spoon the stew over the pastry. —*Juli Roberts*

PER SERVING: 880 CALORIES | 58G PROTEIN | 79G CARB | 34G TOTAL FAT | 7G SAT FAT | 9G MONO FAT | 15G POLY FAT | 80MG CHOL | 860MG SODIUM | 5G FIBER

beef stew with red wine and carrots

SERVES 6

- **1** **3-lb. boneless beef chuck roast**
- **2** **Tbs. extra-virgin olive oil**
- **2** **slices thick-cut bacon, cut into ½-inch pieces**
- **Kosher salt and freshly ground black pepper**
- **8** **oz. shallots (8 to 10 medium), thinly sliced (about 2 cups)**
- **2** **Tbs. brandy, such as Cognac**
- **2** **Tbs. tomato paste**
- **2** **to 3 cloves garlic, finely chopped (2 to 3 tsp.)**
- **2** **tsp. herbes de Provence**
- **2** **cups hearty red wine, such as Côtes de Provence or Côtes du Rhône**
- **1** **14.5-oz. can whole, peeled tomatoes**
- **4** **strips orange zest (2½ inches long, removed with a vegetable peeler)**
- **1** **lb. slender carrots, peeled and cut into ¾- to 1-inch chunks (about 2 cups)**
- **¼** **cup coarsely chopped fresh flat-leaf parsley**

Rather than buying already cut-up stew meat, buy a whole chuck roast and cut it into 1½- to 2-inch cubes. These larger chunks won't dry out during the long braise, and they make the stew more satisfying to eat.

1. Using your fingers and a thin knife, pull the roast apart along its natural seams. Trim off any thick layers of fat. Carve the roast into 1½- to 2-inch cubes and arrange them on a paper-towel-lined tray to dry.

2. Position a rack in the lower third of the oven. Heat the oven to 325°F.

3. Heat the oil and bacon together in a 7- or 8-quart Dutch oven over medium heat, stirring occasionally, just until the bacon is browned but not crisp, 5 to 6 minutes. With a slotted spoon, transfer the bacon to a small plate. Season about one-third of the beef with salt and pepper, and arrange the cubes in a sparse single layer in the pot to brown. Adjust the heat so the beef sizzles and browns but does not burn. Cook until all sides are a rich brown, a total of about 10 minutes. Transfer to a large plate or tray, and season and brown the remaining beef in 2 more batches.

4. When all the beef chunks are browned, pour off all but about 1 Tbs. of drippings, if necessary. Set the pot over medium-high heat, add the shallots, season with a large pinch of salt and several grinds of pepper, and sauté until they just begin to soften, about 1 minute. Add the brandy and let it boil away. Add the tomato paste, garlic, and herbes de Provence, stirring to incorporate, and sauté for another 1 minute. Add the wine, stirring and scraping the bottom of the pan with a wooden spoon to dislodge the caramelized drippings, and bring to a boil. Pour in the liquid from the tomatoes, holding the tomatoes back with your hand. Then one by one, crush the tomatoes with your hand over the pot and drop them in. Add the orange zest, and return the beef (along with any accumulated juices) and bacon to the pot. Finally, add the carrots, bring to a simmer, cover, and slide into the oven.

5. Cook the stew, stirring every 45 minutes, until the meat is fork-tender (taste a piece; all trace of toughness should be gone), 2 to 3 hours. Before serving, skim off surface fat (if there is any), taste for salt and pepper, and stir in the parsley. *—Molly Stevens*

PER SERVING: 580 CALORIES | 49G PROTEIN | 20G CARB | 25G TOTAL FAT | 9G SAT FAT | 12G MONO FAT | 1.5G POLY FAT | 160MG CHOL | 630MG SODIUM | 4G FIBER

Make Ahead

This dish can be made up to 3 days ahead. Reserve the chopped parsley and don't bother skimming the surface fat. Instead, transfer the cooled stew to a bowl or baking dish, cover tightly, and refrigerate. Before reheating, lift off the layer of solid fat that will be on the surface. Reheat gently in a 325°F oven in a covered baking dish, stirring once, for about 30 minutes, or until hot. Taste for salt and pepper and add the parsley just before serving.

slow-roasted pork shoulder with carrots, onions & garlic

**SERVES 4 WITH LEFTOVERS
(OR 8 WITHOUT)**

Kosher salt and freshly
ground black pepper

1   6¾- to 7-lb. boneless
    pork shoulder roast

1   large yellow onion, cut
    into ½-inch-thick rings

3   medium carrots, cut
    into sticks ½ inch wide
    and 2 to 2½ inches long

10 cloves garlic, peeled

1   cup dry white wine

Start this recipe at least a day ahead. Serve the pork and vegetables with mashed potatoes or with beans (like cranberry or cannellini) seasoned with pounded garlic, extra-virgin olive oil, and sage.

1. Combine 2 Tbs. salt and 2 tsp. pepper in a small bowl and rub the mixture all over the pork. Put the pork, fat side up, in a large roasting pan (about 12x16x3 inches). Cover and refrigerate overnight or for up to 3 days.

2. Remove the pork from the refrigerator and let sit at room temperature for 1 to 1½ hours before cooking.

3. Position a rack in the center of the oven and heat the oven to 300°F. Uncover the pork and roast until tender everywhere but the very center when pierced with a fork, 4 to 4½ hours. Add the onion, carrots, garlic, wine, and 1 cup water to the roasting pan and continue to roast, stirring the vegetables occasionally, until the pork is completely tender, about 1 hour more.

4. Remove the roast from the oven and raise the oven temperature to 375°F. Using tongs, separate the pork into 8 to 10 large, rustic chunks and spread out on the pan. If most of the liquid has evaporated, add a splash more water to the pan to create a little more juice. (It shouldn't be soupy.) Return the pork to the oven and continue to roast until nicely browned on the newly exposed surfaces, about 15 minutes. Remove the pan from the oven, transfer the meat and vegetables to a serving platter, and tent loosely with foil. Let rest for 20 minutes. Skim the excess fat from the juices and serve the juices with the vegetables and meat.   —*Tasha DeSerio*

PER SERVING: 630 CALORIES | 75G PROTEIN | 6G CARB | 29G TOTAL FAT | 11G SAT FAT | 13G MONO FAT | 3.5G POLY FAT | 235MG CHOL | 1,090MG SODIUM | 1G FIBER

alsatian stuffed cabbage

YIELDS ABOUT 8 SMALL
STUFFED CABBAGES; SERVES 4

FOR THE STUFFING

- ¾ lb. ground veal
- ½ lb. sausage meat, removed from casing
- ¼ lb. lightly smoked bacon, finely chopped
- 3 Tbs. finely chopped fresh flat-leaf parsley
- 6 medium shallots, finely chopped (about ¾ cup)
- 2 cloves garlic, finely chopped
- 1 cup fresh breadcrumbs
- 2 eggs, lightly beaten
  Dash of ground nutmeg (freshly grated, if possible)
- 1½ tsp. salt
  Freshly ground black pepper

FOR THE CABBAGE

- 1 head Savoy or green cabbage (about 3 lb.) or 2 smaller cabbages
- 2 Tbs. butter
- 1 large onion, chopped
- 1 large carrot, thinly sliced
- 2 cloves garlic, finely chopped
- 1 cup white wine (preferably slightly sweet)
- 2 cups homemade or lower-salt canned vegetable, chicken, or beef stock; more if needed
- 4 sprigs fresh thyme
- 2 sprigs fresh flat-leaf parsley
- 1 bay leaf
  Salt and freshly ground black pepper

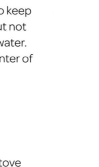

Aidells chicken-and-apple sausage is great in this recipe, but any sausage will do.

FOR THE STUFFING
In a large bowl, combine all of the stuffing ingredients. Mix well and refrigerate.

PREPARE THE CABBAGE
Bring a large pot of salted water to a boil. Fill a large bowl with ice water. Core the cabbage and peel and discard any loose outer leaves. Separate the leaves, taking care to keep them intact. Plunge into the boiling water and boil until they're limp but not mushy, 6 to 8 minutes. Drain the leaves and refresh them in the cold water. Spread the leaves to dry on paper towels. Cut the stiff rib from the center of each leaf.

STUFF THE CABBAGE
Follow the method shown below.

FINISH THE DISH
Heat the oven to 350°F. In a heavy casserole, melt the butter on the stove over medium heat. Add the onion, carrot, and garlic. Cover the casserole and cook until the vegetables are soft but not browned, about 5 minutes. Uncover, add the wine, stock, thyme, parsley, and bay leaf. Bring to a boil; cook until the liquid is reduced by about one-third. Season lightly with salt and pepper. Arrange the stuffed cabbages in the casserole side by side. Check that the broth covers at least the bottom third of the rolls. Cover the casserole and bake until the rolls are somewhat firm to the touch, 50 to 60 minutes. Serve with a little broth to moisten them. —*Hubert Keller*

PER SERVING: 680 CALORIES | 42G PROTEIN | 40G CARB | 40G TOTAL FAT | 15G SAT FAT | 17G MONO FAT | 4G POLY FAT | 230MG CHOL | 1,870MG SODIUM | 14G FIBER

how to make perfectly round stuffed cabbage

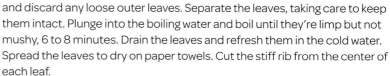

A coffee cup is the perfect size. Line the cup with a 12-inch square of plastic wrap, letting the excess hang over the edge. Line the plastic with a large cabbage leaf (or two overlapping smaller leaves). Pack in ⅓ cup of stuffing and then fold the leaves over the top.

Twist the plastic for a tight bundle. After pulling the plastic-wrapped cabbage out of the cup, hold the excess plastic in one hand and twist the stuffed cabbage in the other, stretching the plastic around the cabbage tightly.

A compact little globe. The leaves stay tightly closed after the plastic is removed.

mustard, sage & maple–glazed pork roast with garlic-roasted potatoes

SERVES 6

FOR THE PORK

1 **6-bone center-cut pork roast (about 5½ pounds), chine bone removed**

Kosher salt and freshly ground black pepper

Mustard, Sage & Maple Glaze (recipe facing page)

FOR THE POTATOES

2 **pounds medium red or yellow potatoes, rinsed (you can use a combination, but they may cook at slightly different rates)**

1 **head garlic, cloves separated and peeled**

3 **Tbs. olive oil**

Kosher salt and freshly ground black pepper

4 **Tbs. unsalted butter, cut into small pieces**

1 **Tbs. chopped fresh flat-leaf parsley**

When buying the pork, be sure to have the backbone (called the chine bone) removed so you'll be able to slice the roast between the rib bones. But since most people love to chew the crusted meat and crackling pork fat off the rib bones, don't have them scraped clean (butchers call this frenching).

1. Position racks in the center and bottom of the oven and heat the oven to 425°F. Let the roast sit at room temperature while the oven heats. Season the meat generously with salt and pepper. Put the pork in a small roasting pan, bone side down, and roast on the center oven rack to an internal temperature of 115°F, 50 to 60 minutes. Remove the roast from the oven and let it rest for 20 minutes. (This rest will give the juiciest results.)

2. Meanwhile, shortly before the pork hits 115°F, cut the potatoes lengthwise into wedges 1½ to 1¾ inches wide at their thickest part. In a medium bowl, toss the potatoes with the garlic cloves, olive oil, 1 tsp. salt, and several grinds of pepper. Arrange in a roasting pan or rimmed baking sheet, one cut side down, evenly spaced. Sprinkle with the pieces of butter. When you take the roast out of the oven, put the potatoes on the bottom rack and reduce the oven temperature to 350°F.

3. After 20 minutes of resting, cover the roast evenly with the mustard glaze and return it to the center oven rack. At this time, turn the potatoes with a metal spatula onto their other cut side. Roast the pork until the internal temperature is 140°F. Roast the potatoes until they're golden and crisp on the outside and fork-tender inside. Both should take about 30 minutes (check the potatoes at 20 minutes and, if necessary for even browning, flip them back to their other cut side.) Transfer the roast to a carving board and tent with foil.

4. Let the pork rest for at least 20 minutes before carving. Set the potatoes aside in a warm place, uncovered (so they stay crisp and don't steam), until ready to serve. To serve, slice the roast between the bones into individual chops. Toss the potatoes with the chopped parsley. Arrange the meat and potatoes on a platter and serve with vegetables, like braised cabbage, if desired. *—Ris Lacoste*

PER SERVING: 800 CALORIES I 64G PROTEIN I 49G CARB I 38G TOTAL FAT I 13G SAT FAT I 18G MONO FAT I 3.5G POLY FAT I 190MG CHOL I 1,390MG SODIUM I 3G FIBER

mustard, sage & maple glaze

YIELDS ABOUT 1½ CUPS

1 Tbs. olive oil

1 small-medium yellow onion (6 ounces), cut into medium dice (to yield 1 cup)

4 cloves garlic, coarsely chopped

⅓ cup coarsely chopped fresh sage (about 1½ bunches)

½ cup Dijon mustard

½ cup pure maple syrup

1 Tbs. soy sauce

¼ tsp. kosher salt

Pinch of freshly ground black pepper

This glaze can be made up to 2 days ahead and refrigerated. You could also use this glaze on pork tenderloin or even roast chicken; put it on chicken halfway through cooking.

Heat the oil in a medium sauté pan over medium heat. Add the onion and garlic and cook, stirring frequently, until the onion softens, about 5 minutes. Set aside until cooled to room temperature. Purée the onion and garlic with all of the remaining ingredients in a blender or food processor until somewhat smooth. Keep covered in the refrigerator until ready to use on the pork roast.

calabrese pork ragù with fennel

YIELDS 8 CUPS OF SAUCE,
ENOUGH FOR ABOUT 1 LB. OF
PASTA; SERVES 8

- **3 lb. pork butt or shoulder (from about a 7-lb. bone-in shoulder) or 3 lb. packaged ground pork**
- **2 Tbs. olive oil; more as needed**
- **6 oz. pancetta, finely chopped**
- **1 large yellow onion, chopped**
- **1 Tbs. finely chopped garlic**
- **1 Tbs. fennel seeds, crushed**
- **Kosher salt and freshly ground black pepper**
- **1 tsp. sugar**
- **1 tsp. dried oregano**
- **1 bay leaf**
- **1 tsp. dried red pepper flakes**
- **1 cup dry white wine**
- **2 cups canned puréed tomatoes**
- **¾ cup tomato paste**
- **Unsalted butter, ½ Tbs. per serving; more to taste**
- **1 lb. pasta, cooked al dente**
- **Freshly grated Parmesan (optional)**

Pancetta, cured Italian bacon, is available at many supermarkets; you'll also find it at specialty stores and in Italian markets.

1. If using pork butt or shoulder, cut off any skin and discard, and then cut the meat off the bone into chunks about 1 inch or so. In a food processor, pulse the pork in batches, about five times for a few seconds each time; set aside.

2. Heat the olive oil in a large heavy-based pot over medium heat. Add the pancetta and onion and sauté, stirring occasionally, until browned, 12 to 15 minutes.

3. Add the garlic and crushed fennel and stir for about 2 minutes. Transfer to a large bowl.

4. Increase the heat to medium high. In the same pot, add just enough of the ground pork to make one layer. If using packaged ground meat, don't crumble it; instead, break it into pieces (about 1 inch) to brown. Season with salt and pepper. Brown the meat all over, stirring occasionally, 3 to 5 minutes. Transfer the first batch of meat to the bowl and sear the remaining pork in batches, if necessary; add more olive oil as needed.

5. Return all the seared pork and the onion mixture to the pot. Add the sugar, oregano, bay leaf, red pepper, 2 tsp. salt, and 1½ tsp. pepper, and stir to combine. Pour in the wine to deglaze the pot, stirring up any browned bits stuck to the bottom of the pan. Let the wine reduce by at least half. Add the tomato purée and tomato paste and bring the sauce to a boil (the mixture will be thick).

6. Add ½ cup of water, reduce the heat, and simmer the sauce, stirring occasionally, for 1½ to 2 hours. As it cooks, juices will evaporate; add more water periodically, letting it reduce after each addition, to total 1½ to 2 cups. After 1½ hours, the meat should be tender and the flavors melded. Remove and discard the bay leaf. Immediately before serving, whisk ½ Tbs. butter per serving into the sauce and toss with the pasta. Serve sprinkled with Parmesan, if you like. *—Suzette Gresham-Tognetti*

PER SERVING: 600 CALORIES I 45G PROTEIN I 57G CARB I 20G TOTAL FAT I 8G SAT FAT I 9G MONO FAT I 2G POLY FAT I 120MG CHOL I 960MG SODIUM I 4G FIBER

sweet-and-sour pork chops with pickled fennel

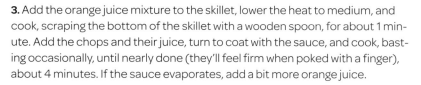

SERVES 4

- 1 cup freshly squeezed orange juice; more as needed
- 2 Tbs. packed dark brown sugar
- 4 1-inch-thick bone-in pork chops (about 2 lb.)
- Kosher salt and freshly ground black pepper
- 1 Tbs. olive oil
- 1 pint Pickled Fennel with Mustard and Peppercorns (recipe below)

Here, pickled fennel brightens up a simple weeknight pork chop supper. Serve with sautéed spinach or chard.

1. In a small bowl, mix the orange juice and sugar until dissolved.

2. Season the pork chops on both sides with salt and pepper. Heat the oil in a 12-inch skillet over medium-high heat. Brown the chops on both sides, about 5 minutes total. Transfer to a plate.

3. Add the orange juice mixture to the skillet, lower the heat to medium, and cook, scraping the bottom of the skillet with a wooden spoon, for about 1 minute. Add the chops and their juice, turn to coat with the sauce, and cook, basting occasionally, until nearly done (they'll feel firm when poked with a finger), about 4 minutes. If the sauce evaporates, add a bit more orange juice.

4. With tongs, pull the pickled fennel from the jar and add it to the pan, leaving the liquid behind. Cook until the pork reaches 145°F on an instant-read thermometer. Serve immediately. —*Eugenia Bone*

PER SERVING: 500 CALORIES | 29G PROTEIN | 18G CARB | 35G TOTAL FAT | 12G SAT FAT | 16G MONO FAT | 3G POLY FAT | 105MG CHOL | 430MG SODIUM | 1G FIBER

pickled fennel with mustard and peppercorns

YIELDS ABOUT 2 PINTS

- ½ tsp. yellow mustard seeds
- ½ tsp. whole black peppercorns
- 1 1-lb. fennel bulb, trimmed, cored, and thinly sliced
- 1 cup white-wine vinegar
- ½ cup granulated sugar
- 3 Tbs. olive oil
- Kosher salt

Tangy pickled fennel is a good match for fish and seafood and roasted lean meats like chicken and pork.

1. Have ready 2 sterilized wide-mouth pint jars, bands, and lids. Toast the mustard seeds and peppercorns in a small dry skillet over medium heat until fragrant, 1 to 2 minutes. Grind to a medium-coarse texture in a spice grinder or with a mortar and pestle. Pack the fennel into the jars, layering it with the spice mixture.

2. In a medium saucepan, bring the vinegar, sugar, oil, 1 Tbs. salt, and ½ cup water to a boil over medium heat. Pour the liquid over the fennel until it reaches the top of the jars. Screw on the lids, cool to room temperature, and refrigerate for 3 days before using. The fennel will keep in the refrigerator for at least 2 weeks.

PER ½ CUP: 20 CALORIES | 1G PROTEIN | 4G CARB | 0.5G TOTAL FAT | 0G SAT FAT | 0G MONO FAT | 0G POLY FAT | 0MG CHOL | 65MG SODIUM | 1G FIBER

fresh ham with rosemary, garlic & lemon

FOR THE HAM

- **1** 8½-lb. bone-in fresh half ham, preferably shank end, rind (skin) removed
- **1** medium lemon
- **¼** cup olive oil
- **¼** cup fresh rosemary leaves
- **6** medium cloves garlic, halved

  Kosher salt and freshly ground black pepper
- **¼** cup white-wine vinegar

FOR THE PAN SAUCE

- **¼** cup dry white wine
- **½** cup lower-salt chicken broth
- **2** tsp. unsalted butter, softened
- **2** tsp. unbleached all-purpose flour
- **1** Tbs. cherry jam

With just a few seasonings rubbed on a day ahead, a slow-roasted fresh ham becomes a juicy, fork-tender, and fragrant holiday centerpiece. Serve with roasted sweet potatoes and lightly sautéed green beans. Use leftover ham to make the Croque-Madame Sandwiches on p. 186.

PREPARE THE HAM

1. Set the ham fat side up in a large heavy-duty roasting pan. Use a sharp knife to score the fat in a 1-inch diamond pattern, cutting only about three-quarters of the way through the fat.

2. Peel the zest from the lemon with a vegetable peeler, avoiding the white pith. Put the zest, olive oil, rosemary, garlic, 1 Tbs. salt, and 1 tsp. pepper in a food processor and pulse to a coarse paste. Rub this mixture all over the ham. Cover the pan tightly with foil and refrigerate for 12 to 24 hours.

3. Position a rack in the oven so that the ham will sit as high as possible but still have at least 2 inches head space for air circulation. Heat the oven to 350°F.

4. Keep the ham covered with the foil and roast for 3 hours.

5. Uncover the pan and drizzle the vinegar over the ham, taking care not to wash off the coating. Continue roasting, basting every 15 minutes or so, until the ham is well browned and an instant-read thermometer inserted in the center of the meat without touching bone registers 170°F (check in several places), 1 to 1½ hours more. If the ham or drippings begin to brown too much, cover loosely with foil to prevent burning. Transfer the ham to a carving board to rest while you make the sauce.

MAKE THE SAUCE

1. Pour the pan drippings into a bowl, let sit until the fat rises to the top, and then skim off the fat. Return the skimmed drippings to the roasting pan and set the pan over medium heat. Whisk in the wine, scraping up any particles stuck to the pan's bottom. Whisk in the broth, add ½ cup water, and continue to boil until the liquid is reduced by one-third, about 2 minutes. Meanwhile, use a fork to mash the butter with the flour in a small bowl or ramekin to create a thick paste. Whisk the cherry jam into the sauce, then add the butter paste in parts, whisking until the paste is fully dissolved and the sauce is simmering and thickened.

2. Carve the ham and serve with the sauce. Leftover ham will keep in the refrigerator for up to 3 days and in the freezer for up to 2 months.
—*Bruce Weinstein and Mark Scarbrough*

PER SERVING: 760 CALORIES I 57G PROTEIN I 4G CARB I 54G TOTAL FAT I 21G SAT FAT I 26G MONO FAT I 4.5G POLY FAT I 215MG CHOL I 680MG SODIUM I 0G FIBER

ham and polenta spoonbread

SERVES 6 TO 8

- 2 oz. (4 Tbs.) unsalted butter; more for the pan
- 3 cups milk (whole or low-fat)

  Kosher salt
- ⅔ cup quick-cooking polenta
- 1 large yellow onion, chopped
- ½ lb. leftover roasted fresh ham (recipe facing page), chopped (about 2 cups)
- 4 oz. fontina, grated (1 cup)
- 2 oz. Asiago, grated (½ cup)
- 2 large eggs, separated
- 2 Tbs. chopped fresh basil
- 2 tsp. chopped fresh oregano
- 2 tsp. chopped fresh thyme
- 3 dashes hot pepper sauce, such as Tabasco

  Freshly ground black pepper

Traditionally served in the South, spoonbread is a savory pudding-like dish that's great for dinner or breakfast. Here, it's livened up with a dose of fresh herbs.

1. Position a rack in the center of the oven and heat the oven to 375°F. Lightly butter a 6-cup baking dish, preferably oval.

2. Bring the milk and ½ tsp. salt to a simmer in a 4-quart saucepan over medium heat. Whisk in the polenta. Continue whisking until thick, 3 to 5 minutes. Transfer to a large bowl and set aside.

3. Melt 2 Tbs. of the butter in a 12-inch skillet over medium-low heat. Add the onion and a pinch of salt and cook, stirring occasionally, until golden and soft, about 15 minutes. Add the ham and stir often until warmed through, about 2 minutes.

4. Stir the ham mixture, cheeses, egg yolks, basil, oregano, thyme, hot pepper sauce, ½ tsp. salt, and ½ tsp. pepper into the polenta; mix well.

5. In a medium bowl, beat the egg whites with an electric mixer on high speed until soft peaks form. Fold the beaten egg whites into the polenta and then spread the mixture in the prepared baking pan. Cut the remaining 2 Tbs. butter into pieces and dot on top.

6. Bake until brown and puffed, 30 to 35 minutes. Cool on a wire rack for 10 minutes before serving with a large spoon.
—*Bruce Weinstein and Mark Scarbrough*

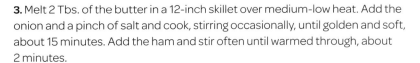

PER SERVING: 330 CALORIES | 19G PROTEIN | 16G CARB | 21G TOTAL FAT | 11G SAT FAT | 6G MONO FAT | 1G POLY FAT | 125MG CHOL | 400MG SODIUM | 1G FIBER

braised lamb shanks with garlic and vermouth

SERVES 6

- **6 lamb shanks (¾ to 1 lb. each)**
- **Kosher salt and freshly ground black pepper**
- **2 Tbs. extra-virgin olive oil**
- **1 cup dry white vermouth, preferably Vya® or Noilly Pratt®**
- **2 bay leaves**
- **2 heads garlic, separated into cloves (unpeeled)**
- **2 tsp. freshly squeezed lemon juice; more as needed**
- **¼ cup chopped fresh herbs, preferably a mix of mint and parsley (chervil and chives are also good)**

Make Ahead

The dish can be made up to 3 days ahead. After braising, transfer the shanks to a baking dish. Strain and season the sauce as directed in the recipe. Pour a little strained sauce over the shanks to moisten them. Refrigerate the shanks and the sauce separately, both tightly covered. Before serving, reheat the chilled sauce, pour it over the shanks in the baking dish, cover the dish with foil, and warm in a 325°F oven for about 30 minutes. Finish with the herbs and black pepper, and serve.

After the long braise, the garlic cloves are tender enough to push through a sieve, creating a flavorful purée that thickens the pan sauce. Don't forget to scrape the pulp clinging to the bottom of the strainer.

1. Position a rack in the lower third of the oven and heat the oven to 325°F. If needed, trim any excess fat from the lamb shanks, but don't trim away the thin membrane that holds the meat to the bone. Season the shanks all over with salt and pepper.

2. Heat the oil over medium heat in a large Dutch oven or other heavy braising pot large enough to accommodate the lamb shanks in a snug single layer. When the oil is shimmering, add half the shanks and brown them on all sides, 12 to 15 minutes total. Set the browned shanks on a platter. Repeat with the remaining shanks. When all the shanks are browned, pour off and discard the fat from the pan.

3. Set the pan over medium-high heat and add the vermouth. As it boils, stir with a wooden spoon to dissolve any drippings. Return the shanks to the pan, arranging them as best you can so they fit snugly. Tuck the bay leaves in between the shanks and scatter the garlic over them. Cover and braise in the oven, turning the shanks every 45 minutes, until fork-tender, 1½ to 2 hours.

4. Transfer the shanks to a platter and cover with foil to keep warm. Tilt the braising pot to pool the juices at one end and skim off and discard any surface fat. Pour what remains in the pot into a medium-mesh sieve set over a bowl. Discard the bay leaves. With a rubber spatula, scrape over and press down on the garlic cloves so the pulp goes through but not the skins; be sure to scrape the pulp clinging to the bottom of the strainer into the sauce. Whisk in the lemon juice. Taste and add salt, pepper, and more lemon juice if needed. To serve, pour the sauce over the shanks and shower them with the chopped herbs and a little freshly ground pepper. —*Molly Stevens*

PER SERVING: 360 CALORIES | 32G PROTEIN | 1G CARB | 20G TOTAL FAT | 7G SAT FAT | 10G MONO FAT | 1.5G POLY FAT | 120MG CHOL | 360MG SODIUM | 0G FIBER

lamb tagine with honey, prunes, onions & toasted almonds

SERVES 6

- **16** pearl onions
- **2** Tbs. olive oil
- **2** lb. lamb stew meat cut into 1-inch cubes, or ½ leg of lamb cut into 1-inch cubes, bone reserved
- **1** medium onion, finely diced
- **10** threads Spanish saffron
- **1½** cups homemade or lower-salt beef broth or water
- **⅓** cup honey
- **1** tsp. ground turmeric
- **½** tsp. ground cinnamon
- **⅛** tsp. ground mace
- **1** cup (about 24) pitted prunes
- **20** sprigs fresh cilantro, chopped
- **¼** cup whole almonds
   Kosher salt and freshly ground black pepper

Serve this Moroccan stew over couscous or with chunks of warm, crusty bread.

1. Heat the oven to 375°F. In a small saucepan filled with boiling water, blanch the pearl onions for 1 minute. Drain and let cool. Peel the onions and set aside.

2. In a medium Dutch oven, heat the olive oil over medium-high heat. Brown the meat in batches on all sides. Transfer the meat to a platter. Add the diced onion to the pot and cook, stirring occasionally, until softened, about 5 minutes.

3. Grind the saffron in a mortar and pestle (or rub it between your fingers) and add it to the beef broth. Return the meat to the pot. Stir the broth into the pot with the lamb, along with any bones. Stir in the honey, turmeric, cinnamon, mace, and prunes. Add the cilantro. Cover the pot tightly with foil and then with a lid. Put the pot in the oven and bake until the lamb is tender, about 50 minutes. Add the pearl onions, cover, and cook for another 5 minutes.

4. Meanwhile, in a small dry nonstick frying pan, toast the almonds until golden. Set aside.

5. Remove the foil and lid. Carefully spoon off any grease. Add 1 tsp. salt and 1½ tsp. pepper. Return the pot, uncovered, to the oven, and let the sauce reduce slightly, about 5 minutes. Sprinkle the tagine with the toasted almonds. Serve on rimmed plates or in shallow bowls. *—Kitty Morse*

PER SERVING: 480 CALORIES | 41G PROTEIN | 41G CARB | 18G TOTAL FAT | 6G SAT FAT | 10G MONO FAT | 2G POLY FAT | 125MG CHOL | 480MG SODIUM | 4G FIBER

pistachio-crusted lamb chops

SERVES 4 TO 6

- 1 **cup unsalted shelled pistachios**

  Kosher salt
- 3 **Tbs. honey**
- 1 **Tbs. fresh lemon juice**
- 1 **tsp. ground cumin**
- ¼ **tsp. cayenne**

  Freshly ground black pepper
- 12 **lamb rib chops (about 1½ lb.)**
- 2 **Tbs. extra-virgin olive oil**

Serve the lamb chops with lentils and rice and plain Greek yogurt mixed with chopped mint.

1. Position a rack about 4 inches from the broiler and heat the broiler on high.

2. Finely chop the pistachios in a food processor. Combine the pistachios and ½ tsp. salt in a small bowl. Set aside. In another small bowl, use a fork to mix the honey and lemon juice. Set aside. In a third small bowl, mix the cumin, cayenne, 1 tsp. salt, and ½ tsp. pepper.

3. Brush the lamb chops with the oil and season on both sides with the spice mixture.

4. Arrange the chops on a foil-lined rimmed baking sheet. Broil until lightly browned, 1 to 2 minutes. Flip and broil until the second sides are lightly browned, 1 to 2 minutes. Remove the baking sheet from the oven, and lower the rack to about 6 inches from the broiler. Using a pastry brush, spread about half of the honey mixture on the top sides of the chops. Sprinkle with about half of the nuts, pressing so that they adhere. Broil until the nuts are lightly toasted, about 30 seconds.

5. Flip the chops and repeat the honey-nut coating on the other side. Broil until the nuts are lightly browned and the lamb is medium rare, about 30 seconds. Let the chops rest for about 2 minutes, and then serve, sprinkling any nuts that may have fallen off the lamb onto each portion. —*Dina Cheney*

PER SERVING: 300 CALORIES I 19G PROTEIN I 15G CARB I 19G TOTAL FAT I 3.5G SAT FAT I 10G MONO FAT I 3.5G POLY FAT I 45MG CHOL I 320MG SODIUM I 2G FIBER

seared lamb shoulder chops
with mustard-dill pan sauce

4   bone-in lamb shoulder chops
    (2 to 2½ lb. total)

    Kosher salt and freshly
    ground black pepper

1   Tbs. extra-virgin olive oil

2   small shallots, finely chopped

½   cup lower-salt chicken broth

½   cup dry white wine

1   Tbs. Dijon mustard

2   tsp. freshly squeezed lemon
    juice

2   Tbs. cold unsalted butter,
    cut into small pieces

1   Tbs. finely chopped fresh dill

If you like, substitute pork chops or chicken breasts for the lamb; this sauce is equally delicious on both.

1. Season the lamb chops all over with 1½ tsp. salt and ½ tsp. pepper. Heat the oil in a large skillet over medium-high heat. Put 2 of the chops in the skillet and cook, flipping once, until deep golden-brown and medium rare (130°F), about 10 minutes. Transfer to a large plate, cover loosely with foil, and keep warm. Repeat with the remaining 2 chops.

2. Add the shallots to the skillet and cook, stirring, until softened, about 1 minute. Add the broth and wine and cook, scraping up any browned bits, until reduced by half, 4 to 5 minutes. Reduce the heat to medium low, stir in the mustard and lemon juice, and cook for 1 minute more. Add the butter a piece or two at a time, swirling the skillet to melt it into the sauce. Remove the skillet from the heat and stir in the dill. Season to taste with salt and pepper. Serve the lamb with the sauce. *—Liz Pearson*

PER SERVING: 330 CALORIES | 29G PROTEIN | 3G CARB | 19G TOTAL FAT | 7G SAT FAT | 8G MONO FAT | 1G POLY FAT | 105 MG CHOL | 600MG SODIUM | 0G FIBER

spicy red lentil dal with winter vegetables and lamb

SERVES 4

- 1 lb. boneless leg of lamb, trimmed and cut into 1-inch pieces
- 5 tsp. garam masala or curry powder
- Kosher salt and freshly ground black pepper
- 1 medium yellow onion, coarsely chopped (1½ cups)
- 4 medium cloves garlic, chopped
- 2 Tbs. peeled and chopped fresh ginger (from a 2-inch piece)
- 1 fresh serrano chile, stemmed and chopped
- 3 Tbs. vegetable oil
- 1½ tsp. brown mustard seeds
- 1½ cups dried red lentils, picked through
- ½ small head of cauliflower, cut into 1½-inch pieces (about 3 cups)
- 4 medium carrots, peeled and cut into 1-inch pieces (about 2½ cups)
- 2 large Yukon Gold potatoes (about 8 oz. each), peeled and cut into 1-inch chunks (1¼ cups)
- 1 tsp. ground turmeric
- 1 cup chopped fresh cilantro

Dal is a thick, spicy Indian stew made with legumes like chickpeas and lentils. Serve with basmati rice.

1. In a medium bowl, mix the lamb with 2 tsp. of the garam masala, 1 tsp. salt, and ½ tsp. pepper.

2. In a food processor, pulse the onion, garlic, ginger, and chile in 1-second intervals until finely chopped. (Don't run the processor constantly or the mixture will become too watery.)

3. Heat 2 Tbs. of the oil in a 4- to 5-quart pot over medium heat. When the oil is hot, add the mustard seeds. When the seeds begin to pop and turn gray, about 1 minute, stir in the remaining 3 tsp. garam masala, the onion mixture, lentils, cauliflower, carrots, potatoes, turmeric, 6 cups of water, and 1½ tsp. salt.

4. In a 12-inch skillet, heat the remaining 1 Tbs. oil over medium-high heat and brown the lamb, about 2 minutes per side. Transfer the meat to a bowl. Deglaze the skillet with ½ cup water, let it reduce by half, and add it to the bowl.

5. Add the lamb and its liquid to the dal. Bring to a boil over medium-high heat, reduce to medium low, and cover. Simmer until the vegetables and meat are tender, stirring occasionally, about 30 minutes. Season to taste with salt and pepper and stir in the cilantro. *—Ivy Manning*

PER SERVING: 320 CALORIES | 16G PROTEIN | 51G CARB | 6G TOTAL FAT | 0.5G SAT FAT | 2G MONO FAT | 2G POLY FAT | 0MG CHOL | 610MG SODIUM | 11G FIBER

seared scallops with cauliflower, brown butter & basil

SERVES 4

- 3 Tbs. extra-virgin olive oil
- 1 small head cauliflower (1 lb.), trimmed and cut into bite-size florets (about 4 cups)
- 1 lb. all-natural (dry-packed) sea scallops
- 2 Tbs. unsalted butter
- 1 large shallot, minced
- ½ cup dry vermouth

  Kosher salt and freshly ground black pepper
- 8 large fresh basil leaves, thinly sliced

In this easily assembled meal, vermouth-laced brown butter imbues cauliflower with deep flavor, while a basil garnish adds color and freshness.

1. Heat 1 Tbs. of the oil in a 12-inch nonstick skillet over medium-high heat until shimmering hot. Add the cauliflower and cook, stirring often, until lightly browned, about 4 minutes. Transfer to a bowl.

2. Add the remaining 2 Tbs. oil to the skillet. When shimmering hot, add the scallops in a single layer. Cook until golden-brown, about 2 minutes. Flip and cook until the scallops are barely cooked through, about 2 minutes more (if you cut into one, it should still be slightly translucent in the center). Transfer to another bowl.

3. Swirl the butter into the skillet, add the shallot and cook, stirring often, until the shallot softens and the butter begins to brown, about 1 minute.

4. Add the vermouth and bring it to a boil, scraping up any bits on the bottom of the skillet with a wooden spoon. Return the cauliflower to the skillet and season with ¼ tsp. each salt and pepper. Cover the skillet and reduce the heat to medium. Cook, stirring once or twice, until the cauliflower florets are tender, about 6 minutes.

5. Return the scallops to the pan and toss to heat through, about 1 minute. Remove from the heat, sprinkle with the basil, and serve.
—*Bruce Weinstein and Mark Scarbrough*

PER SERVING: 300 CALORIES | 21G PROTEIN | 8G CARB | 17G TOTAL FAT | 5G SAT FAT | 9G MONO FAT | 1.5G POLY FAT | 55MG CHOL | 270MG SODIUM | 2G FIBER

red curry with shrimp and sugar snap peas

SERVES 4

- 2 Tbs. vegetable oil
- 2 Tbs. Red Curry Paste (recipe facing page) or jarred
- 1 15-oz. can unsweetened coconut milk
- 1 cup lower-salt chicken broth, fish broth, or water
- 1 lb. shrimp (21 to 25 per lb.), peeled and deveined
- 2 cups sugar snap peas (7 to 8 oz.), trimmed
- 5 wild lime leaves, torn or cut into quarters (optional)
- 2 Tbs. fish sauce
- 1 Tbs. palm sugar or light brown sugar
- ½ tsp. kosher salt

  A handful of fresh Thai or Italian basil leaves

  Hot cooked rice or rice noodles, for serving
- 1 long, slender fresh red chile (such as red jalapeño or serrano), thinly sliced on the diagonal (optional)

Omit the wild lime leaves if you can't find them—there isn't a good substitution.

1. Heat the oil in a 2- to 3-quart saucepan over medium heat until a bit of curry paste just sizzles when added to the pan. Add all the curry paste and cook, pressing and stirring with a wooden spoon or heatproof spatula to soften the paste and mix it in with the oil, until fragrant, about 2 minutes.

2. Add the coconut milk and broth and bring to a simmer. Simmer, stirring often, for 5 minutes, allowing the flavors to develop.

3. Increase the heat to medium high and let the curry come to a strong boil. Add the shrimp, sugar snap peas, and half the lime leaves (if using), and stir well. Cook, stirring occasionally, until the shrimp curl and turn pink, about 2 minutes. Add the fish sauce, sugar, and salt and stir to combine. Remove from the heat.

4. Tear the basil leaves in half (or quarters if they are large), and stir them into the curry, along with the remaining lime leaves (if using). Let rest for 5 minutes to allow the flavors to develop.

5. Serve hot or warm with rice or noodles, garnished with the chile slices (if using). —*Nancie McDermott*

PER SERVING: 430 CALORIES | 24G PROTEIN | 18G CARB | 31G TOTAL FAT | 21G SAT FAT | 4.5G MONO FAT | 4G POLY FAT | 170MG CHOL | 1,240MG SODIUM | 4G FIBER

braised red snapper puttanesca

SERVES 4

- 4 5-oz. skinless red snapper fillets (about ¾ inch thick)

   Kosher salt and freshly ground black pepper

- 3 Tbs. extra-virgin olive oil

- 3 medium cloves garlic, minced (about 1 Tbs.)

- 2 14½-oz. cans petite-diced tomatoes

- 2 anchovy fillets, minced

- ½ cup pitted Kalamata olives, halved lengthwise (about 3 oz.)

- 3 Tbs. coarsely chopped fresh basil leaves

- 1 Tbs. capers, rinsed

- ¼ tsp. crushed red pepper flakes

- 1 Tbs. coarsely chopped fresh mint

- 2 tsp. red-wine vinegar

Black sea bass is a good substitute for snapper in this recipe. Serve with polenta or couscous.

1. Position a rack in the center of the oven and heat the oven to 325°F. Season the snapper all over with salt and pepper. Let sit at room temperature while you prepare the sauce.

2. Heat 2 Tbs. of the olive oil in a 12-inch ovenproof skillet over medium-low heat. Add the garlic and cook, stirring, until softened but not golden, about 1 minute. Add the tomatoes and their juice, anchovies, olives, 2 Tbs. of the basil, capers, and pepper flakes to the pan. Bring the sauce to a brisk simmer and cook, stirring occasionally, until the tomatoes are tender and the juices have reduced to a saucy consistency, about 8 minutes.

3. Nestle the snapper fillets into the sauce, spooning some on top to keep the fish moist. Drizzle with the remaining 1 Tbs. olive oil. Tightly cover the pan with a lid or aluminum foil and braise in the oven until the fish is almost cooked through, 10 to 15 minutes depending on thickness.

4. With a slotted spatula, transfer the snapper to 4 shallow serving bowls. If the sauce seems too thin, simmer over medium-high heat until thickened to your liking. Stir the remaining 1 Tbs. basil and the mint and vinegar into the sauce and spoon it over the fish. *—Allison Ehri Kreitler*

PER SERVING: 320 CALORIES | 31G PROTEIN | 12G CARB | 17G TOTAL FAT | 2.5G SAT FAT | 12G MONO FAT | 2.5G POLY FAT | 50MG CHOL | 1,360MG SODIUM | 0G FIBER

To check if your fish is done, use a paring knife to peek between two bits of flesh in the center of the fillet. The very middle should look ever-so-slightly translucent, which means it's almost cooked through. The fish will continue to cook as you finish your sauce, so it will be perfectly done by the time you're ready to serve it.

indian summer gratin with butternut squash, potatoes, corn & bacon

SERVES 4 AS A MAIN DISH,
6 AS A SIDE DISH

- **1** Tbs. plus ½ tsp. unsalted butter
- **4** slices bacon
- **1½** cups fresh breadcrumbs
- **½** cup plus 2 Tbs. finely grated Parmigiano-Reggiano
- **1** Tbs. extra-virgin olive oil
- **1½** tsp. chopped fresh thyme leaves
- Kosher salt
- **1** large or 2 medium leeks (white and light green parts only), halved and sliced ¼ inch thick
- **2** tsp. minced fresh garlic
- **1¾** to 2 cups fresh corn kernels (from 3 to 4 large ears)
- Freshly ground black pepper
- **⅔** cup heavy cream
- **¾** cup lower-salt chicken broth
- **½** tsp. finely grated lemon zest
- **12** oz. peeled, seeded butternut squash, cut into ½-inch dice (about 2½ cups)
- **8** oz. Yukon Gold potatoes, cut into ⅓-inch dice (about 1½ cups)

This seasonal gratin gets even heartier with the addition of bacon. You can make this a day ahead, if you like; the flavors will develop even more overnight. Reheat at 375°F, covered, for 20 minutes.

1. Position a rack in the center of the oven and heat the oven to 400°F. Rub a 2-quart shallow gratin dish with ½ tsp. of the butter.

2. In a 12-inch nonstick skillet over medium heat, cook the bacon until crisp, about 8 minutes. Transfer the bacon to paper towels. Reserve 2 Tbs. of the fat in the skillet; discard the remainder. When the bacon is cool, crumble or mince it.

3. In a small bowl, combine 1 Tbs. of the crumbled bacon with the breadcrumbs, 2 Tbs. of the Parmigiano, the olive oil, ½ tsp. of the thyme, and a large pinch of salt. Mix well.

4. Add the remaining 1 Tbs. butter to the skillet with the bacon fat and melt over medium heat. Add the leeks and a pinch of salt, and cook, stirring, until softened and just starting to turn golden, 6 to 7 minutes. Add the garlic and stir well. Add the corn, ¼ tsp. salt, and a few grinds of pepper. Cook, stirring, until the corn has lost its raw look and is slightly shrunken, 2 to 3 minutes. Cool slightly.

5. Combine the cream and chicken broth in a 2-cup liquid measure. Add the lemon zest, ½ tsp. salt, and a few grinds of pepper. Stir to mix well.

6. In a large bowl, combine the remaining bacon, the corn-leek mixture, the diced squash, potatoes, and remaining 1 tsp. thyme. Toss lightly to combine. Spread the mixture evenly in the gratin dish. Sprinkle the remaining ½ cup Parmigiano on top. Stir the cream mixture one more time and pour it over everything as evenly as possible. (Be sure to scrape out any seasonings left in the cup.) Press down on the vegetables with a spatula so that the liquid surrounds them and everything is evenly distributed. Sprinkle the breadcrumb mixture evenly over all.

7. Cover with foil and bake for 20 minutes. Remove the foil and continue to bake until the crumb topping is deeply golden and the squash and potatoes are tender when pierced with a fork, about 25 minutes more. The liquid should have bubbled below the surface of the vegetables, leaving browned bits around the edge of the pan. Let cool for 20 to 25 minutes before serving. *—Susie Middleton*

PER SERVING: 350 CALORIES I 8G PROTEIN I 32G CARB I 23G TOTAL FAT I 11G SAT FAT I 8G MONO FAT I 2G POLY FAT I 55MG CHOL I 390MG SODIUM I 4G FIBER

mushroom paprikás

SERVES 8

1 lb. medium to large fresh mushrooms, such as cremini

2 Tbs. unsalted butter or oil

1 large onion, finely chopped

Kosher salt and freshly ground black pepper

1 tsp. paprika

½ cup sour cream

Cooked egg noodles, for serving

This dish is quick to throw together yet it's comforting, filling, and delicious. If you want it to be more colorful, sauté thin strips of red pepper with the onion.

1. Wipe the mushrooms clean and slice them about ⅛ inch thick.

2. Melt the butter in a large frying pan. Add the onion and cook slowly until tender, about 8 minutes. Transfer to a plate. Increase the heat to medium high and add a third of the mushrooms, a sprinkle of salt, and a dash of black pepper. Stir constantly and cook the mushrooms quickly so that they exude and evaporate their juices and brown nicely, about 10 minutes. Remove from the pan and set aside. Continue browning the mushrooms in batches. Lower the heat and stir in the onion and paprika.

3. Return the mushrooms to the pan, stir in the sour cream, taste, and add salt if necessary. Cook over low heat to heat through; don't boil or the sour cream may separate. Serve over the noodles. —*Maria and Lorant Nagyszalanczy*

All about Cremini Mushrooms

Also called baby bella mushrooms, cremini mushrooms are closely related to common white mushrooms, but they have a darker hue and richer flavor. Large cremini mushrooms are called portobello mushrooms. If you don't have creminis, you can substitute white, button, or portobello mushrooms instead.

Warm Maple and Cinnamon
Bread Pudding
(recipe on p. 172)

breakfast & brunch

cheese omelet

SERVES 1

½ Tbs. unsalted butter;
   more as needed

2 large eggs

⅛ tsp. sea salt or kosher salt

Freshly ground black pepper

¼ cup loosely packed grated
   Gruyère

If you prefer firmer eggs or if undercooked eggs are a concern, cook the omelet for another minute before adding the cheese. It will get a little brown, but the eggs will be cooked through.

1. Melt the butter in an 8-inch nonstick skillet over medium heat.

2. In a small bowl, lightly beat the eggs, salt, and a couple of grinds of pepper with a fork until the whites and yolks are completely mixed and the eggs are frothy. Pour the eggs into the skillet and let them sit, undisturbed, until the eggs are just beginning to set around the edges, 30 to 60 seconds.

3. Gently scramble the eggs with a silicone spatula while shaking the pan back and forth. Scramble and shake just until the eggs have set on the bottom but are still undercooked on top, 45 to 60 seconds. Turn off the heat and give the pan a few shakes to evenly distribute the eggs. Tap it once firmly on the stove to smooth the bottom of the omelet (use a heatproof cutting board if your stovetop is glass).

4. Sprinkle the cheese down the center third of the omelet and run a spatula around the edge. You can use the spatula to smooth the top of the eggs if necessary. Let it sit for about 1 minute. The top of the omelet will still be loose and the bottom should have no color.

5. Fold a third of the omelet over the cheese. Shake the unfolded third of the omelet up the side and slightly out of the pan. Invert the pan onto a plate to complete the final fold of the omelet. It should be folded in three, like a letter. Rub the top with cold butter for shine, if desired. Serve immediately.
—*Allison Ehri Kreitler*

PER SERVING: 310 CALORIES I 21G PROTEIN I 1G CARB I 24G TOTAL FAT I 12G SAT FAT I 8G MONO FAT I 2G POLY FAT I 470MG CHOL I 370MG SODIUM I 0G FIBER

how to make a perfect omelet

A classic French omelet is pale on the outside (no browning at all) and creamy—ever so slightly undercooked inside.
Although it's a simple egg dish, you do have to pay attention to a few key steps to get it just right.

Cook until just set around the edge.

Scramble gently.

Turn off the heat as soon as the bottom has set.

Sprinkle the cheese down the middle.

Fold one-third of the omelet toward the center.

Fold again and flip onto a plate.

salmon hash with dilled crème fraîche

SERVES 4

FOR THE DILLED CRÈME FRAÎCHE

- 1 cup crème fraîche or sour cream
- 1 Tbs. chopped fresh dill or 1½ tsp. dried dill
- Pinch of salt
- Freshly squeezed lemon juice (optional)

FOR THE HASH

- 1½ Tbs. unsalted butter
- 1½ Tbs. vegetable oil
- 1 lb. Yukon Gold or red-skinned potatoes, unpeeled, cut into ½-inch dice
- ½ medium onion, diced (about 1 cup)
- 2 Tbs. half-and-half or cream
- 1 tsp. Dijon mustard
- Kosher salt and freshly ground black pepper
- 1 lb. cooked skinless salmon fillet or hot-smoked salmon, flaked
- 3 Tbs. snipped fresh chives or thinly sliced scallion tops
- 1 Tbs. chopped fresh dill or 1½ tsp. dried dill

FOR THE GARNISH

- 4 fried or poached eggs
- Drained capers
- Fresh dill sprigs
- Prepared horseradish (optional)

This hash has a luscious contrast of crusted potatoes and tender, moist salmon. An egg topping is the crowning touch, although it's just as good without.

MAKE THE DILLED CRÈME FRAÎCHE

In a small bowl, stir together the crème fraîche, dill, salt, and lemon juice, if using. Taste and adjust the seasonings; set aside.

MAKE THE HASH

In a 10-inch cast-iron or other large heavy skillet, heat the butter and oil over medium-low heat. Add the potatoes, stirring to coat them with the fat. Cover and cook until the potatoes begin to turn golden and a bit tender with browned edges here and there, about 15 minutes (you should hear only a faint sizzling). Uncover the potatoes and turn them with a spatula. Raise the heat to medium and cook until uniformly soft with some crisp brown spots, about 5 minutes. Stir in the onion and pat the mixture down with the spatula. Cook until the onion is soft and the mixture begins to stick in a few spots and browns on the bottom, about 5 minutes. In a small bowl, whisk together the half-and-half, mustard, a pinch of salt, and a generous grinding of pepper. Scrape up the hash and stir in the mustard mixture. Raise the heat to medium high. Continue cooking the hash, scraping it up and patting it back down another time or two until browned, another 5 to 8 minutes. Mix in the salmon, chives, and dill and cook until heated through, another 2 minutes. Serve hot, topping each portion with a fried or poached egg and a sprinkling of capers. Garnish with dill sprigs or a bit of horseradish on the side, if you like. Top each portion with a dollop of the dilled crème fraîche, passing the rest at the table.

—Cheryl Alters Jamison and Bill Jamison

PER SERVING: 590 CALORIES | 33G PROTEIN | 26G CARB | 39G TOTAL FAT | 18G SAT FAT | 11G MONO FAT | 8G POLY FAT | 170MG CHOL | 540MG SODIUM | 4G FIBER

Salmon Tips

This recipe calls for plain salmon fillet in the hash, cooked as simply as possible. Use whichever method you like best and cook the salmon until it's cooked through: roasted, broiled, poached, steamed, pan-seared, and even microwaved are all fine. Roasting is the most straightforward: Heat the oven to 400°F, coat the salmon with a little olive oil, season it with salt and pepper, and roast it on a rimmed baking sheet until the flesh inside has lost its deep pink color, 15 to 18 minutes.

If you don't feel like cooking salmon, hot-smoked works well, too (look for it in Cryovac® packages in the supermarket seafood section). Don't use cold-smoked fish: It's too oily and strongly flavored.

baked eggs with chives and cream

SERVES 2

- **2** tsp. unsalted butter, softened
- **4** large eggs
  Kosher salt and freshly ground black pepper
- **1½** tsp. chopped fresh chives
- **2** Tbs. heavy cream

These eggs are surprisingly easy, plus they're ready in about 10 minutes.

1. Position a rack in the center of the oven and heat the oven to 425°F. Butter 2 oven-safe 6-inch gratin dishes with 1 tsp. butter each.

2. Crack 2 eggs into each gratin dish. Season with a pinch of salt and pepper, and sprinkle with the chives. Drizzle 1 Tbs. cream in each dish, starting over the yolks and working around the dish. Bake until the eggs are bubbly and browned on the edges but not quite set in the middle, 5 minutes. (For firmer eggs, bake for an additional 1 minute.)

3. Heat the broiler on high. Broil the eggs, still on the center rack of the oven, until the center is just set, about 2 minutes. Remove from the oven immediately—the eggs will continue to set.   —*Nicole Rees*

PER SERVING: 230 CALORIES I 13G PROTEIN I 1G CARB I 19G TOTAL FAT I 9G SAT FAT I 6G MONO FAT I 1.5G POLY FAT I 455MG CHOL I 290MG SODIUM I 0G FIBER

candied bacon

SERVES 2

- **6** slices thick-cut bacon
- **2** Tbs. plus 1 tsp. pure maple syrup
- **1½** Tbs. light brown sugar

Make this maple-syrup-coated, brown-sugar-crusted bacon and then keep it warm while the eggs bake.

Position a rack in the center of the oven and heat the oven to 425°F. Arrange the bacon slices on a rimmed baking sheet. Drizzle both sides with the maple syrup and then sprinkle both sides evenly with the sugar. Bake until browned and crisp, 20 to 22 minutes.

PER SLICE: 70 CALORIES I 2G PROTEIN I 9G CARB I 2.5G TOTAL FAT I 1G SAT FAT I 1G MONO FAT I 0G POLY FAT I 5MG CHOL I 150MG SODIUM I 0G FIBER

blueberry muffins

YIELDS 12 MUFFINS

Vegetable oil or cooking spray for the pan

1 lb. (3½ cups) unbleached all-purpose flour

4 tsp. baking powder

½ tsp. baking soda

½ tsp. table salt

1⅓ cups granulated sugar

5 oz. (10 Tbs.) unsalted butter, melted and cooled slightly

1 cup whole milk, at room temperature

1 cup crème fraîche or sour cream, at room temperature

2 large eggs, at room temperature

1 large egg yolk, at room temperature

2 tsp. finely grated lemon zest

1½ cups fresh (washed, dried, and picked over) or frozen (no need to thaw) blueberries

Overfilling the muffin cups gives you those great big bakery-style muffin tops. This muffin batter is also delicious with the flavoring variations that follow the recipe. Be sure to add the fruit before the batter is fully mixed to avoid overmixing.

1. Position a rack in the center of the oven and heat the oven to 350°F. Lightly oil (or spray with cooking spray) the top of a standard 12-cup muffin tin and then line with paper or foil baking cups. (Spraying the pan keeps the muffin tops from sticking to the pan's surface.)

2. In a large bowl, sift together the flour, baking powder, baking soda, and salt; mix well. In a medium bowl, whisk the sugar, butter, milk, crème fraîche or sour cream, eggs, egg yolk, and zest until well combined.

3. Pour the wet ingredients into the dry and fold gently with a rubber spatula just until the dry ingredients are mostly moistened; the batter will be lumpy, and there should still be quite a few streaks of dry flour. Sprinkle the blueberries on the batter and fold them in until just combined. (The batter will still be lumpy; don't try to smooth it out or you'll overmix.)

4. If you have an ice cream scoop with a "sweeper" in it, use it to fill the muffin cups. Otherwise, use two spoons to spoon the batter in, distributing all of the batter evenly. The batter should mound higher than the rim of the cups by about ¾ inch.

5. Bake until the muffins are golden brown and spring back lightly when you press the middle, 30 to 35 minutes. (The muffin tops will probably meld together.) Let the muffin tin cool on a rack for 15 to 20 minutes. Use a table knife to separate the tops, and then invert the pan and pop out the muffins.
—*Joanne Chang*

PER MUFFIN: 480 CALORIES | 7G PROTEIN | 72G CARB | 19G TOTAL FAT | 12G SAT FAT | 5G MONO FAT | 1G POLY FAT | 95MG CHOL | 320MG SODIUM | 1G FIBER

Variations

Cranberry-Orange Muffins In place of the lemon zest and blueberries in the batter, add orange zest and chopped fresh cranberries.

Banana-Walnut Muffins Don't add any zest to the batter. Instead add 1½ cups thinly sliced ripe banana and ¾ cup coarsely chopped toasted walnuts.

buttermilk pancakes

YIELDS ABOUT 17 PANCAKES

3   Tbs. unsalted butter; more for serving

9   oz. (2 cups) unbleached all-purpose flour

¼   cup granulated sugar

2½ tsp. baking powder

½   tsp. baking soda

½   tsp. kosher salt

2   cups buttermilk

2   large eggs

Vegetable oil for the griddle

Pure maple syrup, for serving

Make Ahead

Cooked pancakes will keep, sealed in freezer bags, for up to 2 days in the refrigerator and up to 1 month in the freezer. Defrost in the refrigerator overnight and reheat in a 350°F oven for 5 minutes.

You can add fresh berries, thinly sliced fruit, or even crumbled crisp bacon to this batter for an extra hit of flavor. Or substitute ½ cup wheat germ, cornmeal, or whole-wheat flour for ½ cup of the all-purpose flour. This recipe can be easily doubled or tripled.

1. Heat the oven to 200°F. Melt the butter in a small bowl in the microwave or in a small saucepan on the stove and set aside to cool briefly.

2. In a large bowl, whisk the flour, sugar, baking powder, baking soda, and salt. In a medium bowl, whisk the buttermilk and eggs. Pour the wet ingredients into the dry ingredients. Whisk gently until the dry ingredients are almost incorporated; stop before the batter is evenly moistened. Add the cooled melted butter and mix just until the batter is evenly moistened (there will be lumps). Let the batter rest while you heat the griddle.

3. Heat a griddle or a large skillet over medium heat (or set an electric griddle to 375°F) until drops of water briefly dance on the surface before evaporating. Lightly oil the griddle. Working in batches, pour ¼ cup of the batter onto the griddle for each pancake, spacing them about 1 inch apart. Let cook undisturbed until bubbles rise to the surface and the edges look dry, 1 to 2 minutes. Check the underside of each pancake to make sure it's nicely browned; then flip. Cook until the second side is nicely browned, about 1 minute more. Transfer the pancakes to a baking sheet and keep warm in the oven while you repeat with the remaining batter.

4. Serve hot with butter and maple syrup. —*Denise Mickelsen*

PER PANCAKE: 110 CALORIES | 3G PROTEIN | 16G CARB | 3.5G TOTAL FAT | 1.5G SAT FAT | 1G MONO FAT | 0G POLY FAT | 30MG CHOL | 170MG SODIUM | 0G FIBER

Buttermilk Stand-Ins

These pancakes get their tangy flavor and light-as-air texture from buttermilk. But in a pinch, you can use any of these substitutions:

Powdered buttermilk Use according to package directions, adding water to the wet ingredients and the powder to the dry.

"Sour milk" Add 2 Tbs. white vinegar or lemon juice to 2 cups whole milk and let it stand for 10 minutes to thicken slightly; add to the wet ingredients.

Yogurt and milk Add 1 cup plain yogurt and 1 cup milk (both can be full-fat or low-fat) to the wet ingredients.

pork and potato hash with poached eggs and avocado

SERVES 4

1½ lb. russet potatoes, peeled and cut into small dice (about 3¾ cups)

Kosher salt

2 Tbs. extra-virgin olive oil; more as needed

1 medium yellow onion, cut into small dice (about 1¼ cups)

2¼ cups leftover finely shredded Slow-Roasted Pork Shoulder (recipe p. 138)

2 medium cloves garlic, finely chopped

½ tsp. white-wine vinegar or lemon juice

4 large eggs

1 large ripe avocado, sliced

¼ cup coarsely chopped fresh cilantro

Piment d'Espelette or other medium-hot red pepper flakes (optional)

For a finishing touch, sprinkle this hash with cilantro and piment d'Espelette.

1. Put the potatoes in a medium saucepan, add water to cover by about ¾ inch, and add 1 Tbs. salt. Bring to a boil over high heat, reduce the heat to maintain a simmer, and cook until the potatoes are tender but not falling apart, about 5 minutes. Drain the potatoes, transfer to a plate, and set aside.

2. Heat the oil in a 10-inch straight-sided sauté pan over medium-high heat. Add the onion and ½ tsp. salt and cook, stirring occasionally until soft, 5 to 7 minutes. Add the pork and continue to cook until the pork is warm, about 3 minutes. Add the garlic and cook, stirring, until the raw garlic aroma subsides, about 1 minute. Add the potatoes, toss gently to combine, and continue to cook, stirring, until heated through, 1 to 3 minutes more. Season to taste with salt. If the hash is a little dry, add a drizzle of olive oil. Keep warm.

3. Fill a medium saucepan with 3 inches of water. Add the vinegar or lemon juice and a pinch of salt, and bring the water to a simmer. Crack the eggs one at a time into a small bowl or teacup and then gently slide each egg into the water. Poach the eggs, gently turning once or twice until the whites are completely opaque but the yolks are still soft, 3 to 4 minutes. Using a slotted spoon, remove the eggs from the water and gently blot dry with a paper towel.

4. Evenly distribute the hash among 4 plates. Prop a poached egg and a few slices of avocado next to each portion. Sprinkle the egg and avocado with salt. Sprinkle the cilantro and piment d'Espelette (if using) over the hash, and serve immediately. —*Tasha DeSerio*

PER SERVING: 510 CALORIES | 27G PROTEIN | 43G CARB | 26G TOTAL FAT | 6G SAT FAT | 15G MONO FAT | 3G POLY FAT | 265MG CHOL | 910MG SODIUM | 8G FIBER

What Is Piment d'Espelette?

Piment d'Espelette chiles come from a group of ten villages (one of which is called Espelette) in the Basque region of southwestern France. After harvesting, the chiles are strung together and dried outside houses and shops in the villages—the image of a chile-festooned building is in the logo used to designate this product.

The slightly sweet, mildly spicy chiles are most commonly ground into a coarse power. In the Basque region, the spice is often used in place of black pepper. In addition to using it as a finishing touch on dishes, it is a nice addition to spice rubs and sauces.

Store piment d'Espelette as you would any other spice—in an airtight container in a cool, dry place for up to 6 months.

sour cream coffee cake with brown sugar streusel

YIELDS ONE 8-INCH-SQUARE CAKE; SERVES 9

FOR THE STREUSEL

- 3⅜ oz. (¾ cup) unbleached all-purpose flour; more for the pan
- ½ cup packed light brown sugar
- ½ tsp. ground cinnamon
- ⅛ tsp. table salt
- 2¼ oz. (4½ Tbs.) unsalted butter, melted; more if needed

FOR THE CAKE

- 4 oz. (½ cup) very soft unsalted butter; more for the pan
- ½ cup sour cream, at room temperature
- 1 tsp. pure vanilla extract
- 2 drops pure almond extract
- ¾ cup granulated sugar
- 1 large egg yolk, at room temperature
- 1 large egg, at room temperature
- ¼ plus ⅛ tsp. table salt
- 5¼ oz. (1⅓ cups) cake flour
- 1 tsp. baking powder
- ⅛ tsp. baking soda

No mixer required: This quick, easy cake comes together with just a wooden spoon and a whisk.

MAKE THE STREUSEL

In a small bowl, stir the flour, brown sugar, cinnamon, and salt. Drizzle the melted butter over the dry ingredients and stir until well combined. The streusel should feel clumpy, not sandy, when gently squeezed between your fingertips. If it seems dry, add more melted butter.

MAKE THE CAKE

1. Position a rack in the center of the oven and heat the oven to 350°F. Lightly butter the bottom and sides of an 8-inch-square metal cake pan. Line the bottom of the pan with parchment and butter the parchment. Dust the pan with flour, tapping out any excess.

2. In a small bowl, whisk the sour cream, vanilla, and almond extract.

3. In a large bowl, cream the butter, granulated sugar, and egg yolk with a wooden spoon until blended, about 20 seconds. Using a whisk, whisk in the whole egg and salt and continue to whisk until the batter is smooth and the sugar begins to dissolve, about 30 seconds. Whisk in the sour cream mixture. Sift the cake flour, baking powder, and baking soda directly onto the batter. Whisk until the mixture is smooth and free of lumps.

4. Spread the batter evenly in the pan. Sprinkle the streusel over the batter, squeezing it with your fingertips to form small clumps. Bake until puffed and golden and a skewer inserted in the center of the cake comes out with only moist crumbs clinging to it, 28 to 30 minutes. Set the pan on a rack to cool for 15 minutes.

5. Run a knife between the cake and the sides of the pan. Invert the cake onto the rack and remove the parchment. Invert again onto a serving plate, so the streusel is on top. Let cool for at least 10 minutes before serving. This cake is best served warm. —*Nicole Rees*

PER SERVING: 400 CALORIES | 4G PROTEIN | 51G CARB | 20G TOTAL FAT | 12G SAT FAT | 5G MONO FAT | 1G POLY FAT | 95MG CHOL | 210MG SODIUM | 1G FIBER

herbed buttermilk biscuits

YIELDS ABOUT EIGHT 3-INCH
OR TWELVE 2-INCH BISCUITS

- 9 oz. (2 cups) unbleached all-purpose flour
- 2 tsp. baking powder
- ¾ tsp. table salt
- ½ tsp. baking soda
- 2 Tbs. chopped fresh dill or 2 tsp. dried dill
- 2 Tbs. chopped fresh flat-leaf parsley
- 3 Tbs. vegetable shortening or lard, well chilled and cut into small chunks
- 2 Tbs. unsalted butter, well chilled and cut into small chunks
- ¾ cup plus 2 Tbs. buttermilk

Other delicate fresh herbs (tarragon, chives, chervil) will work in this recipe in place of the dill. For a browner crust, brush the tops of the biscuits with melted butter before baking.

1. Position a rack in the center of the oven and heat the oven to 450°F. Lightly flour a small cutting board and set aside (this portable surface is easy to transfer to the refrigerator). Sift the flour, baking powder, salt, baking soda, and dried dill (if using) into a large, preferably shallow bowl. Mix in the fresh dill (if using) and the parsley. Add the shortening and butter to the dry ingredients. Combine with a pastry blender or two table knives just until a coarse meal forms. Make a well in the center and pour in the buttermilk. With your fingers (or a wooden spoon) and using just a few swift strokes, blend the dough just until combined (it will be a sticky mess; this is fine). Turn it out onto the floured cutting board. Wash, dry, and flour your hands. Gently pat out the dough and fold it back over itself about half a dozen times, just until smooth. Pat it out again, this time into a round or oval that's an even ½ to ¾ inch thick. Cover the dough lightly with plastic wrap and refrigerate for about 20 minutes.

2. Remove the cutting board with the dough from the refrigerator. Cut the dough with a sharp biscuit cutter—avoid twisting the cutter—trying to get as many rounds as possible (the dough will toughen a bit each time you work it). Lightly pat the remaining dough scraps together, pat down evenly, and cut again. Position the biscuits at least ½ inch apart on a parchment-lined baking sheet. Bake, rotating the pan halfway through to ensure even cooking, until raised and golden brown (10 to 12 minutes total for 3-inch biscuits, 9 to 11 minutes for 2-inch biscuits). —*Cheryl Alters Jamison and Bill Jamison*

PER BISCUIT: 130 CALORIES | 3G PROTEIN | 17G CARB | 5G TOTAL FAT | 2G SAT FAT | 2G MONO FAT | 1G POLY FAT | 5MG CHOL | 300MG SODIUM | 1G FIBER

shaggy dough makes a tender biscuit

Scrape the sticky dough out of the bowl and onto a small, floured cutting board.

After gently kneading the dough, patting it out, and chilling it briefly, use a sharp cutter to punch out the biscuits. Try to avoid twisting the cutter so the biscuits rise as much as possible.

asparagus, ham & mushroom strata

SERVES 8

2 Tbs. unsalted butter, more for the pan

1 lb. asparagus, ends snapped off, cut into 1½-inch pieces

1 tsp. kosher salt

1 tsp. freshly ground black pepper

3½ oz. fresh oyster mushrooms (or shiitake or white mushrooms), stemmed and thinly sliced

6 scallions, trimmed and thinly sliced, white and green parts separated (½ cup green, 2 Tbs. white)

9 large eggs, beaten

2¾ cups milk (preferably whole)

1 large loaf (about 1 lb.) rustic white bread (like ciabatta), cut into 1-inch cubes

8 oz. thinly sliced deli ham, cut into 1-inch strips

3 cups grated extra sharp Cheddar (about 8 oz.)

A strata is like an Italian quiche, but instead of an involved pastry crust, left-over bread forms the egg custard base. As with a bread pudding, assemble this dish ahead of time and bake it just before serving. It's up to you whether or not to trim the bread crust. When entertaining, trim it for a neat and pretty dish or leave it intact for a heartier texture.

1. Melt the butter in a large (12-inch) skillet over medium-high heat. Add the asparagus, sprinkle with ½ tsp. each salt and pepper, and cook, stirring occasionally, until the spears start to brown and soften, about 3 minutes. Add the mushrooms and scallion whites and cook, stirring occasionally, until the mushrooms soften and cook through, about 2 minutes. Remove from the heat and let cool for a couple of minutes.

2. Butter a 9x13-inch baking dish. Whisk the eggs with the milk and the remaining ½ tsp. each salt and pepper. Spread half the bread in a single layer on the bottom of the baking dish. Top with half the egg mixture and then cover with half the ham, cheese, and asparagus mixture, and sprinkle with half the scallion greens. Repeat with the remaining egg mixture, ham, cheese, asparagus mixture, and scallions. Cover with plastic wrap, pressing down so the bread is completely submerged in the egg mixture, and refrigerate for at least 4 hours and up to 2 days before baking.

3. Position a rack in the center of the oven and heat the oven to 350°F. Let the strata sit at room temperature while the oven heats. Bake until the custard sets and the top browns, about 30 minutes. Loosely cover with foil and bake for another 20 minutes. Let cool for 10 minutes, cut into square pieces, and serve. —*Tony Rosenfeld*

spiced yogurt waffles with toasted-pecan maple syrup

YIELDS ABOUT 10 WAFFLES

- **9** oz. (2 cups) unbleached all-purpose flour
- **⅓** cup granulated sugar
- **2** tsp. ground cinnamon
- **1½** tsp. baking powder
- **1** tsp. baking soda
- **½** tsp. kosher salt
- **¼** tsp. ground nutmeg
- **⅛** tsp. ground cloves
- **1½** cups plain full-fat or low-fat yogurt
- **¾** cup whole milk
- **2** large eggs, separated
- **3** Tbs. vegetable oil; more for the waffle iron
- **½** tsp. pure vanilla extract
- **1** cup pure maple syrup
- **½** cup toasted pecans, coarsely chopped

Yogurt gives waffles a rich texture and a slightly tangy flavor, which is complemented here by warm spices. Whipped egg whites folded into the batter ensure light, tender results.

1. Heat the oven to 200°F and heat a waffle iron, preferably a Belgian-waffle iron.

2. In a small bowl, combine the flour, sugar, cinnamon, baking powder, baking soda, salt, nutmeg, and cloves. In a large bowl, combine the yogurt, milk, egg yolks, vegetable oil, and vanilla.

3. In a medium bowl, with a wire whisk or electric hand mixer, beat the egg whites to soft peaks.

4. With a spatula, gently fold the dry ingredients into the yogurt mixture until just combined (the batter should be a little lumpy). Fold the whipped egg whites into the batter until just incorporated.

5. Brush the waffle iron with a little vegetable oil. Working in batches, cook the batter in the waffle iron according to the manufacturer's instructions until crisp and golden. Set the waffles directly on the oven rack to keep warm. Do not stack them.

6. Meanwhile, in a 2-quart saucepan, warm the maple syrup over medium heat. Stir in the pecans and keep warm.

7. Serve the waffles with the syrup. *—Samantha Seneviratne*

PER SERVING: 330 CALORIES | 6G PROTEIN | 52G CARB | 11G TOTAL FAT | 2.5G SAT FAT | 5G MONO FAT | 3.5G POLY FAT | 50MG CHOL | 280MG SODIUM | 2G FIBER

spinach, cheese & caramelized red onion frittata

SERVES 8

- ¼ cup olive oil
- 1 large red onion, thinly sliced (about 1 cup)
- 1¼ tsp. kosher salt
- 1 fresh jalapeño, cored, seeded, and finely diced (about 2 Tbs.)
- 10 oz. whole leaf spinach, trimmed, washed, and spun dry
- 10 large eggs, beaten
- 1¼ cups freshly grated Grana Padano
- 3 oil-packed sun-dried tomatoes, finely diced (about 2 Tbs.)
- 8 fresh basil leaves, torn into small pieces
- 1 tsp. freshly ground black pepper

This Italian omelet is perfect for brunch or a quick weeknight dinner. It also reheats nicely in the microwave as a midday snack. To add heft, fold diced boiled potatoes into the spinach mixture before adding it to the eggs. Incorporating strips of roasted red peppers adds more color.

1. Position a rack in the center of the oven and heat the oven to 450°F.

2. Heat 2 Tbs. oil in a large (12-inch), oven-proof, nonstick skillet over medium-high heat. Add the onion, sprinkle with ½ tsp. salt, and cook, stirring until it starts to color and soften, about 2 minutes. Reduce the heat to medium, add the jalapeño, and continue cooking until the onion softens almost completely, about 5 minutes. Add the spinach, sprinkle with ½ tsp. salt, increase the heat to high, and cook, tossing, until the spinach just wilts, about 2 minutes. Remove from the heat and let cool for a couple of minutes.

3. In a large bowl, whisk the eggs with the Grana Padano, sun-dried tomatoes, basil, pepper, and ¼ tsp. salt. Add the vegetables from the skillet to the egg mixture and stir to combine.

4. Wipe the skillet with a paper towel and heat the remaining 2 Tbs. oil in it over medium heat. Add the egg mixture and cook, running a spatula along the bottom of the pan to prevent sticking, until the eggs begin to set around the edges, about 3 minutes. Transfer the skillet to the oven and bake until the eggs puff and are firm to the touch and browned on top, about 12 minutes. Let cool for a couple minutes, then slide onto a cutting board, cut into wedges, and serve. *—Tony Rosenfeld*

What Is Grana Padano?

Like Parmigiano-Reggiano, Grana Padano is a well-aged, semi-fat, hard cheese made from cow's milk. To be labeled as Grana Padano, like Parmigiano-Reggiano, the cheese must be made in certain areas of northern Italy, following strict quality guidelines, and aged for a considerable amount of time (up to 18 months). Grana Padano tends to have a milder flavor and less grainy texture than Parmigiano-Reggiano.

warm maple and cinnamon bread pudding

SERVES 8 TO 10

Unsalted butter for the pan

3 **cups whole milk**

8 **large eggs, beaten**

1 **tsp. pure vanilla extract**

Kosher salt

1 **cup walnuts (about 4 oz.), toasted**

½ **cup light brown sugar**

1 **tsp. ground cinnamon**

1 **lb. rustic white bread (like ciabatta), cut into ¾-inch-thick slices**

¾ **cup pure maple syrup**

Confectioners' sugar, for sprinkling (optional)

Take the flavors of a coffee cake, apply them to a bread pudding, and you get this warming custard, reminiscent of French toast and perfect for brunch or dessert. For the best results, let the custard soak into the bread for at least 4 hours before baking.

1. Butter a 9x13-inch baking dish. In a medium bowl, whisk the milk with the eggs, vanilla, and ¾ tsp. salt. In a mini chopper or food processor, pulse the walnuts with the brown sugar and cinnamon. Arrange half the bread slices in an even layer on the bottom of the dish; cut slices into small pieces to fill in the holes. Cover with half of the egg mixture, a third of the nuts, and a third of the maple syrup. Make another layer with the remaining bread and cover with the rest of the egg mixture, another third of the nuts, and a third of the maple syrup. Sprinkle with the rest of the nut mixture and maple syrup. Cover with plastic wrap, pressing down so the bread is completely submerged in the egg mixture, and refrigerate for at least 4 hours and up to 2 days before baking.

2. Position a rack in the center of the oven and heat the oven to 350°F. Let the bread pudding sit at room temperature while the oven heats. Bake until the custard starts to set, about 30 minutes. Loosely cover the pudding with foil to prevent browning, and cook for another 10 minutes. Let cool for 10 minutes and serve sprinkled with the confectioners' sugar, if desired.

—*Tony Rosenfeld*

Variation

Individual Bread Puddings To make individual bread puddings, butter eight 10-oz. ramekins and fill each halfway with a layer of bread and cover with ⅛ cup of the egg mixture. Sprinkle with the nuts and 1 tsp. maple syrup. Repeat with a second layer of bread and egg mixture, nuts, and syrup; the ramekins should be about three-quarters full. Cover each ramekin with plastic wrap, pressing down so that the bread is submerged in the egg mixture, and refrigerate for at least 4 hours. When ready to bake, put the ramekins on a large rimmed baking sheet lined with parchment paper and bake in the center of a 350°F oven. Start checking for doneness after 30 minutes.

baked cheddar grits with bacon

SERVES 6

 Kosher salt

1 cup hominy grits (not instant or quick), such as Quaker® Old Fashioned Grits

1½ cups grated sharp or extra-sharp white Cheddar (about 5 oz.)

1 Tbs. unbleached all-purpose flour

1 tsp. chopped fresh thyme

 Freshly ground black pepper

1 medium clove garlic

6 strips bacon (about 6 oz.), cooked until crisp and chopped into small bits

3 large eggs, separated

¼ cup heavy cream

Bacon and Cheddar give simple grits a huge flavor boost. Whipped egg whites lighten the grits, making for a soufflé-like texture.

1. Position a rack in the center of the oven and heat the oven to 350°F.

2. Put 4½ cups water and ½ tsp. salt in a 4-quart saucepan, cover, and bring to a boil. Whisk the grits into the pan in a slow stream. Reduce the heat to medium low, cover, and simmer, whisking occasionally, until thickened, 12 to 15 minutes.

3. In a large bowl, toss 1¼ cups of the cheese, the flour, thyme, and several grinds of pepper. Chop the garlic, sprinkle with a generous pinch of salt, and mash it into a paste with the side of a chef's knife. Whisk the mashed garlic, the cheese mixture, and the bacon into the grits until blended and the cheese is melted. Season to taste with salt and pepper.

4. Scrape the grits into the large bowl. In a medium bowl, beat the egg whites and a pinch of salt with a hand mixer until they just hold stiff peaks. In a small bowl, whisk the yolks and cream; whisk this mixture into the grits. With a large spatula, gently stir one-third of the whites into the grits to lighten them and then fold in the remaining whites. Scrape the grits into an 8x8x2-inch glass or ceramic baking dish.

5. Sprinkle the remaining ¼ cup cheese evenly over the grits. Bake until puffed, browned, and bubbling, 50 minutes to 1 hour. *—Tony Rosenfeld*

Keeping Cheese Fresh

Check the cheese's sell-by date before purchase—be sure it's at least a month away. Once you've gotten the Cheddar home and have removed its original packaging, store it in the refrigerator by wrapping it first in parchment or waxed paper and then in a layer of plastic wrap or foil. It will keep for several weeks. If any mold develops, simply cut it away, about ½ inch below the mold. If the cheese emits any off-odors or becomes slimy, discard it.

cornmeal-blueberry pancakes with spiced maple butter

SERVES 4 TO 6

FOR THE MAPLE BUTTER

- 4 oz. (½ cup) unsalted butter, softened
- ¼ cup pure maple syrup

  Kosher salt
- ¼ tsp. chili powder
- ¼ tsp. ground cinnamon

FOR THE PANCAKES

- 7¾ oz. (1¾ cups) unbleached all-purpose flour
- ¾ cup yellow cornmeal
- 1 Tbs. granulated sugar
- 2 tsp. baking powder
- ½ tsp. baking soda
- ½ tsp. table salt
- 2¼ cups buttermilk
- ¼ cup vegetable oil
- 3 large eggs
- 1 tsp. pure vanilla extract

  Unsalted butter for the griddle
- 1 pint blueberries (¾ lb.), rinsed and picked through

While cornmeal gives these pancakes a hearty texture and blueberries offer a fresh tartness, the spicy sweet butter puts them over the top. Add warmed maple syrup for a little more sweetness.

MAKE THE MAPLE BUTTER

Put all the ingredients in a food processor and process, scraping 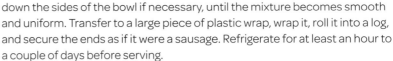 down the sides of the bowl if necessary, until the mixture becomes smooth and uniform. Transfer to a large piece of plastic wrap, wrap it, roll it into a log, and secure the ends as if it were a sausage. Refrigerate for at least an hour to a couple of days before serving.

MAKE THE PANCAKES

1. In a large bowl, mix together the flour, cornmeal, sugar, baking powder, baking soda, and salt. In a medium bowl, whisk the buttermilk with the oil, eggs, and vanilla. Gently whisk the buttermilk mixture into the flour mixture until it's mostly uniform (a few lumps are fine).

2. Heat a large stovetop griddle or large (12-inch) heavy-duty pan (like a cast-iron skillet) over medium heat until a droplet of water immediately evaporates upon hitting the pan. Melt a small pat of butter in the pan, pour in the batter (about ⅓ cup for each pancake), and then sprinkle with the blueberries. Leave space between each pancake so flipping them isn't a problem. Cook the pancakes until bubbles form on top, the cakes set around the edges, and the bottoms brown, 2 to 3 minutes. Flip and cook on the other side until they brown and the cakes become just firm to the touch, about 2 minutes more. Serve immediately topped with a pat of the maple butter. —*Tony Rosenfeld*

apple, sage & fennel breakfast sausage

YIELDS SIXTEEN 2½-INCH
PATTIES; SERVES 8

- 3 Tbs. vegetable oil; more as needed
- 2 tart cooking apples (15 oz. total), like Granny Smith or Pink Lady, peeled, cored, and cut into ¼-inch dice
- 1 bunch scallions, thinly sliced, white and green parts separated
- 2 lb. ground pork (avoid pork labeled "extra tender," if possible)
- ½ cup loosely packed fresh sage leaves, finely chopped
- 1½ tsp. fennel seeds, crushed in a mortar or lightly chopped
- 1 tsp. table salt
- ¾ tsp. freshly ground black pepper

The patties can be kept warm for up to an hour, but the more freshly cooked they are, the juicier they'll taste.

1. Heat the oven to 200°F. In a 10-inch skillet, heat 1 Tbs. of the oil over medium heat. Add the apples and the scallion whites. Cook, stirring occasionally, until the apples soften and just begin to brown, 5 to 8 minutes. Let cool for 10 minutes. In a large bowl, combine the apple mixture with the pork, scallion greens, sage, fennel seeds, salt, and pepper. Mix with your hands until well combined, but don't compact the mixture. Gently shape into 16 patties, about 3 inches in diameter and ¾ inch thick.

2. In a 12-inch heavy skillet, heat the remaining 2 Tbs. oil over medium-low to medium heat. Cook the sausages (in three batches so they're not crowded) until nicely browned and cooked through, about 5 minutes per side. Add more oil only if needed after each batch, and adjust the heat to prevent overbrowning. Keep the sausages warm on a baking sheet in the oven, covered with foil.
—Nicole Rees

PER SERVING: 310 CALORIES | 21G PROTEIN | 6G CARB | 22G TOTAL FAT | 7G SAT FAT | 0G MONO FAT | 4G POLY FAT | 75MG CHOL | 350MG SODIUM | 1G FIBER

cornmeal-cherry muffins

YIELDS ABOUT 20 MEDIUM
MUFFINS

- 3 eggs
- 3 Tbs. lemon zest
- ¼ cup freshly squeezed lemon juice
- 6 oz. (12 Tbs.) unsalted butter, melted
- ¼ cup plus 2 Tbs. vegetable oil
- 3 cups buttermilk
- 15 oz. (3⅓ cups) unbleached all-purpose flour
- 19 oz. (3 cups) medium (polenta-type) cornmeal
- 4½ tsp. baking powder
- 1 tsp. baking soda
- ¾ cup sugar
- 1 tsp. table salt
- 8 oz. (about 2 cups) chopped dried cherries

Medium-grain cornmeal gives these muffins a rustic texture. For a finer texture, use half fine cornmeal and half medium.

Position a rack in the center of the oven and heat the oven to 350°F. In a large mixing bowl, whisk the eggs, lemon zest, juice, butter, oil, and buttermilk. In a separate bowl, whisk the flour, cornmeal, baking powder, baking soda, sugar, and salt. Slowly pour the dry ingredients into the wet and stir until just mixed. Gently fold in the cherries. Grease and flour a muffin tin (or line it with muffin papers, preferably foil). Scoop about ½ cup batter into each muffin cup so that the curve of the batter is even with the rim of the cup. (Refrigerate any extra batter in an airtight container for up to a week.) Bake until firm to the touch, 30 to 35 minutes. Remove the muffins from the tin when they're cool enough to handle. *—Kathleen Stewart*

PER MUFFIN: 370 CALORIES | 7G PROTEIN | 56G CARB | 13G TOTAL FAT | 5G SAT FAT | 4G MONO FAT | 3G POLY FAT | 50MG CHOL | 280MG SODIUM | 3G FIBER

pan-fried southwestern hash

SERVES 4 TO 6

1¼ lb. fingerling potatoes,
     cut into ½-inch pieces

     Kosher salt

⅓   cup canola oil

1   large yellow onion, finely diced
     (about 1 cup)

½   large red bell pepper, cut into
     ¼-inch dice (about ¾ cup)

½   medium green bell pepper, cut
     into ¼-inch dice (about ½ cup)

1   tsp. chili powder

1   tsp. fresh oregano

     Freshly ground black pepper

Buttery fingerling potatoes and a healthy punch of spice wake up your basic breakfast hash. This technique—parboiling the potatoes and then sautéing them and the onions and peppers separately—ensures the potatoes have a soft interior and crisp exterior.

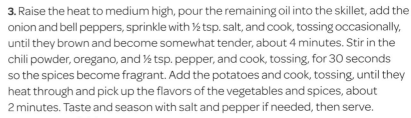

1. Put the potatoes in a 3-quart saucepan, cover with cold water by a couple of inches, stir in 1 Tbs. salt, and bring to a boil. Reduce to a simmer, cover, and cook until the potatoes are tender but still firm, about 10 minutes. Drain well.

2. Heat 3 Tbs. oil in a large (12-inch), heavy-duty skillet over medium-high heat until shimmering. Lower the heat to medium, add the potatoes, sprinkle with ¼ tsp. salt, and cook, stirring occasionally, until they brown and start to crisp, 6 to 8 minutes. Transfer to a large plate.

3. Raise the heat to medium high, pour the remaining oil into the skillet, add the onion and bell peppers, sprinkle with ½ tsp. salt, and cook, tossing occasionally, until they brown and become somewhat tender, about 4 minutes. Stir in the chili powder, oregano, and ½ tsp. pepper, and cook, tossing, for 30 seconds so the spices become fragrant. Add the potatoes and cook, tossing, until they heat through and pick up the flavors of the vegetables and spices, about 2 minutes. Taste and season with salt and pepper if needed, then serve.

—Tony Rosenfeld

Storing Fingerling Potatoes

Store fingerling potatoes like any other potato: in a cool, dark place away from sunlight. Avoid putting them in the refrigerator, as moisture causes the spuds to sprout. Be mindful that fingerlings will not typically keep as long as full-size potatoes, so check them regularly and immediately discard any that give off an odor or have soft spots.

eggs benedict

SERVES 4

- 2 tsp. white-wine vinegar
- 8 large eggs
- 2 Tbs. salted butter, softened
- 4 English muffins, split in half
- 8 ¼-inch-thick rounds of Canadian bacon
- 1 recipe Hollandaise Sauce (recipe below)

   Pinch of paprika, for garnish (optional)

   Thinly sliced fresh chives, for garnish (optional)

If you can't find Canadian bacon, you can substitute ham in this recipe.

1. Pour enough water into a 10- to 12-inch skillet so that it's three-quarters full. Add the vinegar and bring to a simmer over medium-high heat. Gently break the eggs into the water around the edge of the skillet, which will help keep the eggs together. Lower the heat to medium low and simmer until the eggs are just set, about 3 minutes; the yolks should still be runny. (Alternatively, add the eggs to the simmering water, turn off the heat, cover the skillet, and let them sit for 4 to 5 minutes.) Remove the eggs from the skillet with a slotted spoon and set aside on a warm paper-towel-lined plate. If the eggs have any feathery edges, you can trim them if you like.

2. Meanwhile, toast and butter the muffin halves.

3. Heat a 10-inch skillet over medium-high heat and cook 4 slices of the bacon, flipping once, until heated through and browned in spots, about 1 minute per side. Transfer to a large plate and repeat with the remaining slices.

4. To serve, put two muffin halves on a warm plate, top each with a slice of the bacon and a poached egg, and spoon over about ¼ cup of the hollandaise sauce. Garnish with a sprinkle of paprika and some chives (if using). Repeat with the remaining ingredients and serve immediately. —*John Ash*

PER SERVING: 650 CALORIES | 30G PROTEIN | 29G CARB | 47G TOTAL FAT | 24G SAT FAT | 15G MONO FAT | 4G POLY FAT | 665MG CHOL | 1,450MG SODIUM | 2G FIBER

hollandaise sauce

YIELDS ABOUT 1½ CUPS

- 4 large egg yolks
- 2 Tbs. freshly squeezed lemon juice
- 1 tsp. Dijon mustard (optional)
- 6 oz. (12 Tbs.) unsalted butter, melted

   Pinch of cayenne or a few drops of hot pepper sauce

   Kosher salt

Here's the trick to making this simple sauce: Whisk it over simmering water so the egg yolks cook gently and don't curdle.

Position a large heatproof bowl over a pot of barely simmering water, making sure the bottom of the bowl doesn't touch the water. In the bowl, whisk the yolks, lemon juice, and mustard (if using) until well combined. Gradually whisk in the butter in a thin stream and keep whisking until the sauce is thick enough for the whisk to leave tracks that hold for a couple of seconds, 1 to 2 minutes. If the sauce is too thick, whisk in a few drops of hot water to thin it. Whisk in the cayenne or hot sauce and season to taste with salt. Keep the sauce warm in its bowl set over the simmering water, whisking occasionally, until ready to use.

PER ¼ CUP: 240 CALORIES | 2G PROTEIN | 1G CARB | 26G TOTAL FAT | 16G SAT FAT | 7G MONO FAT | 1.5G POLY FAT | 200MG CHOL | 170MG SODIUM | 0G FIBER

individual cinnamon coffee cakes with chocolate-cherry-almond swirl

YIELDS 8 COFFEE CAKES

FOR THE DOUGH

½ cup warm whole milk (about 105°F)

1½ tsp. active dry yeast

⅓ cup plus 2 tsp. granulated sugar

9 oz. (2 cups) unbleached all-purpose flour

½ tsp. table salt

1 tsp. ground cinnamon

2 large eggs, lightly beaten

5 oz. (10 Tbs.) very soft unsalted butter

½ cup sliced almonds, toasted

FOR THE FILLING

4 oz. semisweet chocolate

6 oz. (about 1 cup) dried cherries

1 cup sliced almonds, toasted

⅓ cup granulated sugar

½ tsp. ground cinnamon

1 large egg, separated

½ tsp. whole milk

FOR THE GLAZE

1 cup confectioners' sugar

4 to 5 tsp. strong brewed coffee

The rich ingredients of these coffee cakes call for an equally rich and assertive dough to hold them—brioche. Brioche dough is naturally tacky, so working with it cold helps to minimize the stickiness during shaping. This coffee treat is great hot out of the oven, stores well, and freezes like a dream.

MAKE THE DOUGH

1. A day before baking, make the dough: In the bowl of a stand mixer, gently whisk the warm milk with the yeast to combine. Sprinkle with 2 tsp. of the sugar. Let the yeast proof until air pockets float up, making the mixture look spongy, 5 to 10 minutes.

2. Add the remaining dough ingredients and mix with the paddle attachment on medium-low speed until the dough comes together, and then continue mixing for 6 minutes to knead the dough, scraping down the sides of the bowl once or twice. The dough should be loose and seem more like a tacky batter.

3. Immediately scrape the dough into a greased bowl that's at least twice the dough's size, cover tightly with plastic wrap, and refrigerate overnight.

MAKE THE FILLING

The next morning, put the chocolate in a food processor and pulse to chop coarsely. Add the dried cherries, almonds, sugar, and cinnamon and pulse until quite fine. Add the egg white and process just until the ingredients form a rough paste. (Cover and refrigerate the leftover yolk.)

ASSEMBLE THE BREAD

1. Grease 8 cups of a 12-cup muffin pan. Scrape the chilled dough onto a liberally floured surface. Using a well-floured rolling pin, gently roll the dough into a rectangle about 8x12 inches. Work quickly; the warmer the dough gets, the harder it is to handle. Spread the filling by hand over the dough, leaving a 1-inch border on all four sides. It's all right if it's a bit uneven. Starting with a long side, roll the dough into a log shape. If the dough sticks to the work surface, use a bench knife or a spatula to lift it.

2. Brush the excess flour from the top and sides of the dough roll. Using a sharp knife, trim the ends of the roll just enough to expose the spiral of filling. Discard the trimmings. Cut the roll into 8 equal slices (each 1½ to 2 inches wide). Set each slice spiral side up in a greased muffin cup, brushing the flour from the bottom of each piece as you go. Press very gently to be sure each piece reaches the bottom of the cup. Pour a few tablespoons of water into the empty, ungreased cups.

3. Cover the dough with a clean, damp dishtowel or an oversize plastic storage container (to make a little "greenhouse") and let rise until light and billowy, 1½ to 2 hours. (Be patient. Remember your dough is cold and the rate of rising will depend on the temperature of the kitchen.)

4. Meanwhile, heat the oven to 350°F. Make an egg wash by mixing the reserved egg yolk with the ½ tsp. milk. Just before baking, brush the dough with the egg wash. Bake until puffed and deep golden, 20 to 25 minutes. Let cool for 10 to 15 minutes. Carefully siphon or drain the water from the extra cups and wipe dry. Loosen under the edge of the cakes' caps with the tip of a paring knife. If the cakes grew together during baking, cut between them to separate. Turn onto a cooling rack set over paper towels or parchment.

APPLY THE GLAZE

In a cup, mix the confectioners' sugar and coffee to make a smooth paste. It should be thick but still pourable. Drizzle over the cakes after they have cooled slightly. —*Paige Retus*

PER COFFEE CAKE: 660 CALORIES I 12G PROTEIN I 89G CARB I 30G TOTAL FAT I 13G SAT FAT I 11G MONO FAT I 3G POLY FAT I 120MG CHOL I 330MG SODIUM I 6G FIBER

All about Dried Cherries

Dried cherries are fresh cherries that have been dehydrated and may or may not contain added sugar. No preservatives are added in the drying process, but, as with other dried fruits, many of the nutrients are lost due to the loss of water content. Most commercially dried cherries are tart, rather than sweet, cherries because the tart variety tends to fare better in cooking, freezing, canning, and drying processes. They are a lusciously sweet addition to both savory and sweet dishes, and they provide a welcome, slightly tarter substitution for raisins. If you don't have dried cherries, substitute raisins, dried currants, dried cranberries, or any other dried berry.

Keep unopened dried cherries in a cool, dry place, and store opened ones in a tightly sealed bag or container; it is not necessary to refrigerate or freeze them. Use within 12 months of opening.

lemon-glazed banana scones with crystallized ginger

YIELDS 8 SCONES

FOR THE SCONES

- **9 oz. (2 cups) unbleached all-purpose flour; more as needed**
- **¼ cup granulated sugar**
- **2¼ tsp. baking powder**
- **1 tsp. finely grated fresh lemon zest**
- **⅜ tsp. table salt**
- **2¾ oz. (5½ Tbs.) cold unsalted butter, cut into pieces**
- **1 small ripe (but not mushy) banana, cut into ¼-inch dice (½ cup)**
- **1 Tbs. minced crystallized ginger**
- **¾ cup plus 2 Tbs. heavy cream; more for brushing**
- **Coarse white sanding sugar (optional)**

FOR THE GLAZE

- **3 oz. (¾ cup) confectioners' sugar**
- **1½ Tbs. freshly squeezed lemon juice**
- **½ oz. (1 Tbs.) unsalted butter, softened**
- **Pinch of table salt**

Crystallized ginger and lemon zest complement the assertive banana flavor in these scones. While scones are usually best the day they're made, added moisture from the banana will keep these delicious for an extra day.

MAKE THE SCONES

1. Position a rack in the top third of the oven and heat the oven to 375°F. Stack two rimmed baking sheets and line the top one with parchment.

2. In a large bowl, whisk the flour, sugar, baking powder, lemon zest, and salt. With your fingers, rub the butter into the flour mixture until a few pea-size lumps remain. Stir in the banana and the ginger. Add the cream; with a fork, gradually stir until the mixture just comes together.

3. Turn the dough onto a lightly floured surface and pat gently into a 7-inch circle about 1 inch high. Using a chef's knife or bench knife, cut the dough into 8 wedges. Transfer to the baking sheet, spacing the wedges 1 to 2 inches apart. Brush the tops with heavy cream and sprinkle liberally with sanding sugar (if using).

4. Bake until the tops are golden, 19 to 25 minutes, rotating halfway through baking for even browning. Transfer the scones to a wire rack and cool slightly, 3 to 4 minutes.

GLAZE THE SCONES

In a small bowl, stir the confectioners' sugar, lemon juice, butter, and salt until smooth. Drizzle the warm scones with the glaze. Serve warm or at room temperature. —*Nicole Rees*

PER SERVING: 390 CALORIES | 4G PROTEIN | 47G CARB | 21G TOTAL FAT | 13G SAT FAT | 6G MONO FAT | 1G POLY FAT | 65MG CHOL | 250MG SODIUM | 1G FIBER

bananas: a buyer's guide

Although there are hundreds of banana varieties, few are available in the United States. Supermarkets are dominated by a single variety, the yellow, mildly sweet Cavendish. But bananaphiles can take heart: Major companies like Dole® and Chiquita® are bringing more varieties to grocery stores. Ethnic markets are a great source for unusual bananas, too (at right are a few types you might find).

HOW TO BUY When purchasing the common Cavendish, look for a firm, evenly colored yellow peel that is flecked with brown and bruise-free. Bananas that are greenish-yellow will be ready to eat in a couple of days.

HOW TO STORE Store bananas at room temperature. It takes them 5 to 7 days to go from green to yellow with lots of brown spots. To make green bananas ripen faster, put them in a paper bag with fruit like apples or avocados (they give off ethylene gas, which hastens the ripening process). Conversely, prevent bananas from ripening too fast by keeping them away from other aging fruit.

Banana hangers allow air to circulate evenly around the fruit, encouraging ripening and eliminating the bruising that can occur when bananas are left on the counter. Once bananas are ripe, store them in the refrigerator to slow over-ripening.

MANZANO (OR APPLE BANANA) A small, squat variety with tangy apple and strawberry notes that turns dark yellow when ripe.

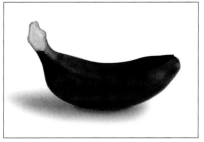

RED BANANA This short variety takes on a purple hue when ripe; its flesh is creamy white to pink, with a faint berry flavor.

LADYFINGER Although it looks like a miniature Cavendish, it's sweeter when ripe.

PLANTAIN Extremely popular in Latin America, Africa, and Asia, this variety is starchy when unripe and is usually cooked (it's delicious fried or stewed). When its peel turns black, it's ripe enough to eat out of hand and is less sweet than the Cavendish.

Oven-Toasted Ham, Brie & Apple Sandwiches (recipe on p. 184)

sandwiches

classic grilled cheese

SERVES 4

- **4 tsp. salted butter, at room temperature**
- **8 ¼-inch-thick slices Italian country bread or sourdough**
- **6 oz. coarsely grated Cheddar**

Don't be timid when pressing the sandwiches after you've turned them. A little muscle power ensures terrific, crisp results.

1. Spread the butter on one side only of each bread slice. Put 4 slices, buttered side down, on a cutting board. Distribute the cheese over the bread. Top with the remaining bread, buttered side up.

2. Heat a large nonstick pan or griddle over medium-high heat for 2 minutes. Put as many sandwiches as will fit in the pan or on the griddle without crowding, cover, and cook until the cheese has just begun to melt and the bread is golden brown, about 2 minutes. Remove the lid and turn the sandwiches, pressing each one firmly with a spatula to flatten it slightly. Cook the sandwiches uncovered until the bottom is golden-brown, about 1 minute. Turn them once more and press with the spatula again to recrisp the bread, about 30 seconds. Cut the sandwiches in half and serve immediately. —*Laura Werlin*

PER SERVING: 250 CALORIES | 12G PROTEIN | 10G CARB | 19G TOTAL FAT | 11G SAT FAT | 5G MONO FAT | 1G POLY FAT | 55MG CHOL | 410MG SODIUM | 0G FIBER

Good Melting Cheeses

Brie	Gruyére
Camembert	Havarti
Cheddar	Monterey Jack
Emmentaler	Mozzarella
Fontina	Swiss

oven-toasted ham, brie & apple sandwiches

SERVES 4

- **1 large baguette (about 1 lb.), cut into 4 pieces**
- **7 oz. Brie, most of the rind trimmed off and thinly sliced**
- **2 Tbs. unsalted butter**
- **1½ medium Granny Smith apples, peeled (optional), cored, and cut into ¼-inch-thick wedges (about 1½ cups)**
- **¾ lb. ham steak, thinly sliced on the diagonal**
- **2 Tbs. whole-grain Dijon mustard**
- **1 Tbs. honey**
- **1 tsp. chopped fresh thyme**

Remove the rind from the Brie while the cheese is still cold, and choose a thinly sliced ham steak rather than deli ham for a meaty flavor and texture. Look for a ham steak that's labeled "ham in natural juices."

1. Position a rack in the center of the oven and heat the oven to 425°F. Split the baguette pieces lengthwise, open them up like a book, and top one side with the Brie. Set on a baking sheet lined with parchment paper or aluminum foil, and bake until the cheese melts and the bread lightly browns, about 5 minutes.

2. Meanwhile, melt the butter in a large (12-inch) heavy-duty skillet over medium-high heat. Add the apples and cook, tossing every minute or so, until they start to soften and brown in places, 3 to 4 minutes. Add the ham and cook, gently tossing, until it warms. Remove from the heat and gently toss with the mustard, honey, and thyme until the ham and apples are evenly coated. Using tongs, distribute the ham mixture into the warm pieces of baguette, secure with 2 toothpicks, cut in half, and serve. —*Tony Rosenfeld*

grilled mozzarella and spinach blts

SERVES 4

12 slices thick-cut bacon

1 medium clove garlic, finely chopped

3 cups lightly packed baby spinach

Kosher salt and freshly ground black pepper

8 slices country-style white bread

8 oz. fresh mozzarella, sliced

1 large tomato (about 8 oz.), cored and thinly sliced

1 Tbs. extra-virgin olive oil

Creamy mozzarella is a good foil for the salty, smoky bacon in this grilled version of a BLT. Before cooking, remove any tough stems from the spinach.

1. Working in batches, cook the bacon in a 12-inch skillet over medium heat until crisp, about 8 minutes per batch. Transfer to a paper-towel-lined plate and drain off all but 1 Tbs. of the fat. Return the pan to medium heat, add the garlic, and cook until fragrant, about 30 seconds. Stir in the spinach and cook until just wilted, about 30 seconds longer. Season to taste with salt and pepper.

2. Heat a panini or sandwich press according to the manufacturer's instructions. (Alternatively, heat a nonstick grill pan over medium-high heat.)

3. While the press is heating, arrange the spinach on 4 pieces of the bread. Top each with some bacon, mozzarella, and tomato, sprinkle lightly with salt, and complete each sandwich with a slice of the remaining bread. Brush both sides of the sandwiches with the oil.

4. Put the sandwiches on the press, pull the top down, and cook until browned and crisp and the cheese is melted, 3 to 6 minutes depending on how hot your machine is. (If using a grill pan, put a heavy pan on top of the sandwiches and cook, turning the sandwiches over once.) Carefully remove from the press and serve. *—Lauren Chattman*

PER SERVING: 570 CALORIES | 29G PROTEIN | 46G CARB | 29G TOTAL FAT | 12G SAT FAT | 11G MONO FAT | 2G POLY FAT | 70MG CHOL | 1,510MG SODIUM | 5G FIBER

croque-madame sandwiches

SERVES 4

- 5 Tbs. unsalted butter
- 2½ Tbs. unbleached all-purpose flour
- 1¾ cup milk (whole or low-fat)
- 2 Tbs. brandy
- 2 tsp. Worcestershire sauce
- ¼ tsp. fresh thyme
- ¼ tsp. grated nutmeg

 Kosher salt and freshly ground black pepper

- 8 slices country-style white sandwich bread
- 4 tsp. Dijon mustard
- 4 oz. Gruyère, grated (1 cup)
- 12 oz. leftover roasted fresh ham (recipe on p. 144), sliced
- ½ oz. Parmigiano-Reggiano, finely grated (½ cup using a rasp-style grater)
- 4 large eggs, at room temperature

In this riff on the classic French croque-madame (a toasted ham and cheese sandwich topped with béchamel and a fried egg), roasted fresh ham replaces the typical cured ham.

1. Melt 2 Tbs. of the butter in a medium saucepan over medium-low heat. Whisk in the flour and continue whisking just until it turns beige, about 20 seconds. Whisk in the milk in a slow, steady stream; continue whisking until smooth, thickened, and slightly bubbling, 2 to 3 minutes. Whisk in the brandy, Worcestershire sauce, thyme, nutmeg, ¼ tsp. salt, and ¼ tsp. pepper. Whisk for 30 seconds; then remove the béchamel sauce from the heat and set aside, whisking occasionally to prevent a skin from forming.

2. Position a rack 4 inches from the broiler element and heat the broiler on high.

3. Spread 4 of the bread slices on one side with 1 tsp. Dijon mustard each. Layer the Gruyère and ham on the bread in this pattern: cheese, ham, cheese. Top with the remaining bread.

4. Melt 1 Tbs. of the butter in a 12-inch skillet over medium heat. Cook 2 of the sandwiches until brown and crisp, turning once halfway through the cooking, about 4 minutes. Transfer to a rimmed baking sheet. Repeat with another tablespoon of butter and the remaining 2 sandwiches.

5. Ladle the béchamel sauce over the sandwiches (it will run down the sides), and then top with the Parmigiano-Reggiano. Broil until bubbling and lightly browned, 3 to 4 minutes.

6. Meanwhile, in a 10-inch nonstick skillet, melt the remaining 1 Tbs. butter over medium heat. Crack the eggs into the skillet and fry them sunny side up until the whites are set but the yolks are still runny, 3 to 4 minutes.

7. Use a large, flat spatula to transfer the sandwiches to serving plates. Place a fried egg on each. Sprinkle with salt and pepper and serve.
—*Bruce Weinstein and Mark Scarbrough*

PER SERVING: 840 CALORIES | 49G PROTEIN | 52G CARB | 45G TOTAL FAT | 21G SAT FAT | 15G MONO FAT | 3G POLY FAT | 365MG CHOL | 1,040MG SODIUM | 4G FIBER

classic maryland crab cakes

SERVES 4

- 1 lb. jumbo lump or backfin lump crabmeat (fresh or pasteurized)
- 1 large egg
- ¼ cup mayonnaise
- 1½ tsp. Dijon mustard
- 1½ tsp. Old Bay seasoning
- 1 tsp. freshly squeezed lemon juice
- ½ tsp. Worcestershire sauce
- Kosher salt
- 1¼ cups fresh breadcrumbs (from soft white sandwich bread, such as Pepperidge Farm®)
- 1 Tbs. chopped fresh flat-leaf parsley
- 2 Tbs. unsalted butter
- 1 Tbs. olive oil
- Lemon wedges, for serving

You can find Old Bay® seasoning in most supermarkets and seafood stores. Use just enough to give a hint of its presence or it will overpower the crab.

1. Drain the crabmeat, if necessary, and pick through it for shells (jumbo lump will not have shells). Put the crab in a medium mixing bowl and set aside.

2. In a small bowl, whisk the egg, mayonnaise, mustard, Old Bay seasoning, lemon juice, Worcestershire sauce, and ¼ tsp. salt. Scrape the mixture over the crab and mix gently until well combined. Gently break up the lumps with your fingers but do not overmix.

3. Sprinkle the breadcrumbs and the parsley over the mixture, and mix them in thoroughly but gently; try not to turn the mixture into a mash—it should still be somewhat loose. Cover with plastic wrap and refrigerate for 1 to 3 hours.

4. Shape the crab mixture into 8 cakes about 1 inch thick. In a 12-inch nonstick skillet, heat the butter with the olive oil over medium heat. When the butter is frothy, add the cakes to the pan (8 should fit comfortably). Cook until dark golden-brown on the underside, about 4 minutes. Flip the cakes, reduce the heat to medium low, and continue cooking until the other side is well browned, 4 to 5 minutes. Serve with lemon wedges on the side for squeezing over the cakes. *—Susie Middleton*

PER SERVING: 340 CALORIES | 23G PROTEIN | 9G CARB | 23G TOTAL FAT | 6G SAT FAT | 7G MONO FAT | 7G POLY FAT | 140MG CHOL | 890MG SODIUM | 0G FIBER

caramelized onion cheeseburgers

SERVES 4

2 Tbs. extra-virgin olive oil; more as needed

1 large sweet onion, thinly sliced (about 2 cups)

Kosher salt and freshly ground black pepper

⅓ cup mayonnaise

1 Tbs. Dijon mustard

1½ tsp. freshly squeezed lemon juice

1 tsp. finely chopped fresh rosemary

1 small clove garlic, minced

1½ lb. ground beef (85% lean)

4 slices Comté or Gruyère

4 good-quality hamburger buns or rolls, split

12 fresh arugula leaves

Burgers just got better with the addition of tender sweet onions, melted cheese, and tangy lemon-Dijon mayonnaise.

1. Prepare a medium-high gas or charcoal grill fire. Alternatively, position an oven rack 5 to 6 inches from the broiler and heat the broiler to high. Line the bottom of a broiler pan with foil and lightly oil the perforated part of the pan.

2. Meanwhile, heat the oil in a 10-inch skillet over medium-high heat. Add the onion, ¼ tsp. salt, and ⅛ tsp. pepper; reduce the heat to medium low and cook, stirring occasionally, until deeply golden-brown and tender, 15 to 18 minutes.

3. Combine the mayonnaise, mustard, lemon juice, rosemary, and garlic in a small bowl. Season to taste with salt and pepper and set aside.

4. In a medium bowl, gently combine the beef with ¼ tsp. salt and ⅛ tsp. pepper. Form the beef into 4 patties (3½ inches in diameter) and make a deep depression in the center of each patty so the burgers keep their shape during cooking. Lightly sprinkle the patties with ¾ tsp. salt and ½ tsp. pepper. Grill or broil them on the prepared pan for about 4 minutes per side for medium, or until desired doneness. Top each burger with 1 slice of the cheese and grill or broil until melted, 30 to 60 seconds.

5. Toast the buns on the grill or under the broiler until golden, 30 to 60 seconds. Serve the burgers on the toasted buns with the caramelized onions, mayonnaise, and arugula. —*David Bonom*

PER SERVING: 740 CALORIES | 43G PROTEIN | 27G CARB | 50G TOTAL FAT | 16G SAT FAT | 20G MONO FAT | 10G POLY FAT | 140MG CHOL | 930MG SODIUM | 2G FIBER

smoky black bean and cheddar burrito with baby spinach

SERVES 4

4 burrito-size (9- to 10-inch) flour tortillas

15 grape tomatoes, quartered lengthwise

2 Tbs. freshly squeezed lime juice; more as needed

¼ cup chopped fresh cilantro

Kosher salt

2 Tbs. extra-virgin olive oil

¼ cup raw pepitas (optional)

1 tsp. seeded and minced chipotle chile plus 1 tsp. adobo sauce (from a can of chipotles en adobo)

¾ tsp. ground cumin

1 19-oz. can black beans, rinsed and drained

½ cup grated sharp Cheddar

1½ oz. baby spinach (about 1½ cups)

¼ to ½ cup sour cream (optional)

Quick and easy, this hearty burrito is lightened with the addition of baby spinach and a hit of tangy lime.

1. Heat the oven to 250°F. Wrap the tortillas in aluminum foil and warm them in the oven. Meanwhile, in a small bowl, toss the tomatoes with 1 Tbs. of the lime juice, about 1½ Tbs. of the cilantro, and a generous pinch of salt. Set aside.

2. If using the pepitas, heat 1 Tbs. of the olive oil and the pepitas in a 12-inch skillet over medium heat. Cook, stirring frequently, until they are puffed and some are golden brown, 1 to 2 minutes. Using a slotted spoon, transfer the pepitas to a plate lined with a paper towel. Sprinkle with a generous pinch of salt and toss.

3. Return the pan to medium heat. Add the remaining 1 Tbs. olive oil. (Or if not using pepitas, heat the 2 Tbs. oil over medium heat.) Add the chipotle, adobo sauce, and cumin. Stir to blend into the oil, and then add the beans and 2 Tbs. water to the pan, stirring to blend. Simmer until warmed through, about 2 minutes. Reduce the heat to low. Mash about half of the beans with a fork. Stir in the Cheddar and the remaining 2½ Tbs. cilantro and 1 Tbs. lime juice. Season to taste with salt. If the beans seem too thick, add 1 to 2 Tbs. water to thin to a soft, spreadable consistency.

4. Working with 1 tortilla at a time, spread about a quarter of the beans along the bottom third of a tortilla. Top with a quarter of the spinach, and sprinkle with about a quarter of the tomatoes and pepitas (if using). If you like, add a little lime juice and sour cream on top. Fold the bottom edge over the filling, fold in the sides, and roll up the burrito. —*Mary Ellen Driscoll*

PER SERVING: 510 CALORIES | 19G PROTEIN | 63G CARB | 21G TOTAL FAT | 6G SAT FAT | 10G MONO FAT | 4G POLY FAT | 15MG CHOL | 1,020MG SODIUM | 9G FIBER

slow cooker
pulled-pork sandwiches

YIELDS 8 CUPS PULLED
PORK, ENOUGH FOR
12 TO 16 SANDWICHES

- **1 large yellow onion, halved and sliced**
- **¾ cup jarred tomato salsa (medium heat)**
- **⅓ cup plus 2 Tbs. cider vinegar**
- **⅓ cup packed light brown sugar**
- **1 Tbs. ground cumin**
- **1 Tbs. chili powder**
- **Kosher salt**
- **1 4- to 4½-lb. bone-in pork shoulder, trimmed**
- **3 Tbs. tomato paste**
- **Toasted hamburger buns, for serving**

An easy version of the classic, this pulled-pork sandwich is great with a side of vinegary coleslaw.

1. In a 4-quart slow cooker, combine the onion, salsa, ⅓ cup of the vinegar, the brown sugar, cumin, chili powder, and 1 tsp. salt. Add the pork shoulder and turn to coat. Cover the slow cooker and cook until the pork is fork-tender, 5 to 6 hours on high or 7 to 8 hours on low.

2. Transfer the pork to a cutting board. Using two forks, shred the pork. Discard the bone and fat. Put 1 cup of the juices and onions in a large bowl. Whisk in the tomato paste, the remaining 2 Tbs. vinegar, and 1 tsp. salt. Add the pulled pork and stir to combine. If the pork seems dry, add more juices as needed. Mound the pork on the toasted hamburger buns. —*Allison Fishman*

PER SERVING: 280 CALORIES | 19G PROTEIN | 28G CARB | 9G TOTAL FAT | 3G SAT FAT | 4G MONO FAT | 1.5G POLY FAT | 55MG CHOL | 480MG SODIUM | 2G FIBER

shrimp salad rolls
with tarragon and chives

SERVES 6

Kosher salt

2 lb. large shrimp (31 to 40 per lb.), preferably easy-peel

¾ cup finely chopped celery with leaves

½ cup mayonnaise

¼ cup thinly sliced fresh chives

1 Tbs. finely chopped fresh tarragon

1 Tbs. freshly squeezed lemon juice; more as needed

Freshly ground black pepper

6 hot dog rolls, preferably New England–style split-top rolls

Check the frozen-food aisle for shrimp; frozen shrimp is often fresher than that sold as "fresh" (which has often been previously frozen).

1. Bring a large pot of well-salted water to a boil over high heat. Add the shrimp and cook, stirring, until bright pink and cooked through, about 2 minutes—the water needn't return to a boil. Drain in a colander and run under cold water to stop the cooking. Shell the shrimp, devein if necessary, and cut into ½- to ¾-inch pieces.

2. In a large bowl, stir the celery, mayonnaise, chives, tarragon, lemon juice, ¼ tsp. salt, and ¼ tsp. pepper. Stir in the shrimp and season to taste with more lemon, salt, and pepper.

3. Position a rack 6 inches from the broiler element and heat the broiler on high. Toast both outside surfaces of the rolls under the broiler, about 1 minute per side. Spoon the shrimp salad into the rolls, using about ⅔ cup per roll, and serve. *—Lori Longbotham*

PER SERVING: 390 CALORIES | 29G PROTEIN | 25G CARB | 18G TOTAL FAT | 3.5G SAT FAT | 1G MONO FAT | 1G POLY FAT | 230MG CHOL | 800MG SODIUM | 1G FIBER

caramelized onion, gruyère & sausage panini

SERVES 4

- **3** Tbs. extra-virgin olive oil
- **1** Tbs. unsalted butter
- **2** large yellow onions, thinly sliced (8 cups)
- **¼** cup Calvados (apple brandy)
-    Kosher salt and freshly ground black pepper
- **½** tsp. chopped fresh thyme
- **4** cooked chicken sausages
- **¼** cup Dijon mustard
- **8** ½-inch-thick slices of crusty, rustic bread
- **4** oz. Gruyère, very thinly sliced

Cooked chicken sausage links meet the flavors of French onion soup in this quick weeknight sandwich.

1. Heat 1 Tbs. of the oil and the butter in a 12-inch skillet over medium-high heat. Add the onions, 3 Tbs. of the Calvados, ¼ tsp. salt, and ⅛ tsp. pepper. Reduce the heat to medium low and cook, stirring occasionally, until the onions are deep golden-brown, 25 to 30 minutes. Add the remaining 1 Tbs. Calvados and the thyme and cook about 1 minute more.

2. Meanwhile, in another 12-inch skillet over medium-high heat, heat 1 Tbs. of the oil until hot. Add the sausages and cook until browned and heated through, 5 to 6 minutes. Cut in half lengthwise. Keep warm.

3. Heat a panini press. (Alternatively, heat a nonstick grill pan over medium heat.) Meanwhile, spread the mustard on the bread and assemble 4 sandwiches, distributing the onions, cheese, and sausage evenly among them.

4. Brush the outside of the sandwiches with the remaining 1 Tbs. oil. Cook them in the panini press until browned and crisp, 3 to 6 minutes. (If using a grill pan, put a heavy pan on top of the sandwiches and cook, flipping the sandwiches once.) Serve immediately. *—Samantha Seneviratne*

PER SERVING: 720 CALORIES I 31G PROTEIN I 57G CARB I 38G TOTAL FAT I 13G SAT FAT I 11G MONO FAT I 1.5G POLY FAT I 120MG CHOL I 1,600MG SODIUM I 5G FIBER

Choose Your Sausage Flavor

Chicken sausages are available in many varieties, and this recipe will work with just about any flavor you choose. Sautéed sausages with cabbage slaw and fruit chutney are a great match for a sweet or hot Italian-style link, and the orzo salad is delicious with roasted red pepper and garlic sausage. Apple or roasted garlic sausages are a perfect match for the panini.

smoked turkey reubens

SERVES 4

- 2 **cups thinly sliced green cabbage (about 4 oz.)**
- ¾ **cup julienned kosher dill pickle (from 1 large)**
- 2 **tsp. cider vinegar**
- **Kosher salt**
- ½ **cup mayonnaise**
- 3 **oil-packed sun-dried tomatoes**
- 2 **Tbs. ketchup**
- 8 **slices whole-wheat bread**
- 12 **thin slices smoked turkey**
- 8 **thin slices Swiss cheese**
- 2 **Tbs. unsalted butter, softened**

In this update on the classic, smoked turkey stands in for corned beef, while a fresh slaw and sun-dried tomato mayo take the place of sauerkraut and Thousand Island dressing.

1. In a medium bowl, toss the cabbage and pickles with the vinegar and ½ tsp. salt. Transfer to a colander, set it in the sink, and let sit for 10 minutes. Meanwhile, pulse the mayonnaise, sun-dried tomatoes, and ketchup in a food processor until the tomatoes are finely chopped.

2. Squeeze the cabbage mixture to remove any excess liquid and return to the bowl. Toss the cabbage with 2 Tbs. of the mayonnaise mixture.

3. Spread the remaining mayonnaise on one side of each slice of the bread. Assemble the sandwiches, layering the turkey, cabbage, and cheese over 4 slices of the bread and topping with the other 4 slices. Spread the outsides of the sandwiches with the butter.

4. Heat a large grill pan, skillet, or stovetop griddle over medium-low heat. Working in batches if necessary, put the sandwiches in the pan, top with a grill press or heavy skillet to weigh them down, and cook until browned, 2 to 4 minutes. Flip and cook the other side until browned and the cheese is melted, 2 to 4 minutes more. Cut the sandwiches in half and serve.

—*Tony Rosenfeld*

PER SERVING: 660 CALORIES I 30G PROTEIN I 33G CARB I 46G TOTAL FAT I 17G SAT FAT I 12G MONO FAT I 13G POLY FAT I 90MG CHOL I 1,370MG SODIUM I 5G FIBER

mexican black bean burgers

SERVES 4

- **3 Tbs. olive oil**
- **½ cup thinly sliced scallions, white and green parts**
- **⅓ cup finely chopped fresh poblano chile (1 small chile)**
- **2 large cloves garlic, finely chopped**
- **1 15-oz. can black beans, drained and rinsed**
- **½ cup coarsely chopped fresh cilantro**
- **½ cup toasted whole-grain breadcrumbs (about 1 slice of bread)**
- **1 large egg, lightly beaten**
- **½ tsp. pure chile powder, such as ancho or New Mexico**
- **½ tsp. ground cumin**
- **Kosher salt**
- **Tomatillo and Avocado Salsa (recipe below)**

It's better to sauté these burgers rather than grill them because they have a fragile texture and lack the protein that meat and fish have to hold everything together.

1. Heat 1 Tbs. of the oil in a 10-inch skillet over medium heat. Add the scallions, poblano, and garlic and cook until beginning to soften, 1 to 2 minutes. Transfer to a food processor. Add the beans and pulse 2 or 3 times to roughly chop. Be careful not to overprocess.

2. Transfer the mixture to a large bowl and gently mix in the cilantro, breadcrumbs, egg, chile powder, cumin, and ¾ tsp. salt. Shape the mixture into four equal ¾-inch-thick patties. Refrigerate, covered, for at least 30 minutes and up to 4 hours.

3. Heat the remaining 2 Tbs. oil in a large skillet over medium heat. Cook the burgers until nicely browned on both sides, flipping carefully, about 5 minutes total.

4. Serve with the Tomatillo and Avocado Salsa. —*John Ash*

PER SERVING: 300 CALORIES | 9G PROTEIN | 26G CARB | 19G TOTAL FAT | 3G SAT FAT | 13G MONO FAT | 2.5G POLY FAT | 55MG CHOL | 490MG SODIUM | 9G FIBER

tomatillo and avocado salsa

YIELDS ABOUT 1 CUP

- **1 medium tomatillo, husked, washed, and coarsely chopped**
- **1 Tbs. thinly sliced scallion**
- **½ tsp. chopped garlic**
- **½ tsp. seeded and minced fresh serrano chile; more as desired**
- **1 large ripe avocado, pitted, peeled, and coarsely chopped**
- **Kosher salt and freshly ground black pepper**

This salsa can be refrigerated in an airtight container for up to 2 days. It's also tasty on pork tacos or with quesadillas.

Put the tomatillo, scallion, garlic, and serrano chile in a food processor and whirl until finely chopped, about 15 seconds. Add the avocado and pulse until just combined. The salsa should be chunky. Season to taste with salt, pepper, and more chile if you like.

PER SERVING: 20 CALORIES | 0G PROTEIN | 1G CARB | 2G TOTAL FAT | 0G SAT FAT | 1G MONO FAT | 0G POLY FAT | 0MG CHOL | 35MG SODIUM | 1G FIBER

salmon burgers with herb aïoli

SERVES 4

- 2 **small cloves garlic**
- **Kosher salt**
- 1½ **cups mayonnaise**
- ⅓ **cup finely chopped fresh chives**
- 2 **Tbs. finely chopped fresh dill**
- 1½ **Tbs. Dijon mustard**
- 1 **Tbs. freshly squeezed lemon juice**
- ⅛ **tsp. cayenne**
- **Freshly ground black pepper**
- 5 **brioche or hamburger buns, 1 cut into large cubes, the other 4 split**
- 1 **lb. skinless salmon fillets, preferably wild, pin bones removed, cut into 1-inch pieces (about 2 cups)**
- 2 **oz. (4 Tbs.) unsalted butter**

Ask your fishmonger to remove the pin bones from the salmon or do it yourself with a pair of small tweezers or pliers. Ripe tomato slices sprinkled with salt and pepper would be a colorful addition to these burgers.

1. Chop the garlic, then using the flat side of a chef's knife, mash the garlic to a paste with a pinch of salt. Transfer the garlic paste to a small bowl and stir in the mayonnaise, chives, dill, mustard, lemon juice, cayenne, ¼ tsp. pepper, and salt to taste. Set the aïoli aside.

2. In a food processor, pulse the cubed bun into crumbs. Reserve ½ cup of the crumbs and save the rest for another use. Pulse the salmon until coarsely chopped, about 5 pulses. Transfer the salmon to a medium bowl and stir in ¾ cup of the aïoli, the reserved breadcrumbs, ¼ tsp. salt, and ⅛ tsp. pepper. Shape into four 1-inch-thick patties.

3. Heat 2 Tbs. of the butter in a 12-inch nonstick skillet over medium-high heat. When melted and hot (but not smoking or brown), add the patties and cook until they are firm and each side is crisp and golden-brown, 3 to 5 minutes per side.

4. Meanwhile, position a rack 6 inches from the broiler and heat the broiler on high. Melt the remaining 2 Tbs. butter in a microwave or on the stovetop. Brush it on the insides of the split buns. Put the buns on a baking sheet, butter side up, and toast under the broiler until light golden-brown, 1 to 2 minutes.

5. Serve the burgers on the buns, spread with the remaining aïoli. —*Dina Cheney*

PER SERVING: 870 CALORIES I 35G PROTEIN I 55G CARB I 53G TOTAL FAT I 22G SAT FAT I 8G MONO FAT I 12G POLY FAT I 265MG CHOL I 1,140MG SODIUM I 1G FIBER

fresh tuna burgers
with ginger and cilantro

SERVES 4

- **1** lb. fresh sushi-grade tuna fillet
- **2** Tbs. chopped fresh cilantro
- **2** Tbs. finely chopped red onion or scallion
- **2** Tbs. mayonnaise
- **1** tsp. minced fresh ginger
- **½** tsp. minced fresh hot green or red chile, such as cayenne, Thai bird, or serrano

    Kosher salt and freshly ground black pepper

- **2** Tbs. canola oil

    Thai-Style Dipping Sauce (recipe below)

The key to a good tuna burger is to avoid overprocessing and overcooking. Cook them on the stovetop so you have better heat control and can ensure that they stay a nice, moist medium rare inside.

1. With a very sharp knife, cut the tuna into ¼-inch dice. Alternatively, cut the tuna into 1-inch chunks and pulse in a food processor until just chopped, about 4 quick pulses—take care not to overprocess. Gently stir in the cilantro, onion, mayonnaise, ginger, chile, ¾ tsp. salt, and ¼ tsp. pepper. Shape the tuna into four 1-inch-thick patties. Refrigerate, uncovered, for at least 20 minutes and up to 4 hours.

2. Heat the oil in a 12-inch skillet over medium-high heat. Cook the tuna burgers until nicely browned on both sides but still pink in the center, 2 to 4 minutes total. Don't overcook or the burgers will be dry.

3. Serve with the Thai-Style Dipping Sauce. —*John Ash*

PER SERVING: 320 CALORIES I 27G PROTEIN I 10G CARB I 18G TOTAL FAT I 2.5G SAT FAT I 6G MONO FAT I 3.5G POLY FAT I 45MG CHOL I 1,000MG SODIUM I 0G FIBER

thai-style dipping sauce

YIELDS ABOUT ½ CUP

- **¼** cup freshly squeezed lime juice
- **2½** Tbs. granulated sugar
- **2** Tbs. fish sauce
- **1½** tsp. rice vinegar
- **1½** tsp. coarsely chopped fresh cilantro
- **1** tsp. minced garlic
- **½** tsp. minced fresh hot red or green chile, such as cayenne, Thai bird, or serrano

Inspired by the Thai tradition of serving dipping sauces with meals, this salty, sweet, tart, and spicy sauce is utterly delicious. It's also fantastic with grilled fish fillets or pork.

Combine all the ingredients in a small bowl and stir until the sugar is dissolved. Let stand for at least 30 minutes before serving to let the flavors develop and blend.

chinese pork and mushroom wraps

6 cups thinly sliced green cabbage (about ¾ lb.)

Kosher salt

2 Tbs. hoisin sauce (Koon Chun® or Lee Kum Kee™ brand), plus ½ cup for serving

1 Tbs. soy sauce

2 tsp. Asian sesame oil

1 tsp. rice vinegar

3 Tbs. canola or peanut oil

2 cups matchstick-cut cooked roasted pork loin (about ½ lb.)

1 bunch scallions, trimmed, white and light green parts thinly sliced and green parts cut into 2-inch pieces (keep separate)

½ lb. fresh shiitake mushrooms, stemmed and thinly sliced (about 4 cups)

2 large eggs, beaten

2 tsp. minced fresh ginger

2 tsp. minced garlic

6 to 8 medium (about 8-inch-diameter) flour tortillas, warmed

Like the Chinese-American restaurant classic mu shu pork, this wrap is an Asian take on a soft burrito.

1. Put the cabbage in a colander over the sink and toss with ½ tsp. salt. Let sit for 10 minutes. Transfer to a baking sheet lined with paper towels and pat dry.

2. In a small bowl, mix 2 Tbs. of the hoisin sauce with the soy sauce, sesame oil, and vinegar. Set aside.

3. In a 12-inch heavy-duty nonstick skillet, heat 1 Tbs. of the canola oil over medium-high heat until shimmering. Add the pork, sprinkle lightly with salt, and cook, stirring, until it starts to brown around the edges, about 3 minutes. Transfer to a large plate. Add another 1 Tbs. oil to the pan and once it's shimmering, add the scallion whites, the mushrooms, and ¼ tsp. salt and cook, stirring occasionally, until they brown and soften, 2 to 3 minutes. Push the mushroom mixture to one side of the pan and add the eggs. Cook, scrambling and breaking up with a wooden spoon or spatula into small pieces, until just set, about 1 minute. Transfer the contents of the skillet to the plate with the pork.

4. Heat the remaining 1 Tbs. oil and add the scallion greens, cabbage, ginger, and garlic. Cook, stirring occasionally, until softened, about 2 minutes. Add the reserved hoisin mixture and the pork mixture to the cabbage and stir to distribute the hoisin. Cook, stirring occasionally, for 1 minute to meld the flavors. Serve family style: Tell diners to spread about 1 Tbs. of the hoisin down the center of a tortilla, arrange a generous amount of the pork mixture over the hoisin, and wrap in the tortilla, burrito-style. —*Tony Rosenfeld*

PER SERVING: 330 CALORIES | 14G PROTEIN | 36G CARB | 14G TOTAL FAT | 2.5G SAT FAT | 7G MONO FAT | 3G POLY FAT | 70MG CHOL | 730MG SODIUM | 4G FIBER

skirt steak tacos with spicy sour cream

SERVES 4

½ cup sour cream

¼ tsp. ground chipotle chile

    Kosher salt

1 Tbs. extra-virgin olive oil

1 tsp. ground cumin

    Freshly ground pepper

1 lb. skirt steak (¾ inch thick)

8 6-inch flour or corn tortillas

¼ small head iceberg lettuce,
    shredded (2 cups)

2 medium ripe tomatoes
    (8 oz. each), cored and
    chopped (2 cups)

1 medium ripe avocado, pitted,
    peeled, and sliced ¼ inch thick

⅓ cup chopped red onion

A chipotle chile is a smoked and dried jalapeño. Ground to a powder, it adds a fiery kick to the creamy sauce for these tacos. Look for ground chipotle in the supermarket spice section. If you don't have a grill, you can cook the steak on a grill pan over medium-high heat.

1. Prepare a medium-hot charcoal or gas grill fire.

2. Combine the sour cream, chipotle, and ¼ tsp. salt in a small bowl. Set aside at room temperature to let the flavors meld.

3. In a small bowl, mix the olive oil, cumin, ½ tsp. salt, and ¼ tsp. pepper. Rub this mixture on all sides of the steak. Grill the steak, covered, flipping once, until medium rare, 3 to 4 minutes per side. Transfer the steak to a large plate to rest for at least 5 minutes.

4. Meanwhile, warm the tortillas on the grill for about 30 seconds per side. Slice the steak across the grain into ¼-inch-thick slices. Fill each tortilla with some of the steak, lettuce, tomato, avocado, and onion. Drizzle with the sauce and serve. —*Adeena Sussman*

PER SERVING: 560 CALORIES | 32G PROTEIN | 42G CARB | 30G TOTAL FAT | 9G SAT FAT | 16G MONO FAT | 3G POLY FAT | 75MG CHOL | 700MG SODIUM | 7G FIBER

rib-eye steak and blue cheese sandwiches

- **4** rib-eye steaks, each ½ inch thick, trimmed
- **5** cloves garlic, minced; plus 2 cloves, sliced
- **1** Tbs. chopped fresh rosemary

  Kosher salt and freshly ground black pepper
- **4** Tbs. unsalted butter
- **2** shallots, minced
- **16** medium fresh cremini mushrooms (about 8 oz.), sliced
- **¼** cup sweet Marsala
- **1** medium onion, sliced
- **1** Tbs. extra-virgin olive oil
- **4** to 6 oz. Cambozola cheese, rind removed (or creamy Gorgonzola)
- **8** ½-inch-thick slices pugliese-style bread, lightly toasted
- **1½** Tbs. Dijon mustard

Pugliese is an Italian country bread with a very crisp crust and a soft interior; a good substitute is ciabatta or another artisan Italian loaf. Cambozola is like a cross between Camembert and Gorgonzola—it has a white rind and a creamy, blue-streaked interior.

1. Cut each steak in half crosswise. In a small bowl, combine 4 cloves of the minced garlic, the rosemary, 1½ tsp. salt, and pepper to taste. Rub all over the steaks.

2. In a 12-inch skillet, heat 2 Tbs. of the butter over medium-high heat. Add the shallots and remaining minced garlic and sauté until fragrant, about 2 minutes. Add the mushrooms and Marsala; season with salt and pepper. Cook, stirring frequently, until the mushrooms are cooked through and the liquid has evaporated, about 5 minutes. Transfer to a bowl. Melt another 1 Tbs. butter in the pan. Add the onion, season with salt and pepper, and sauté over medium-high heat until browned but still crunchy, 3 to 5 minutes. Add the sliced garlic and cook until it begins to brown, about 1 minute. Transfer to the bowl with the mushrooms.

3. Add the oil and the remaining 1 Tbs. butter to the pan over high heat. In 2 batches, sear the steaks until well browned, about 2 minutes per side for medium.

4. To serve, stir the Cambozola in a small bowl until spreadable. Put 2 pieces of the toasted bread on each of 4 plates; spread lightly with the mustard and some of the Cambozola. Set a piece of steak on top of each toast and drizzle with any accumulated juices. Return the mushroom mixture to the pan to reheat briefly. Top each steak with some of the mushrooms and a dollop of the Cambozola and serve. *—Kara Adanalian*

PER SERVING: 710 CALORIES | 50G PROTEIN | 23G CARB | 45G TOTAL FAT | 21G SAT FAT | 20G MONO FAT | 4G POLY FAT | 220MG CHOL | 1,150MG SODIUM | 2G FIBER

turkey and corn quesadillas with guacamole

**SERVES 4 FOR DINNER;
8 FOR A LIGHT LUNCH**

- 2 **medium ripe avocados**
- ¼ **cup finely chopped red onion**
- 1 **medium lime, one half juiced and the other cut into wedges**
- 1 **fresh serrano chile, seeded and minced**
- **Kosher salt and freshly ground black pepper**
- 4 **cups shredded roast turkey or chicken**
- 2 **cups fresh corn kernels, blanched, or frozen corn, cooked according to package directions and drained**
- ½ **cup packed coarsely chopped fresh cilantro**
- 8 **7-inch flour tortillas**
- 2 **cups (5 oz.) grated pepper Jack cheese**
- 2 **Tbs. canola oil**

These quesadillas make great use of leftover turkey. Serve them with a mango and jícama salad.

1. Position a rack in the center of the oven and heat the oven to 200°F.

2. Halve and pit the avocados. Scoop the flesh into a medium bowl and mash with a potato masher. Stir in the onion, 1 Tbs. of the lime juice, the chile, ½ tsp. salt, and ½ tsp. pepper. Season to taste with more salt and lime juice. Put a piece of plastic wrap directly on the surface of the guacamole to prevent browning.

3. In a large bowl, toss the turkey, corn, and cilantro with 1 tsp. salt. Top half of each tortilla with one-eighth of the filling mixture and ¼ cup of the cheese. Fold the uncovered half of each tortilla over the filling.

4. Heat 1½ tsp. of the oil in a large nonstick skillet over medium heat. Add 2 of the quesadillas to the pan and weigh down with a lid. Cook until golden-brown and a bit crisp, 2 to 3 minutes. With a spatula, carefully flip each quesadilla and cook until golden-brown and the cheese has melted, about 2 minutes more. Transfer the quesadillas to a baking sheet and put in the oven.

5. Wipe out the pan. Repeat, cooking the remaining quesadillas in 3 more batches, using 1½ tsp. oil for each batch.

6. Cut the quesadillas into wedges and serve with the guacamole and lime wedges on the side.   —*Dina Cheney*

PER SERVING: 510 CALORIES | 30G PROTEIN | 39G CARB | 27G TOTAL FAT | 7G SAT FAT |
11G MONO FAT | 4.5G POLY FAT | 75MG CHOL | 600MG SODIUM | 6G FIBER

soft-shell crab sandwiches with spicy tartar sauce

SERVES 4

FOR THE TARTAR SAUCE

- ½ cup mayonnaise
- 1 Tbs. minced red onion
- 1 Tbs. finely chopped dill pickle
- 1 Tbs. rinsed and finely chopped capers
- 1 Tbs. thinly sliced fresh chives
- 1½ tsp. Old Bay Seasoning
- 1 tsp. freshly squeezed lemon juice
- ¼ tsp. hot sauce, such as Tabasco

FOR THE CRABS

- ¼ cup unbleached all-purpose flour
- ¼ cup medium-grind yellow cornmeal
- Kosher salt and freshly ground black pepper
- 4 jumbo soft-shell crabs, cleaned (bodies about 5 inches across; 3 to 3½ oz. each after cleaning)
- 2 Tbs. canola or vegetable oil
- 1 Tbs. unsalted butter

TO ASSEMBLE

- 8 slices white sandwich bread, toasted
- 4 large leaves bibb lettuce
- 4 to 8 slices ripe tomato

Soft-shell crabs cook in minutes and are easier to eat than hard-shell crabs. Their sweet, briny flavor and crunchy-soft, juicy texture can't be beat.

MAKE THE SAUCE

In a small bowl, combine the mayonnaise, onion, pickle, capers, chives, Old Bay, lemon juice, and hot pepper sauce. Set aside.

COOK THE CRABS

1. In a wide, shallow bowl, combine the flour, cornmeal, ½ tsp. salt, and ¼ tsp. pepper. Dredge the crabs to coat on both sides (if the top shells are thicker than a piece of paper, pull them off before dredging).

2. Heat the oil in a 12-inch skillet (preferably cast iron) over medium-high heat until shimmering hot. Add the butter to the skillet and swirl the pan to melt it. Add the crabs top side down and cook, shaking the pan once or twice, until crisp and browned, about 3 minutes. The crabs may pop and splatter, so be careful. Flip the crabs and cook until crisp and just cooked through (an instant-read thermometer inserted in the center of the crab should read 145°F), about another 3 minutes. Transfer the crabs to a large paper-towel-lined plate.

ASSEMBLE THE SANDWICHES

Spread the tartar sauce on each slice of toast. Top 4 of the toast slices, sauce side up, with a piece of lettuce and 1 or 2 slices of tomato. Put 1 crab on each sandwich, top with the remaining toast, sauce side down, and serve.

—*Denise Mickelsen*

PER SERVING: 600 CALORIES I 34G PROTEIN I 35G CARB I 35G TOTAL FAT I 6G SAT FAT I 11G MONO FAT I 15G POLY FAT I 115MG CHOL I 1,380MG SODIUM I 2G FIBER

Classic Scalloped Potatoes
(recipe on p. 206)

sides

roasted fingerling potato crisps with shallots and rosemary

SERVES 4

- **1 lb. fingerling potatoes,
  thinly sliced lengthwise
  (about ⅛ inch thick)**
- **3 Tbs. olive oil**
- **2 large shallots, sliced
  ¼ inch thick and broken
  into individual rings**
- **2 tsp. chopped fresh rosemary**
- **Kosher salt and freshly
  ground black pepper**

Try to cut the fingerlings no larger than ⅛ inch thick, so that the potatoes will crisp in the oven. (Using a mandolin will allow you to cut them even thinner.) These crisps make a great accompaniment to grilled steak or roasted fish.

1. Position a rack in the center of the oven and heat the oven to 425°F. Line a large, rimmed baking sheet with parchment or foil.

2. In a large bowl, toss the potato slices with the oil, shallots, rosemary, 1¼ tsp. salt, and ½ tsp. pepper, and then spread the chips flat on the baking sheet. Bake the potatoes, turning after 10 minutes, until they brown and start to crisp, 25 to 30 minutes; the shallots should be tender and browned. Serve immediately. —*Tony Rosenfeld*

What Are Fingerlings?

Like heirloom tomatoes, fingerling potatoes are an old variety that has been resuscitated by the advent of farmers' markets and organic growers. They get their name from their small, finger-length size and come in a range of colors, from white, yellow, and orange to red and purple. The Russian banana, the most common fingerling variety, has yellow flesh and a buttery texture similar to that of Yukon Gold. Fingerlings are delicious sliced and roasted, pan-fried, or mashed with butter and fresh herbs.

mashed sweet potatoes with mango chutney

YIELDS ABOUT 3 CUPS;
SERVES 4

2 lb. sweet potatoes (about 3 medium), peeled and cut into ½-inch chunks

Kosher salt

⅓ cup jarred Major Grey's mango chutney

½ cup heavy cream

2 small scallions, thinly sliced (white and green parts separated)

1 Tbs. finely chopped crystallized ginger

Freshly ground black pepper

Serve this slightly sweet side dish with roasted chicken, turkey cutlets, or pork chops.

1. Put the sweet potatoes in a large saucepan. Add cool water to barely cover and a large pinch of salt. Boil over high heat until the potatoes are very soft when pierced with a fork, about 10 minutes. Drain the potatoes in a colander and return them to the saucepan. Set the pan over high heat and dry the potatoes, stirring often, until any liquid has evaporated, about 30 seconds. Remove from the heat.

2. If the chutney contains any large chunks, finely chop them. In a small saucepan, bring the cream, chutney, scallion whites, ginger, ½ tsp. salt, and ¼ tsp. pepper to a boil over medium-high heat. Remove from the heat.

3. Force the sweet potatoes through a ricer or a food mill and into a serving bowl (or mash for a chunkier texture). Stir in the warm cream mixture and season to taste with more salt and pepper. Sprinkle with the scallion greens and serve immediately. —*Lori Longbotham*

PER SERVING: 320 CALORIES | 3G PROTEIN | 51G CARB | 11G TOTAL FAT | 7G SAT FAT | 3G MONO FAT | 0.5G POLY FAT | 40MG CHOL | 430MG SODIUM | 5G FIBER

couscous with chickpeas and pistachios

SERVES 6 TO 8

¼ cup whole pistachios or slivered almonds

¼ cup extra-virgin olive oil

1 red bell pepper (about 10 oz.), cut into ¼-inch dice

Kosher salt

10 oz. (1⅔ cups) couscous

⅔ cup cooked or canned chickpeas, rinsed well

3 or 4 drops Tabasco or other hot sauce

You can make the couscous an hour ahead and keep it in a covered stainless-steel bowl over a pot of simmering water.

1. Heat the oven to 325°F. On a baking sheet, toast the pistachios or almonds until golden brown, 12 to 15 minutes.

2. In a small sauté pan, heat 2 Tbs. of the olive oil and sauté the red pepper until slightly soft, 3 to 4 minutes.

3. In a medium pan, bring 3 cups water to a boil. Add 1 tsp. salt and the remaining 2 Tbs. olive oil. Pour in the couscous, turn off the heat, cover, and set aside for 5 minutes.

4. Add the red pepper, pistachios, chickpeas, and Tabasco to the couscous and fluff with a fork. Season with salt to taste. —*Arlene Jacobs*

PER SERVING: 250 CALORIES | 7G PROTEIN | 35G CARB | 9G TOTAL FAT | 1G SAT FAT | 6G MONO FAT | 1G POLY FAT | 0MG CHOL | 250MG SODIUM | 4G FIBER

classic scalloped potatoes

SERVES 10 TO 12

- **2 Tbs. unsalted butter, cut into small pieces; more for the baking dish**
- **1¾ cups heavy cream**
- **1¾ cups whole milk**
- **4 medium cloves garlic, smashed and peeled**
- **2 Tbs. coarsely chopped fresh thyme**
- **¼ tsp. freshly grated nutmeg**
- **Kosher salt and freshly ground black pepper**
- **3½ lb. Yukon Gold potatoes (8 to 10 large), peeled and sliced ⅛ inch thick**

Make Ahead

The dish can be assembled up to 4 hours ahead, covered, and refrigerated. Let sit at room temperature while the oven heats. You can keep the cooked scalloped potatoes, covered, in a warm oven for up to 1 hour before serving.

Equal amounts of heavy cream and whole milk result in the perfect tender texture and creamy consistency. Resist the urge to use lighter versions of either ingredient if it's the real thing you're after.

1. Position a rack in the center of the oven and heat the oven to 375°F. Butter a 3-quart (9x13x2-inch) baking dish.

2. In a 3- to 4-quart saucepan, whisk the cream, milk, garlic, thyme, nutmeg, 2½ tsp. salt, and 1 tsp. pepper. Bring to a simmer over medium heat, stirring occasionally, and then remove from the heat and let cool in the pan to room temperature. Strain through a fine sieve into a large liquid measuring cup.

3. Arrange about a third of the potatoes in an overlapping layer in the baking dish. Give the cream mixture a quick whisk and pour about a third of it over the potatoes. Repeat twice more with the remaining potatoes and cream mixture. Dot the butter over the top and cover with foil.

4. Bake until the potatoes are completely tender when pierced with a paring knife, 45 minutes to 1 hour.

5. Remove the potatoes from the oven and heat the broiler on high. Uncover the potatoes and gently press them down with a flat spatula so the cream mixture mostly covers them. Broil until nicely browned on top, 5 to 8 minutes.

6. Let the potatoes rest for 5 to 10 minutes before serving. *—Tony Rosenfeld*

PER SERVING: 270 CALORIES | 4G PROTEIN | 28G CARB | 16G TOTAL FAT | 10G SAT FAT | 4.5G MONO FAT | 0.5G POLY FAT | 55MG CHOL | 270MG SODIUM | 2G FIBER

tips for the best scalloped potatoes

Creamy, rich scalloped potatoes are truly simple to make: Thinly slice potatoes, infuse milk and cream with seasonings (like garlic, nutmeg, and fresh herbs), then bake the spuds in the cream mixture until tender and browned on top. (A gratin, on the other hand, has a top crust of breadcrumbs and butter or cheese.) Not only is it easy to make, but it goes with almost anything, from a weeknight roast chicken to a Sunday roast beef. Here are the secrets to making this indulgent cold-weather comfort food.

CHOOSE THE RIGHT POTATO
Use buttery, waxy Yukon Golds; they release just the right amount of starch for a creamy sauce and hold their shape for great texture. (Floury potatoes, like russets, will leak too much starch and give you thick and sometimes gloppy results.)

STAY THIN
Slice the potatoes very thinly (about ⅛ inch thick) and uniformly so they cook evenly. This is a great time to break out your mandoline, or use a very sharp chef's knife.

INFUSE
Steep cream and milk with fresh thyme, garlic, and nutmeg to add lots of extra flavor to the finished dish.

COVER UP
Keep the potatoes covered during most of the cooking process to seal in steam, which helps promote even cooking. When they're tender, uncover and broil the potatoes for a browned crust.

LET THEM REST
Once the potatoes come out of the oven, give them 5 to 10 minutes to cool and reabsorb the cream mixture before serving. This results in creamy—not soupy—scalloped potatoes.

classic creamed spinach

SERVES 4 TO 6

- 2 lb. fresh spinach (mature crinkly leaves, not flat baby leaves), stems removed
- Kosher salt
- ½ cup whole milk
- ½ cup heavy cream
- 3 large cloves garlic, smashed and peeled
- Freshly ground black pepper
- Freshly grated nutmeg
- ½ oz. (1 Tbs.) unsalted butter
- 1 Tbs. plus 1 tsp. unbleached all-purpose flour
- ⅓ cup freshly grated Parmigiano-Reggiano

Excess liquid will dilute the béchamel sauce, so drain as much from the wilted spinach as possible. While it's in the colander, firmly press the spinach a couple of times with a dishtowel (but don't squeeze it to death); then blot the spinach again when it's transferred to a cutting board.

With a subtle infusion of garlic and a little bit of Parmigiano-Reggiano, this creamy side dish holds its own against the steakhouse competition.

1. Wash the spinach thoroughly using 2 or 3 changes of water, but don't dry the leaves. Set a 6- to 8-quart Dutch oven over medium-high heat and add half of the wet spinach to it. Season with ¼ tsp. salt, cover, and steam, tossing frequently, until wilted, 3 to 4 minutes. Transfer to a colander in the sink and repeat with the remaining spinach.

2. Allow the spinach to cool in the colander for several minutes. Using a clean, folded dishtowel, press down on the spinach to remove as much water as possible. Let the spinach rest for a few more minutes and then press again to remove more water. Transfer the spinach to a cutting board, blot again with the towel, and chop very coarsely.

3. Put the milk, cream, and smashed garlic in a 1-quart saucepan. Bring to a boil over medium heat; then immediately remove from the heat and let sit for 10 minutes.

4. With a fork, remove most of the smashed garlic from the cream mixture, pressing the garlic against the side of the pan to squeeze out the cream. (It's fine if small pieces of garlic remain.) Transfer the cream mixture to a liquid measuring cup and add ½ tsp. salt, a few grinds of pepper, and a big pinch of nutmeg.

5. Wipe out the saucepan. Melt the butter in the pan over medium-low heat. Add the flour and cook, whisking constantly, until pale and smooth, about 1 minute.

6. Whisk in the cream mixture in a slow, steady stream. Raise the heat to medium and simmer the sauce, whisking constantly, until it thickens and reduces slightly, about 2 minutes. Remove from the heat.

7. Return the chopped cooked spinach to the Dutch oven and set over medium heat. Add the sauce and stir to combine. Add the Parmigiano and mix well. Continue to stir constantly until the spinach is hot, 1 to 2 minutes. Season with more salt and pepper and serve immediately. —*Susie Middleton*

PER SERVING: 140 CALORIES | 5G PROTEIN | 7G CARB | 11G TOTAL FAT | 7G SAT FAT | 3G MONO FAT | 0.5G POLY FAT | 35MG CHOL | 250MG SODIUM | 2G FIBER

sausage-maple bread stuffing

YIELDS ABOUT 12 CUPS;
SERVES 12

- 1½ lb. dense, chewy bread, cut into ¾-inch cubes (about 13 cups)
- 5 oz. (10 Tbs.) unsalted butter, softened
- ⅓ cup chopped fresh thyme leaves (from about 1 oz. thyme sprigs)
- ⅓ cup chopped fresh sage leaves (from about ¾ oz. sage sprigs)
- ¾ tsp. poultry seasoning
- 3 cups medium-diced yellow onion (from 2 medium onions)
- 3 cups medium-diced celery (6 large stalks)
- 7½ cups lower-salt chicken broth
- 2 bay leaves
- 1 smoked ham hock (about 1 lb.)
- 1 lb. bulk pork breakfast sausage
- ⅓ cup maple syrup
- 1½ tsp. freshly ground black pepper
- Kosher salt

The bread can be dried weeks in advance, bagged, frozen, and then thawed when ready to use. The stuffing can be made (but not baked) up to 2 days ahead and refrigerated, covered.

1. Lay the bread cubes in a single layer on two baking sheets. Leave out to dry completely at room temperature, tossing once or twice, for about 2 days.

2. Position a rack in the center of the oven and heat the oven to 375°F.

3. In a heavy-based, 8-quart stockpot or Dutch oven, melt 5 Tbs. of the butter over medium heat until it begins to foam. Stir in the thyme, sage, and poultry seasoning and cook just enough to coat the herbs and season the butter, 30 to 60 seconds. Stir in the onions and celery and cook, stirring occasionally, until soft and fragrant, about 15 minutes. Add the chicken broth, bay leaves, and ham hock and bring to a boil over high heat. Reduce the heat to medium low and simmer until the liquid reduces by one-third, about 30 minutes.

4. Meanwhile, put the sausage on a rimmed baking sheet and break it into quarter-size chunks. Roast until cooked through, about 15 minutes. Let cool, and then chop the sausage into smaller bits.

5. Add the sausage to the broth and simmer just to allow the flavors to meld, about 5 minutes. Remove the ham hock and bay leaves. Discard the bay leaves and set the hock aside to cool. Stir the dried bread, several cups at a time, into the broth until all of the broth is absorbed and the bread cubes are well moistened. Stir in the maple syrup, pepper, and the remaining 5 Tbs. butter.

6. When the hock is cool enough to handle, pick off the meat, chop it into small pieces, and add to the stuffing. Season to taste with salt if necessary (depending on the sausage and ham hock, both of which are salty, there may already be enough).

7. Transfer the stuffing to a 9x13-inch baking dish and bake uncovered until heated through and crisp on top, about 20 minutes if freshly made or about 30 minutes if made ahead. —*Ris Lacoste*

PER SERVING: 430 CALORIES I 17G PROTEIN I 42G CARB I 22G TOTAL FAT I 9G SAT FAT I 7G MONO FAT I 2.5G POLY FAT I 65MG CHOL I 800MG SODIUM I 3G FIBER

shrimp fried rice

SERVES 4 TO 6

- 2 Tbs. soy sauce
- 2 Tbs. gin or high-quality Chinese white rice wine
- 1 Tbs. oyster sauce
- 2 tsp. granulated sugar
- 2 tsp. Asian sesame oil
- ¾ tsp. table salt
- White pepper, freshly ground if possible
- 3 large eggs
- 3 Tbs. peanut oil
- 1½ Tbs. minced fresh ginger
- 1½ Tbs. minced garlic (3 to 4 cloves)
- ½ lb. shrimp, shelled, deveined, and cut into ¼-inch pieces
- 3 cups cooked extra-long-grain white rice, at room temperature
- 3 scallions, trimmed, white and green parts finely sliced (to yield ½ cup)

Gin may seem like a funny addition to fried rice, but it's the better choice over the poor-quality Chinese "cooking wine" that supermarkets offer.

1. In a small bowl, mix the soy sauce, gin or rice wine, oyster sauce, sugar, sesame oil, ½ tsp. salt, and a pinch of white pepper.

2. In another small bowl, beat the eggs with ¼ tsp. salt and a pinch of white pepper.

3. Heat a 12-inch skillet or, even better, a large, well-seasoned carbon-steel wok over high heat for 45 seconds. (A very hot pan prevents sticking.) Swirl 1 Tbs. of the peanut oil in the pan to coat the bottom. Add the eggs and scramble them gently with a spatula as they cook until they're still a little soft and loose. Remove the pan from the heat and cut the egg into small pieces with the spatula; it will finish cooking as you do this. Transfer to a bowl.

4. Wipe the pan and spatula clean with paper towels. Heat the pan over high heat for 45 seconds. Pour in the remaining 2 Tbs. peanut oil and swirl to coat the pan. Add the ginger and garlic. Stir constantly with the spatula until the garlic is light brown, about 10 seconds. Immediately add the shrimp; stir constantly until it's opaque, about 1 minute. Add the cooked rice. Cook, stirring constantly, for 2 minutes. Reduce the heat to low. Give the soy sauce mixture a stir and then drizzle it over the rice. Stir well to completely coat the rice and mix the ingredients. Add the scrambled egg and mix well, then add the scallions and mix well again. Taste and add salt if necessary. Transfer the rice to a bowl and serve. —*Eileen Yin-Fei Lo*

PER SERVING: 280 CALORIES | 13G PROTEIN | 31G CARB | 11G TOTAL FAT | 2G SAT FAT | 5G MONO FAT | 4G POLY FAT | 160MG CHOL | 850MG SODIUM | 1G FIBER

parsnip pancakes with caramelized onions and sour cream

SERVES 4

- 3 **Tbs. olive oil**
- 2 **Tbs. unsalted butter**
- 1 **large or 2 small yellow onions, thinly sliced (to yield about 2 cups)**

  Kosher salt and freshly ground black pepper

- 1 **lb. small to medium parsnips (about 6 medium), peeled (if very thick, halve them lengthwise and core them)**
- 1 **medium leek, white part only, finely chopped (to yield about ½ cup)**
- 1 **large egg, lightly beaten**
- 3 **Tbs. unbleached all-purpose flour**

  Sour cream, for garnish

These pancakes are perfect partners for a simple roast like pork, lamb, or chicken, but they also make a delicious first course.

1. In a medium skillet, heat 1 Tbs. each of the olive oil and butter over medium heat. When the foam subsides, add the onions and cook, stirring occasionally, until very soft and golden, 20 to 25 minutes; reduce the heat if they brown too quickly. Season with salt to taste and set aside.

2. Meanwhile, in a large saucepan, bring about 2 quarts salted water to a boil. Add the parsnips (cut them in half if they don't fit in the pan) and cook for 3 minutes. Drain, run under cold water to cool them quickly, and drain again very well. Grate the parsnips in a food processor fitted with a medium grating disk.

3. In a medium bowl, combine the parsnips, leek, and egg. Stir in the flour, 1 tsp. salt, and ⅛ tsp. pepper.

4. In a 10- to 12-inch heavy skillet, heat the remaining 2 Tbs. oil and 1 Tbs. butter over medium-high heat until the foam subsides. Shape the parsnip mixture into 4 equal balls. Put them in the skillet and press on each with a flat spatula to make cakes about 3½ inches wide. Reduce the heat to medium and cook until browned on one side, 4 to 6 minutes. Turn the cakes over and brown the other side, 4 to 5 minutes. Flip to recrisp the first side, about 30 seconds. Drain briefly on paper towels and then serve while hot, garnished with a large dollop of sour cream and the caramelized onions. —*Eva Katz*

PER SERVING: 320 CALORIES I 5G PROTEIN I 34G CARB I 19G TOTAL FAT I 6G SAT FAT I 11G MONO FAT I 1G POLY FAT I 70MG CHOL I 620MG SODIUM I 6G FIBER

cannellini beans with lemon, roasted red peppers & bacon

SERVES 6

- **1** medium lemon, scrubbed
- **2** oz. thick bacon (about 2 slices), cut crosswise into thin strips
- **2** Tbs. extra-virgin olive oil
- **1** tsp. chopped fresh rosemary
- **1** large clove garlic, minced
- **⅛** tsp. crushed red pepper flakes
- **2** 15½-oz. cans cannellini beans, rinsed and drained
- **¾** cup lower-salt chicken broth
- **2** jarred roasted red peppers, cut into small dice
- **½** tsp. freshly ground black pepper

  Kosher salt (optional)

Smoky bacon, sweet roasted red pepper, and tangy lemon transform canned beans in this easy side dish. Serve with lamb chops or sausages.

1. Using a vegetable peeler, shave six 1-inch-wide strips of zest from the lemon (avoid the white pith). Cut the strips crosswise ¼ inch wide. Juice half of the lemon and reserve the juice and zest separately.

2. In a 3-quart saucepan over medium heat, cook the bacon with 1 Tbs. of the oil, stirring occasionally, until it renders most of its fat and starts to brown, 3 to 5 minutes. Using a slotted spoon, transfer the bacon to a paper-towel-lined plate.

3. Remove the pan from the heat and add the rosemary, garlic, and red pepper flakes; cook, swirling the contents of the pan, until sizzling steadily and fragrant, about 30 seconds. Return the pan to medium heat and add the beans, chicken broth, roasted peppers, and lemon zest. Bring to a boil; then reduce the heat to maintain a steady simmer. Cook, stirring occasionally, until the broth thickens and the flavors meld, 10 to 15 minutes. Stir in 1 Tbs. of the lemon juice and the pepper. Season to taste with more lemon juice or salt. Serve drizzled with the remaining 1 Tbs. oil and sprinkled with the bacon.
—*Tony Rosenfeld*

PER SERVING: 200 CALORIES | 8G PROTEIN | 23G CARB | 8G TOTAL FAT | 1.5G SAT FAT | 4.5G MONO FAT | 1.5G POLY FAT | 5MG CHOL | 460MG SODIUM | 6G FIBER

cauliflower sformato

SERVES 6 TO 8

- **1 small head cauliflower (about 2 lb.)**
- **2 Tbs. olive oil; more for the gratin dish**
- **Kosher salt**
- **1¾ oz. freshly grated Parmigiano-Reggiano (⅔ cup grated on the small holes of a box grater)**
- **3¾ cups whole milk**
- **4 oz. (½ cup) unsalted butter**
- **2¼ oz. (½ cup) unbleached all-purpose flour**
- **3 large eggs**
- **2 large egg yolks**
- **2 Tbs. extra-virgin olive oil**
- **Freshly ground black pepper**

A sformato is an Italian version of a soufflé. If you like, you can bake the cauliflower mixture in individual ramekins or gratin dishes; just reduce the baking time.

1. Position a rack in the center of the oven and heat the oven to 375°F.

2. Core the cauliflower and separate it into florets. Cut the florets into ¼-inch-thick slices. Put the cauliflower on a rimmed baking sheet and toss with the olive oil. Spread in an even layer, season with ½ tsp. salt, and roast until tender, 30 to 35 minutes. Let cool.

3. Raise the oven temperature to 400°F. Brush an 8x10-inch (2-quart) gratin dish with olive oil and evenly coat with about half of the Parmigiano-Reggiano. Set aside.

4. Heat the milk in a 2-quart saucepan over medium heat until just about to boil.

5. Meanwhile, melt the butter in a 4-quart saucepan over medium-low heat. Whisk in the flour and cook, whisking constantly, until the mixture turns light golden, 2 to 4 minutes. Slowly add the hot milk, whisking constantly until very smooth. Bring just to a boil and reduce the heat to maintain a simmer. Add 1 tsp. salt and cook, stirring frequently, for 10 minutes to develop the flavor. Transfer to a large bowl.

6. In a small bowl, whisk the eggs, yolks, and extra-virgin olive oil. Roughly chop ½ cup of the cauliflower, and purée the rest in a food processor. Stir the chopped cauliflower, cauliflower purée, egg mixture, and the remaining cheese into the sauce. Season to taste with salt and pepper. Pour the mixture into the prepared gratin dish and bake until the sformato is just set and browned around the edges, about 30 minutes. It should jiggle just a little when you remove it from the oven. Let rest for 10 to 15 minutes before serving.
—*Tasha DeSerio*

PER SERVING: 330 CALORIES I 10G PROTEIN I 16G CARB I 26G TOTAL FAT I 12G SAT FAT I 10G MONO FAT I 2G POLY FAT I 175MG CHOL I 320MG SODIUM I 2G FIBER

twice-baked potatoes with sour cream

SERVES 8

8   large Yukon Gold or medium russet potatoes (about 8 oz. each), scrubbed and dried

6   Tbs. unsalted butter

2   cups sour cream

1   cup thinly sliced chives or scallions

1   cup freshly grated Parmigiano-Reggiano

4   tsp. good-quality balsamic vinegar

    Kosher salt and freshly ground black pepper

These potatoes are stuffed with sour cream, butter, and cheese, but the secret ingredient isn't dairy—it's a splash of balsamic vinegar, which gives the filling a sweet-tangy note. Scooping the baked potato flesh while it's still hot helps the butter and cheese melt easily into the filling.

1. Position a rack in the center of the oven and heat the oven to 425°F. Put the potatoes on the oven rack and bake for 30 minutes. Prick each potato on all sides with a fork. Continue to bake until the potatoes are tender when pierced with a fork, about 15 minutes more. Carefully remove the potatoes from the oven.

2. While the potatoes are still hot, hold each one with a clean kitchen towel and cut off about one-quarter lengthwise from the top. With a spoon, gently scoop the potato flesh into a large bowl, leaving enough flesh attached to the skin so that it holds its shape. Scrape any flesh from the tops and discard the skin (or eat it as a snack).

3. With a fork, mash 4 Tbs. of the butter into the potatoes until melted. Add the sour cream, chives or scallions, ¾ cup of the cheese, and the vinegar. Season to taste with salt and pepper. Don't overmix—it's fine if the mixture has a few lumps.

4. Spoon the filling into the reserved potato shells, mounding it nicely and making sure the filled shells are resting upright. (The potatoes may be prepared to this point up to 1 day ahead; wrap each in plastic and refrigerate.)

5. When ready to serve, arrange the potatoes on a baking sheet or in a baking dish. Cut the remaining 2 Tbs. of butter into small pieces and dot the potatoes with the butter. Sprinkle the potatoes with the remaining cheese. Bake at 425°F until heated through and starting to brown on the top, 20 to 25 minutes. (If baking straight from the refrigerator, allow an additional 10 to 15 minutes for the potatoes to heat through.) *—Bruce Aidells and Nancy Oakes*

PER SERVING: 370 CALORIES | 8G PROTEIN | 42G CARB | 20G TOTAL FAT | 12G SAT FAT | 5G MONO FAT | 1G POLY FAT | 45MG CHOL | 210MG SODIUM | 4G FIBER

acorn squash with rosemary and brown sugar

SERVES 4

- **1 2-lb. acorn squash (unpeeled), halved lengthwise, seeded, and cut into 8 wedges**
- **1 Tbs. unsalted butter**
- **1 Tbs. extra-virgin olive oil**
- **½ cup dry white wine**
- **3 Tbs. packed dark brown sugar**
- **1 Tbs. chopped fresh rosemary**
- **1 Tbs. freshly squeezed lemon juice**
- **Kosher salt and freshly ground black pepper**

If you don't have a sauté pan large enough to brown all of the squash at once, brown it in batches, and then return it all to the pan to simmer.

1. Using a paring knife, score each wedge of squash lengthwise down the middle of the flesh. Heat the butter and oil in an 11- to 12-inch straight-sided sauté pan over medium-high heat. Arrange the squash in the pan in a single layer and cook, flipping occasionally, until deep golden-brown on all cut sides, about 10 minutes.

2. Carefully pour the wine into the pan, then quickly scatter the brown sugar, rosemary, lemon juice, ½ tsp. salt, and ⅛ tsp. pepper over the squash. Cover the pan, reduce the heat to low, and simmer until the squash is almost tender, about 10 minutes more.

3. Uncover the pan and increase the heat to medium. Flip the squash and cook until the liquid is thick and the squash is tender, about 5 minutes more. Transfer the squash to a platter, season with salt and pepper to taste, drizzle any remaining liquid over the top, and serve. —*Liz Pearson*

PER SERVING: 190 CALORIES | 1G PROTEIN | 29G CARB | 6G TOTAL FAT | 2.5G SAT FAT | 3G MONO FAT | 0.5G POLY FAT | 10MG CHOL | 150MG SODIUM | 3G FIBER

roasted winter vegetables with a maple-ginger glaze

SERVES 4

½ lb. parsnips, peeled and cut into ½ x 2-inch sticks

½ lb. carrots (about 3 or 4), peeled and cut into 1½ x 2-inch sticks

½ lb. turnips (about 2 medium or 1 large), peeled and cut into thin wedges

½ lb. Brussels sprouts, ends trimmed and any wilted leaves pulled off; large sprouts halved

1 2-inch piece fresh ginger, peeled and sliced into very thin matchsticks (about ⅓ cup)

3 Tbs. unsalted butter, melted

Kosher salt and freshly ground black pepper

1 tsp. grated fresh ginger

1½ Tbs. pure maple syrup

Thin matchsticks of ginger roast along with the vegetables, absorbing the butter and maple syrup so that they caramelize and become soft, chewy, and irresistible. Some minced ginger is also tossed in at the end to add a fresh, sharp finishing note.

Heat the oven to 425°F. Spread the vegetables and the ginger matchsticks in a large, low-sided roasting pan or a heavy rimmed baking sheet. Drizzle with the butter and season with salt and pepper. Toss to evenly coat the vegetables and spread them so that they're just one layer deep. Roast the vegetables, tossing a couple of times, until tender and golden brown in spots, about 30 minutes. Combine the grated ginger and maple syrup. Drizzle the vegetables with the maple-ginger mixture, toss, and roast for another 5 minutes. The vegetables should be very tender and browned in spots. Serve warm. —*Eva Katz*

PER SERVING: 210 CALORIES I 4G PROTEIN I 31G CARB I 9G TOTAL FAT I 5G SAT FAT I 3G MONO FAT I 1G POLY FAT I 25MG CHOL I 320MG SODIUM I 8G FIBER

garlic-roasted green beans and shallots with hazelnuts

SERVES 4

6 medium shallots

1 lb. green beans, trimmed

5 cloves garlic, coarsely chopped

3 Tbs. extra-virgin olive oil

1 tsp. kosher salt

½ tsp. freshly ground black pepper

¼ cup finely chopped fresh flat-leaf parsley

¼ cup coarsely chopped toasted hazelnuts

1 tsp. finely grated lemon zest

Roasting is not the first method that comes to mind for green beans, but it's a delicious one. A sprinkle of lemon zest and parsley post-roast give the dish a bright feel.

1. Position a rack in the center of the oven and heat the oven to 450°F. Cut each shallot lengthwise into ¼-inch slices. Put the shallots, green beans, and garlic in a large bowl; toss with the oil. Sprinkle the salt and pepper over the vegetables and toss again. Transfer to a 10x15-inch Pyrex® dish and roast until the vegetables are tender and very lightly browned, stirring once, 18 to 20 minutes.

2. Meanwhile, combine the parsley, hazelnuts, and lemon zest in a small bowl. Sprinkle the parsley mixture over the roasted vegetables and toss to coat. Serve immediately. —*Juliana Grimes Bottcher*

PER SERVING: 230 CALORIES I 5G PROTEIN I 22G CARB I 15G TOTAL FAT I 2G SAT FAT I 11G MONO FAT I 2G POLY FAT I 0MG CHOL I 480MG SODIUM I 5G FIBER

creamy mashed yukon golds

SERVES 4 TO 6

1¾ to 2 lb. yellow-fleshed potatoes, peeled and cut into large chunks (1½ to 2 inches)

2 cloves garlic, peeled

Kosher salt

3 Tbs. unsalted butter, softened

1 cup milk, hot but not boiling

Freshly ground black pepper

Yellow-fleshed potatoes have a rich, almost buttery taste. If you like a slightly tangy edge to your mash, substitute buttermilk for the milk. You can also embellish these by adding a whole heap of fresh herbs (up to ½ cup each of chopped parsley and basil) and some toasted pine nuts, too.

1. Put the potatoes and garlic in a large saucepan and cover with cold water by at least an inch. Add a generous ½ tsp. salt and bring to a boil. Lower the heat to maintain a steady simmer, cover the pot partially, and cook until the potatoes are quite tender when tested with a metal skewer, 15 to 20 minutes.

2. Drain the potatoes and garlic—reserving some of the cooking water—and dump them back into the pan. Dry the potatoes over medium heat, shaking the pan and stirring until the potatoes look floury and leave a light film on the bottom of the pan.

3. If using a ricer, dump the potatoes into a bowl and then rice them back into the pot set over very low heat. If using a hand masher, mash them in the pot until completely smooth.

4. Using a wooden spoon, beat in the butter and then beat in the hot milk in ¼-cup increments. If the potatoes are still too thick, beat in a bit of the cooking water until they reach the consistency you want. Season well with salt and pepper and serve right away. —*Roy Finamore and Molly Stevens*

PER SERVING: 170 CALORIES I 4G PROTEIN I 26G CARB I 6G TOTAL FAT I 4G SAT FAT I 2G MONO FAT I 0G POLY FAT I 15MG CHOL I 210MG SODIUM I 2G FIBER

tips and techniques for perfect mashed potatoes

Regardless of the type of potato or the type of mash you're after, use the right tool for the potatoes at hand and follow these tips.

- For quick, even cooking, cut potatoes into pieces and simmer—don't boil. Begin by peeling the potatoes (unless you're making the smashed red-skinned ones) and cutting them into large chunks. A potato boiled in its jacket will absorb less water during cooking, but then you have to play hot potato, peeling it while it's steaming. The key is to mash the potatoes while they're as hot as possible. There's a trick for drying them below.

- Start the potatoes in a generous amount of cold water, and be sure to add salt at the outset or they'll never be quite as tasty as they should. When the water boils, lower the heat to a steady simmer, covering the pot partially to maintain an even temperature. Don't let the water boil vigorously or the potatoes will bang around, break up, and get waterlogged.

- The best way to know when a potato is done is to stick it with a thin metal skewer. (A fork will poke the potato full of holes and invite water in.) A potato is tender enough to mash when the skewer slides into the center with no resistance and slides out just as easily. You don't want the potatoes falling apart, but if they're too firm in the center, you'll have hard bits in the mash.

- Waterlogged potatoes make a dense, soggy mash, so here's the trick for drying them out: After you drain them, put them back in the empty pot and set it over medium heat; shake the pot and stir the potatoes with a wooden spoon so they don't stick. They'll break up a bit and become noticeably drier, brighter, and more starchy looking. Medium- and high-starch potatoes will leave a floury film in the pot when they're dry enough.

- For really great classic mashed potatoes, reach for the ricer. It's a bit more trouble than a hand masher, but it makes the lightest, smoothest mashed potatoes ever.

- You can get good results with a hand masher as long as you're methodical. Start mashing by pressing down firmly and steadily at the 12 o'clock position in the pot and then move just slightly clockwise to 1 o'clock, 2 o'clock, and so on, until you've worked your way around the pot. If there are unmashed potatoes in the center, give them a mash, too. Repeat the circle, pressing with a bit more energy and giving the masher a little twist as you press. As the potatoes start to come together, work the masher even more quickly, almost like a whisk, and whip the potatoes into a smooth mass. Be sure to get to all corners of the pot, and keep going until the potatoes are as smooth as you want.

- Low-starch, waxy salad or boiling potatoes are best coarsely "smashed." A big metal spoon is the best tool to get this job done.

- Use a wooden spoon to beat in enrichments. If you want perfectly smooth mashed potatoes, then get them completely mashed before you start adding enrichments like butter, cheese, or milk. (Lumps somehow manage to elude the masher once you add liquid and fat to the potatoes.) Beat in enrichments with a sturdy wooden spoon, which ensures that the ingredients are evenly distributed.

- When it's time to add ingredients, be sure they're warm or at room temperature so they don't cool the potatoes and make them stiff. Butter should be soft but not oily. Cheeses and olive oil should be at room temperature. And the liquid—milk, cream, or potato water—has to be hot (a microwave is handy).

- Butter or olive oil goes in first. Then add the liquid in small additions, no more than ¼ cup at a time. This lets you best judge how much you need—potatoes vary in how thirsty they are. And remember to beat the potatoes as you go so they come out extra fluffy.

smashed red-skinned potatoes with boursin and scallions

SERVES 4 TO 6

1¾ to 2 lb. red-skinned potatoes, scrubbed and cut into large chunks (1½ to 2 inches)

Kosher salt

2 Tbs. unsalted butter, cut into pieces and softened

4 oz. Boursin cheese (with garlic and herbs), cut into pieces and at room temperature

3 scallions (white parts with some green), chopped

Freshly ground black pepper

Smashing low-starch potatoes into a rustic side dish is the way to go to avoid gumminess. Besides, don't we all know someone who loves lumps? If you can find it, try substituting Gorgonzola dolce for the Boursin®. Gorgonzola dolce is soft and yellowish ivory with greenish-blue striations; it's much less overbearing than the white, crumbly Gorgonzola typically sold in supermarkets.

1. Put the potatoes in a large saucepan and cover with cold water by at least an inch. Add a generous ½ tsp. salt and bring to a boil. Lower the heat to maintain a steady simmer, cover the pot partially, and cook until the potatoes are quite tender when tested with a metal skewer, 15 to 20 minutes.

2. Drain the potatoes—reserving some of the cooking water—and dump them back in the pot. Dry the potatoes over medium heat, shaking the pan and stirring, until most of the moisture has steamed off. Reduce the heat to very low.

3. Use the side of a big metal spoon to cut through the skins and flesh of the potatoes, reducing the chunks to a very coarse mash. Stir in the butter and then the Boursin. If you want, loosen the mash with cooking water: Depending on the potatoes, you might need a few tablespoons of cooking water or as much as ½ cup. Don't beat vigorously or the potatoes may turn gummy. Stir in the scallions, add salt and pepper to taste, and serve right away.

—Roy Finamore and Molly Stevens

PER SERVING: 130 CALORIES | 5G PROTEIN | 10G CARB | 8G TOTAL FAT | 6G SAT FAT | 1G MONO FAT | 1G POLY FAT | 25MG CHOL | 280MG SODIUM | 4G FIBER

creamy parmesan swiss chard gratin

SERVES 4 TO 6

- **2 Tbs. unsalted butter; more for the gratin pan**
- **½ cup toasted or stale coarse breadcrumbs**
- **1 cup heavy cream**
- **2 cloves garlic, smashed and peeled**
- **Freshly ground black pepper**
- **½ tsp. kosher salt**
- **3 strips bacon (about 2½ oz.)**
- **1 lb. (about 1 bunch) Swiss chard, washed and drained, stems removed and cut crosswise into ¼-inch slices, leaves cut into ½-inch-wide ribbons (to yield about 2¾ cups stems and 7 to 8 cups leaves)**
- **⅓ cup freshly grated Parmigiano-Reggiano**

The chard leaves just need wilting for this gratin, but be sure to sauté the stems until lightly browned; this softens their texture.

1. Heat the oven to 400°F. Butter a shallow 5- or 6-cup ceramic gratin dish. Melt 1 Tbs. of the butter and toss it with the breadcrumbs; set aside.

2. In a medium saucepan, bring the cream and garlic to a boil. Immediately lower the heat, and simmer vigorously for 5 minutes, reducing the cream to about ¾ cup. Take the pan off the heat and remove the garlic cloves with a slotted spoon; discard the garlic. Let the cream cool slightly, stirring occasionally to loosen. Season it with a few grinds of fresh pepper and ¼ tsp. of the salt.

3. Meanwhile, in a 12-inch nonstick skillet, cook the bacon over medium heat until crisp and browned. With tongs, transfer it to paper towels; crumble when cool. Leave the bacon fat in the pan (if there's more than 2 Tbs., drain a little off). Add the remaining 1 Tbs. butter to the skillet and let it melt. Add the chard stems and sauté them over medium to medium-high heat until they're somewhat softened and browned on the edges, about 10 minutes. Reduce the heat to medium, add the chard leaves, and toss them with the contents of the skillet. Season them with the remaining ¼ tsp. salt. (You can add the leaves in two batches for easier handling.) Sauté until all the leaves are wilted, about 2 minutes. Use tongs to transfer the contents of the pan to the gratin dish (leave behind any excess liquid in the sauté pan), spreading them evenly.

4. Sprinkle the crumbled bacon and then the cheese over the chard. Pour the seasoned cream over all and top with the buttered breadcrumbs. Bake until the gratin is brown and bubbly, about 25 minutes. Let rest for 10 to 15 minutes before serving. *—Susie Middleton*

PER SERVING: 310 CALORIES | 7G PROTEIN | 11G CARB | 28G TOTAL FAT | 15G SAT FAT | 9G MONO FAT | 2G POLY FAT | 75MG CHOL | 600MG SODIUM | 1G FIBER

Cleaning and Storing Swiss Chard

When you get your greens home, remove any wires or rubber bands from the bunch and discard any yellowed or slimy leaves; trim away tough stem ends. You can also remove tough stems at this point with scissors, a sharp knife, or your hands, or you can leave the stems on and remove them before cooking. Save the chard stems for cooking.

Fill a large bowl or the sink with cool water and swish the greens around in it. Lift out the greens and empty the silty water from the bowl or sink.

Repeat this one or two more times, depending on how dirty the greens are. Let the greens drip-dry on dishtowels and then spin them in a salad spinner (in batches if necessary).

Line the largest zip-top bags you can find with paper towels. Lay the greens in the bags between the paper towels, close the bag tightly, and refrigerate. The paper towels help absorb excess water to prevent rot, while the sealed bag keeps the greens just moist and crisp enough so they don't dry out and go limp.

braised carrots and shallots

SERVES 4

6 medium carrots
(about 1½ lb.), peeled

2 Tbs. olive oil

1½ Tbs. unsalted butter

6 to 8 shallots (about ½ lb.
total), thinly sliced (to yield
1½ cups thin rings)

1 tsp. kosher salt

3 whole canned tomatoes, cut
into ½-inch pieces; plus ½ cup
of the juice

3 large cloves garlic, sliced

3 long strips orange zest
(from 1 small orange)

1 bouquet garni (1 sprig
fresh thyme, 1 bay leaf, and
4 parsley stems, tied with
twine)

Pinch of cayenne

3 Tbs. chopped fresh flat-leaf
parsley

The combination of sweet carrots, shallots, and tangy tomato is an intriguing one. This dish is delicious with all kinds of main courses, from pork chops to braised veal shanks.

1. Heat the oven to 350°F. Halve the carrots lengthwise and cut them into 2-inch-long pieces.

2. Heat the olive oil and butter in a medium (9-inch) Dutch oven over medium heat. When the oil is hot and the butter has melted, add the sliced shallots and cook, stirring occasionally, until softened and slightly browned, about 5 minutes. Remove the shallots from the pot with a slotted spoon and set them aside. Add the carrots and salt. Cook, stirring occasionally, until the carrots are lightly browned, about 12 minutes. Add the tomatoes and their juices, along with the garlic, orange zest, bouquet garni, and cayenne. Stir in the shallots and ¼ cup water. Cover the pot, put it in the oven, and let cook until very tender, 20 to 25 minutes.

3. To serve, discard the orange zest and bouquet garni. Arrange the vegetables on a platter, sprinkle with the parsley, and serve. —*Jean-Pierre Moullé*

PER SERVING: 200 CALORIES | 3G PROTEIN | 24G CARB | 11G TOTAL FAT | 4G SAT FAT | 6G MONO FAT | 1G POLY FAT | 10MG CHOL | 750MG SODIUM | 4G FIBER

roasted brussels sprouts with dijon, walnuts & crisp crumbs

SERVES 6 TO 8

- ¼ **cup plus 1 Tbs. extra-virgin olive oil**
- 2 **Tbs. Dijon mustard**
- 1 **tsp. Worcestershire sauce**
- ½ **tsp. caraway seeds, toasted lightly and crushed**
- ¾ **tsp. kosher salt**

  Freshly ground black pepper
- 2 **lb. Brussels sprouts, ends trimmed, cut through the core into quarters**
- 1 **Tbs. unsalted butter**
- 1 **cup coarse fresh breadcrumbs**
- ½ **cup chopped walnuts**

The mustard-Worcestershire seasoning is a tangy counterpoint to the sprouts, which—despite people's remembrances from childhood—are essentially sweet and nutty. You can fry the crumb topping up to 2 hours before serving.

1. Position racks in the top and bottom thirds of the oven and heat the oven to 400°F. Line two rimmed baking sheets with parchment.

2. In a large bowl, whisk ¼ cup of the olive oil with the mustard, Worcestershire sauce, caraway seeds, ½ tsp. of the salt, and about 10 grinds of pepper. Add the Brussels sprouts and toss to thoroughly distribute the mustard mixture. Spread the sprouts in an even layer on the two baking sheets.

3. Roast until the cores of the sprouts are just barely tender and the leaves are browning and crisping a bit, 20 to 25 minutes (if your oven heat is uneven, rotate the pans midway through cooking).

4. While the sprouts are roasting, make the topping: Line a plate with two layers of paper towel. Heat the remaining 1 Tbs. oil with the butter in a medium (10-inch) skillet over medium-high heat. When the butter has stopped foaming, add the breadcrumbs all at once; toss to coat with the fat. Reduce the heat to medium, add the walnuts and the remaining ¼ tsp. salt, and cook, stirring constantly, until the crumbs are browned and slightly crisp and the nuts are golden, 4 to 6 minutes. (The crumbs will start to sound "scratchy" as they get crisp.) Dump the breadcrumb mixture onto the paper towels to drain the excess fat.

5. Transfer the sprouts to a serving bowl and season to taste with salt and pepper if necessary. Sprinkle the crumbs over the sprouts just before serving.
—*Martha Holmberg*

PER SERVING: 200 CALORIES I 5G PROTEIN I 14G CARB I 15G TOTAL FAT I 2.5G SAT FAT I 7G MONO FAT I 4.5G POLY FAT I 5MG CHOL I 270MG SODIUM I 4G FIBER

Quartered Brussels sprouts are best for roasting. The oven's heat penetrates the quarters well; plus, they have a lot of surface area to come in contact with the roasting pan, so they get browned for deeper flavor.

apple, bacon & caramelized onion stuffing

SERVES 8

Unsalted butter for the pan

½ lb. sliced bacon, cut into 1-inch pieces

1 large onion, diced (about 1½ cups)

1 Tbs. granulated sugar

2 large Granny Smith apples, peeled, cored, and diced (about 2½ cups)

3 large ribs celery, chopped (about 1½ cups)

⅔ cup chopped fresh flat-leaf parsley

1 Tbs. chopped fresh thyme

1 Tbs. chopped fresh sage

1 tsp. kosher salt

Freshly ground black pepper

1 loaf (15 to 16 oz.) stale rustic-style white bread, cut into 1-inch cubes

3 large eggs, lightly beaten

3½ cups homemade or lower-salt chicken broth

If you're assembling this ahead, wait until just before baking to add the eggs and chicken broth.

1. Butter a 9x13-inch or similarly sized baking dish.

2. In a large skillet over medium heat, cook the bacon until crisp, about 15 minutes. With a slotted spoon, transfer the bacon to a plate lined with paper towels. Pour off all but 2 Tbs. of fat from the skillet; reserve the extra. Put the onion in the pan and sauté over medium-high heat until soft and lightly browned, about 5 minutes. Sprinkle the sugar over the onion and sauté, stirring constantly to prevent sticking or burning, until the onion turns deep golden and the edges caramelize, 3 to 5 minutes. Scrape the onion into a large bowl.

3. Return the pan to medium heat and add 2 Tbs. of the reserved bacon fat. Add the apples and celery. Sauté until softened, 5 to 7 minutes. Add the parsley, thyme, sage, ½ tsp. of the salt, and a few grinds of pepper; sauté for another 1 minute. Scrape the contents of the pan into the bowl with the onion.

4. When you're ready to bake the dressing, heat the oven to 350°F. Add the bread cubes and bacon to the bowl of sautéed vegetables and toss. Add the beaten eggs, broth, the remaining ½ tsp. salt, and a few more grinds of pepper; mix well. Transfer to the prepared baking dish and bake uncovered until the top is light and crusty, about 1 hour. *—Diane Morgan*

PER SERVING: 330 CALORIES | 12G PROTEIN | 41G CARB | 13G TOTAL FAT | 5G SAT FAT | 6G MONO FAT | 2G POLY FAT | 95MG CHOL | 810MG SODIUM | 4G FIBER

rustic mashed potatoes

SERVES 12

5 lb. medium russet (Idaho) potatoes, scrubbed

2½ cups half-and-half

Kosher salt and freshly ground black pepper

5 oz. (10 Tbs.) butter, cut into ½-inch pieces and softened

These are the real deal—creamy, buttery potatoes that get great texture from leaving the skins on. If you use a ricer or food mill to mash the potatoes, there will be small bits of skin in the finished dish. If you use a stand mixer, the skin will be in larger pieces.

1. Put the whole unpeeled potatoes in an 8-quart pot and add enough water to cover. Cover and bring to a boil over high heat. Reduce the heat to medium low and simmer until the potatoes are tender when pierced with a skewer or toothpick, 25 to 30 minutes.

2. Cut the potatoes into chunks and pass them through a food mill or a ricer into a large heatproof bowl. Alternatively, put them in a stand mixer fitted with the paddle attachment. Cover the mixing bowl with a towel to contain any splashes and mix on low speed until mostly smooth, about 1 minute.

3. Add the half-and-half, 1 Tbs. salt, and 1 tsp. pepper and mix the potatoes by hand with a wooden spoon until smooth, light, and fluffy. Stir in the butter until melted. Season to taste with salt and pepper.

4. To keep warm for up to 2 hours, cover the bowl with plastic wrap and set it over (but not in) a pan of barely simmering water. *—Pam Anderson*

PER SERVING: 290 CALORIES | 6G PROTEIN | 33G CARB | 16G TOTAL FAT | 10G SAT FAT | 4G MONO FAT | 0.5G POLY FAT | 45MG CHOL | 340MG SODIUM | 3G FIBER

How a Food Mill Works

A food mill is one of those tools you may not use very often, but you'll be glad to have one when you need it. Making mashed potatoes is one of the three main uses for a food mill (the others are making applesauce or butter and separating seeds and skins from tomatoes).

A food mill has a bowl-shaped hopper that holds the food to be milled. A hook and a handle help secure the hopper over a separate bowl to catch the milled food. A hand-driven crank pushes an angled paddle, which smears and forces the food through a disk. The disk, perforated with colander-like holes, strains the food, separating out the unwanted bits.

The best model food mill features a deep hopper and paddle that fits snugly against the disk. The mill should come apart easily for cleaning and have interchangeable disks with various hole sizes, so you can control how finely you strain your food.

Southern Devil's Food Cake
(recipe on p. 226)

desserts

southern devil's food cake

SERVES 8 TO 10

FOR THE GANACHE

- **1 lb. semisweet chocolate (preferably 58% cacao), finely chopped**
- **2 cups heavy cream**
- **1 oz. (2 Tbs.) unsalted butter, softened**

FOR THE CAKE

- **6 oz. (¾ cup) unsalted butter, softened; more for the pans**
- **8 oz. (1¾ cups) unbleached all-purpose flour; more for the pans**
- **2 cups packed dark brown sugar**
- **2 tsp. pure vanilla extract**
- **3 large eggs, at room temperature**
- **2¼ oz. (¾ cup) unsweetened Dutch-processed cocoa powder**
- **1¼ tsp. baking soda**
- **1 tsp. baking powder**
- **1 tsp. kosher salt**
- **1½ cups buttermilk, preferably low-fat, at room temperature**
- **¼ cup mayonnaise**

This four-layer Southern classic is made with cocoa powder, not chocolate, with a generous spoonful of mayonnaise in the batter to keep the cake moist and rich. A simple, luscious ganache of semisweet chocolate, cream, and butter does double duty as filling and frosting.

MAKE THE GANACHE

Put the chopped chocolate in a medium bowl. Bring the cream to a boil in a 2-quart saucepan over medium-high heat. Pour the hot cream directly over the chocolate and let it sit without stirring for 5 minutes. Using a whisk, stir in the center of the mixture in a small, tight circular motion until fully combined. Add the butter and stir until it is fully incorporated. Put a piece of plastic wrap directly onto the surface of the ganache and set aside at room temperature for at least 8 hours or overnight.

MAKE THE CAKE

1. Position a rack in the center of the oven and heat the oven to 350°F.

2. Butter two 8x2-inch round cake pans and line each with a parchment round. Butter the parchment, dust with flour, and tap out any excess.

3. In a stand mixer fitted with the paddle attachment, beat the butter, brown sugar, and vanilla on medium-high speed until lighter in color and slightly increased in volume, 3 to 5 minutes. Lower the speed to medium and add the eggs, one at a time, mixing until each is fully incorporated before adding the next.

4. Sift the flour, cocoa powder, baking soda, and baking powder onto a piece of parchment. Add the salt to the dry ingredients after sifting.

5. Using the parchment as a chute, add one-quarter of the dry ingredients to the batter and mix on low speed until incorporated. Add about ½ cup of the buttermilk and mix on low speed until incorporated. Continue to alternate dry ingredients and buttermilk, mixing until incorporated after each addition and stopping to scrape the bowl and beater as necessary. Using a whisk, fold the mayonnaise into the batter.

6. Divide the batter evenly between the prepared pans and bake until a toothpick inserted in the center of the cakes comes out clean and the sides of the cake have begun to pull away from the pan slightly, 40 to 45 minutes. Remove the pans from the oven and cool on a rack for 15 minutes. Invert the cakes onto the rack and remove the pans and parchment. Cool the cakes completely. (The cakes may be made 1 day ahead; wrap well and store at room temperature.)

ASSEMBLE THE CAKE

With a serrated knife, cut each cake in half horizontally. Put one of the base layers on a cake plate and tuck strips of waxed paper under the cake to keep the plate clean while icing the cake. Top the cake with about ⅓ cup of the ganache, spreading it evenly over the top. Add another cake layer, top with ganache, and repeat until the last layer is in place. Spread a thin layer of ganache over the top and sides of the cake and refrigerate for 15 minutes to seal in any crumbs. Spread the remaining ganache over the top and sides. Remove the waxed paper. The cake may be refrigerated, covered, for up to 2 days. Return to room temperature 2 hours before serving. *—David Guas*

PER SERVING: 890 CALORIES I 11G PROTEIN I 98G CARB I 53G TOTAL FAT I 30G SAT FAT I 15G MONO FAT I 4.5G POLY FAT I 175MG CHOL I 440MG SODIUM I 6G FIBER

blueberry cheesecake with gingersnap crust

SERVES 8 TO 10

FOR THE CRUST

- 3 oz. (6 Tbs.) unsalted butter, melted; more for the pan
- 2 cups ground gingersnap cookies (about 35 cookies)
- 2 Tbs. granulated sugar

FOR THE FILLING AND TOPPING

- 1½ lb. blueberries (about 4 cups), rinsed, dried, and picked through
- 1½ cups granulated sugar
- Finely grated zest and juice of 1 lemon
- ¼ tsp. freshly grated nutmeg
- 2 tsp. cornstarch
- 3 8-oz. packages cream cheese, softened
- 1 cup sour cream (not low- or nonfat)
- 2 large eggs
- 2 large egg yolks
- 1 tsp. pure vanilla extract

Blueberries pair perfectly with the gingersnap crust. The cheesecake needs to chill for about 8 hours in the refrigerator, so you may want to make it a day ahead.

Position a rack in the center of the oven and heat the oven to 350°F. Butter a 9-inch springform pan.

PREPARE AND BAKE THE CRUST

In a medium bowl, toss the gingersnap crumbs with the melted butter and sugar. Pour the crumbs into the prepared pan and, using your fingers and the bottom of a flat glass, tamp down the crust so it's even on the bottom and goes about an inch up the sides of the pan. Bake the crust until it browns lightly and puffs slightly, 10 to 15 minutes. Transfer to a rack to cool to room temperature.

MAKE THE FILLING AND TOPPING

1. Combine the blueberries, ½ cup of the sugar, the lemon zest and juice, and nutmeg in a large (12-inch) sauté pan and let sit for 5 minutes so the blueberries start to release their juices. Cook over medium-high heat, shaking the pan, until the blueberries start to soften and their juices boil, 3 to 4 minutes. Whisk the cornstarch with 2 Tbs. water and stir into the blueberry mixture so it thickens. Remove from the heat and let cool to room temperature. Transfer 1½ cups of this mixture to a blender and purée. Strain the puréed mixture through a fine-mesh sieve, discard the solids, and reserve the liquid. Put the remaining blueberries in an airtight container in the refrigerator.

2. Beat the cream cheese and the remaining 1 cup sugar in a stand mixer with the paddle attachment (or in a large bowl with electric beaters) on medium speed until the mixture is well combined (you may need to use a spatula to free the paddle of the cheese). Reduce to low speed and, one at a time, add the sour cream, eggs, egg yolks, puréed blueberry mixture, and vanilla, and beat until just incorporated. Pour the batter into the gingersnap crust. Wrap the bottom and sides of the springform pan in aluminum foil, making sure the foil goes about three-quarters up the sides of the pan, and then put the springform pan in a large roasting pan. Pour hot water into the roasting pan so it reaches about halfway up the sides of the springform pan (the foil will prevent water from seeping into the pan).

3. Carefully transfer the roasting pan to the oven and bake until the top of the cake sets but the center still jiggles slightly when shaken, about 1 hour. Using a metal spatula and an oven mitt, carefully remove the springform pan from the water bath, discard the foil, and transfer to a cooling rack to cool to room temperature, about 1 hour. Refrigerate the cake uncovered until completely chilled, about 8 hours. Run a paring knife along the sides of the cake to separate it from the pan and then unlatch and remove the sides of the springform pan. Use a metal spatula to loosen the bottom crust from the pan, and then, using two spatulas, transfer the cake to a serving plate. Spoon the refrigerated blueberries on top of the cake. Cut into slices and serve. *—Tony Rosenfeld*

classic carrot cake with vanilla cream cheese frosting

YIELDS ONE 9-INCH LAYER CAKE; SERVES 12 TO 14

The flavors of this moist cake only improve with time, so feel free to bake and frost the cake up to a few days ahead.

FOR THE CAKE

- **1** cup canola, corn, or vegetable oil; more for the pans
- **2** cups (9 oz.) unbleached all-purpose flour; more for the pans
- **2** tsp. ground cinnamon
- **1¾** tsp. baking soda
- **¾** tsp. ground nutmeg
- **¾** tsp. ground ginger
- **¾** tsp. table salt
- **4** large eggs
- **2½** cups (8½ oz.) lightly packed, finely grated carrots
- **2** cups packed light brown sugar
- **¾** cup chopped walnuts, toasted
- **½** cup raisins
- **1½** tsp. pure vanilla extract

FOR THE FROSTING

- **1** lb. cream cheese, softened
- **12** oz. (1½ cups) unsalted butter, softened
- **1** lb. (4 cups) confectioners' sugar
- **4** tsp. pure vanilla extract
- **¾** tsp. table salt

MAKE THE CAKE

1. Position a rack in the center of the oven and heat the oven to 350°F. Lightly oil and flour the sides of two 9x2-inch round cake pans, tapping out any excess flour. Line the bottoms of the pans with parchment.

2. In a medium bowl, whisk the flour, cinnamon, baking soda, nutmeg, ginger, and salt. In a large bowl with a hand mixer or in a stand mixer fitted with the paddle attachment, mix the oil, eggs, carrots, brown sugar, walnuts, raisins, and vanilla on medium speed until well blended, about 1 minute. Add the dry ingredients and mix on low speed until just blended, about 30 seconds. Divide the batter evenly between the prepared pans.

3. Bake until the tops of the cakes spring back when lightly pressed and a cake tester inserted into the centers comes out clean, 28 to 30 minutes.

4. Let cool in the pans on a rack for 15 minutes. Run a knife around the inside edge of the pans to loosen the cakes, invert them onto the rack, remove the pans, and carefully peel away the parchment. Set the cakes aside to cool completely before frosting.

how to ice a cake

Set a cake plate on a rotating cake stand or lazy Susan. Position your first layer of cake upside down on the plate. If necessary, level the cake layer with a long serrated knife. Slide strips of parchment or waxed paper under the edge of the cake to keep the plate clean as you frost.

Gently brush any crumbs from the cake. Using an offset spatula, spread the frosting across the surface of the cake in an even layer.

Place the second cake layer on the frosting, aligning the layers in a perfectly vertical column. If using split layers that were cut unevenly, match the layers so the cake stays flat. If the cake is three or more layers, continue to fill between the layers, ending with the top layer unfrosted.

Frosting the cake is easier if you first seal the crumbs in a thin layer of frosting, called a crumb coat. With an offset spatula, spread about ½ cup of frosting in a thin, even layer over all of the cake. Smooth any frosting protruding between the layers and use that extra frosting as part of the crumb coat. It's fine if the cake is still visible through the thin crumb coat. Refrigerate the cake to firm up the crumb coat, about 20 minutes.

Spread the remaining frosting evenly over the chilled crumb coat. Once the cake is frosted, you can decorate the surface in a variety of ways, using a spoon or offset spatula to create swoops or stripes. If you prefer a smooth look, dip the spatula in hot water, wipe it dry, and hold it against the surface as you rotate the cake. Keep dipping the spatula in water and wiping it dry.

MAKE THE FROSTING

In a large bowl, beat the cream cheese and butter with the mixer on medium speed until very smooth and creamy, about 1 minute. Add the confectioners' sugar, vanilla, and salt and beat on medium high until blended and fluffy, about 2 minutes. Cover the frosting and set aside at room temperature until the layers are completely cool.

ASSEMBLE THE CAKE

1. Carefully set one cake upside down on a large, flat serving plate. Using a metal spatula, evenly spread about 1½ cups of the frosting over the top of the cake. Top with the remaining cake layer, upside down. Spread a thin layer (about ⅓ cup) of frosting over the entire cake to seal in any crumbs and fill in any gaps between layers. Refrigerate until the frosting is cold and firm, about 20 minutes. Spread the entire cake with the remaining frosting. For more tips on how to frost a layer cake, see the sidebar above.

2. Refrigerate the cake for at least 4 hours or up to 2 days. The cake is best served slightly chilled or at room temperature. *—Abigail Johnson Dodge*

PER SERVING: 840 CALORIES | 8G PROTEIN | 86G CARB | 54G TOTAL FAT | 22G SAT FAT |
20G MONO FAT | 9G POLY FAT | 150MG CHOL | 550MG SODIUM | 2G FIBER

yogurt cake with chocolate ganache frosting

SERVES 12

FOR THE CAKE

4	oz. (½ cup) unsalted butter, softened; more for the pan
9	oz. (2 cups) unbleached all-purpose flour
1	tsp. baking powder
1	tsp. baking soda
¼	tsp. table salt
1	cup granulated sugar
3	large eggs
1½	cups plain yogurt (low-fat or full-fat)
2	tsp. pure vanilla extract

FOR THE GANACHE FROSTING

¾	cup heavy cream
8	oz. semisweet chocolate, broken into small pieces
1	Tbs. light corn syrup

Yogurt adds moisture to this dense cake's crumb and a light tartness that breaks up the richness of the ganache frosting. Dairy tends to dull the flavor of cocoa, so a vanilla cake is used instead of a chocolate one. Chocolate lovers can still get their fix from the cake's heavenly chocolate ganache icing.

MAKE THE CAKE

1. Position a rack in the center of the oven and heat the oven to 350°F. Butter a 9-inch cake pan. Line the pan with a piece of parchment cut to size.

2. In a medium bowl, whisk together the flour, baking powder, baking soda, and salt. In a stand mixer fitted with a paddle attachment or in a large bowl with an electric hand mixer, cream the sugar and butter on medium speed until smooth and fluffy. Reduce the speed to low, add the eggs, and then add the yogurt and vanilla, scraping down the sides of the bowl as needed. Add the dry ingredients and mix until just incorporated.

3. Transfer the batter to the prepared pan and bake until a toothpick inserted into the center comes out clean, about 45 minutes. Let cool completely on a rack before turning the cake out of the pan.

MAKE THE GANACHE FROSTING

Bring the cream to a simmer in a small saucepan over medium heat. Reduce the heat to low, add the chocolate and corn syrup, and whisk until the chocolate is completely melted. Remove from the heat and let cool for 15 minutes. Transfer to a large bowl and refrigerate uncovered, stirring every 30 minutes or so, until it firms to a spreadable texture, about 45 minutes.

TO SERVE

Transfer the cake to a cake plate. Frost the cake and serve right away, or refrigerate for up to 5 days in an airtight cake container (return to room temperature before serving). —*Tony Rosenfeld*

Baking and Cooking (and More) with Yogurt

In many recipes, yogurt is a lower-fat substitution for richer ingredients like butter or oil. And like buttermilk or sour cream, yogurt not only adds tang to cakes but also helps to create a moist texture. Beyond that, yogurt is a great base for fruit smoothies and parfaits mixed with fresh fruit and granola.

apple crisp with pecans and orange

SERVES 8

1 tsp. softened butter for the baking dish

FOR THE TOPPING

4½ oz. (1 cup) unbleached all-purpose flour

⅓ cup old-fashioned rolled oats

¼ cup plus 2 Tbs. lightly packed light brown sugar

¼ cup plus 2 Tbs. granulated sugar

½ tsp. ground cinnamon

¼ tsp. kosher salt

4 oz. (½ cup) cold unsalted butter, cut into 8 pieces

1 cup lightly toasted, coarsely chopped pecans

FOR THE FILLING

3 lb. Granny Smith apples (6 large or 8 medium), peeled, cored, and sliced ¼ inch thick

½ cup granulated sugar

2 Tbs. freshly squeezed orange juice (from 1 orange)

1 Tbs. finely grated orange zest (from 1 orange)

1½ tsp. unbleached all-purpose flour

¾ tsp. ground cinnamon

⅛ tsp. kosher salt

Apple season and the pecan harvest coincide, and the two ingredients combine deliciously in this cinnamon-accented crisp.

Position a rack in the center of the oven and heat the oven to 350°F. Lightly butter a 9x9x2-inch pan or other 10-cup ovenproof baking dish.

MAKE THE TOPPING

In a food processor, pulse the flour and the oats until the oats are finely ground. Add the brown sugar, granulated sugar, cinnamon, and salt and pulse until just combined. Add the butter and pulse in short bursts until the mixture just starts to form crumbs and has a streusel-like consistency. When squeezed together with light pressure, the mixture should just clump. Add the pecans and pulse just to blend; you don't want to chop the nuts further. (You can make and refrigerate this topping up to 2 days ahead, or freeze for up to 2 months. Bring to room temperature before using.)

ASSEMBLE AND BAKE THE CRISP

1. In a large bowl, combine all of the filling ingredients and gently toss until well combined. Transfer the mixture to the prepared baking dish. Press down to compact slightly into an even layer. Sprinkle the topping in a thick, even layer all over the filling.

2. Bake until the topping is golden brown, the juices are bubbling around the edges, and the apples are soft when pierced with the tip of a knife, 55 to 60 minutes. Transfer to a rack to cool for 20 to 30 minutes before serving. The crisp can be served warm or at room temperature, but it's best served the day it's made. —*Karen Barker*

PER SERVING: 480 CALORIES | 4G PROTEIN | 70G CARB | 23G TOTAL FAT | 9G SAT FAT | 9G MONO FAT | 3.5G POLY FAT | 30MG CHOL | 60MG SODIUM | 6G FIBER

What to Look for when Buying Pecans

Hand-shelling pecans is time-consuming and messy, so look for shelled pecans, which are usually vacuum-packed in cans, jars, or cellophane bags to protect against humidity and oxidation. You might also find pecans sold in bulk, but make sure they're fresh, since they can become rancid if they've been sitting around in storage for too long. Taste one—if it's rancid, the nut will have an unpleasant, bitter flavor. A fresh pecan, on the other hand, will be faintly sweet and buttery. Look for plump ones that are uniform in color and size.

coffee-toffee pecan pie

SERVES 8

- **3** oz. (6 Tbs.) unsalted butter
- **¾** cup packed dark brown sugar
- **¾** cup light or dark corn syrup
- **½** cup Lyle's Golden Syrup
- **3** large eggs, at room temperature
- **2** Tbs. bourbon
- **1** Tbs. instant espresso powder
- **1** tsp. pure vanilla extract
- **¾** tsp. table salt
- **⅓** cup very finely chopped toasted pecans
- **2** cups toasted pecan halves
- **1** blind-baked All-Butter Piecrust (recipe below)
- **½** cup crushed chocolate toffee candy pieces, such as Heath® or Skor®

With notes of butterscotch, espresso, and bourbon, this is a pecan pie like no other.

1. Position a rack in the center of the oven, set a heavy-duty rimmed baking sheet on the rack, and heat the oven to 375°F.

2. In a medium saucepan over medium heat, melt the butter and cook, swirling the pan occasionally, until the butter is brown, 3 to 5 minutes. Immediately whisk in the brown sugar, corn syrup, and Lyle's Golden Syrup until smooth. Remove the pan from the heat and let cool slightly. One at a time, whisk in the eggs. Whisk in the bourbon, espresso powder, vanilla, and salt. Stir in the chopped pecans.

3. Sprinkle half of the pecan halves in the piecrust, followed by the toffee candy pieces, and then the remaining pecan halves. Pour the syrup mixture over all.

4. Put the pie on the heated baking sheet and reduce the oven temperature to 350°F. Bake until set, 45 to 55 minutes, rotating the pan halfway through baking. When the pan is nudged, the center of the pie will no longer wobble, but the whole pie will jiggle just slightly, and the filling will bubble at the edges.

5. Transfer to a rack and cool completely before serving. The pie can be stored at room temperature for up to 2 days. *—Nicole Rees*

PER SERVING: 810 CALORIES | 8G PROTEIN | 87G CARB | 49G TOTAL FAT | 17G SAT FAT | 19G MONO FAT | 8G POLY FAT | 135MG CHOL | 430MG SODIUM | 4G FIBER

all-butter piecrust

YIELDS ONE 9-INCH PIECRUST

- **6** oz. (1⅓ cups) unbleached all-purpose flour
- **1** tsp. granulated sugar
- **⅜** tsp. table salt
- **4** oz. (8 Tbs.) cold unsalted butter, preferably European style, cut into ¾-inch pieces
- **3** to 4 Tbs. ice water

This pie dough can be made ahead and refrigerated overnight or frozen (before or after rolling) for up to 3 months. Simply transfer the dough to the refrigerator the night before you plan to make pie, and it'll be ready to go.

MAKE THE DOUGH

1. Put the flour, sugar, and salt in a medium bowl and stir with a rubber spatula or a fork to combine. Add the butter to the bowl. Rub the cold chunks of butter between your fingertips, smearing the butter into the flour to create small (roughly ¼-inch) flakes of fat.

2. Drizzle 3 Tbs. ice water over the flour mixture. Stir with the spatula or fork, adding 1 Tbs. more water if necessary, until the mixture forms a shaggy dough that's moist enough to hold together when pressed between your fingers.

3. With well-floured hands, gently gather and press the dough together, and then form it into a disk with smooth edges. Wrap the dough in plastic and chill for at least 1 hour, but preferably 2 to 4 hours, before rolling.

TO ROLL THE DOUGH

1. Let the chilled dough sit at room temperature to soften slightly—it should be cold and firm but not rock hard. Depending on how long the dough was chilled, this could take 5 to 20 minutes. When ready to roll, lightly flour the countertop or other surface (a pastry cloth, silicone rolling mat, or parchment on a counter also works great) and position the rolling pin in the center of the dough disk. Roll away from you toward 12 o'clock, easing the pressure as you near the edge to keep the edge from becoming too thin. Return to the center and roll toward 6 o'clock. Repeat toward 3 and then 9 o'clock, always easing the pressure at the edges and picking up the pin rather than rolling it back to the center.

2. Continue to "roll around the clock," aiming for different "times" on each pass, until the dough is 13 to 14 inches in diameter and about ⅛ inch thick. Try to use as few passes of the rolling pin as possible. After every few passes, check that the dough isn't sticking by lifting it with a bench knife (dough scraper). Reflour only as needed—excess flour makes a drier, tougher crust. Each time you lift the dough, give it a quarter turn to help even out the thickness.

LINE THE PIE PLATE

1. Gently transfer the dough to a 9-inch pie plate, preferably metal, by folding it in half and unfolding it into the plate. Do not stretch the dough as you line the pan, or it will spring back when baked. Gently lift the outer edges of the dough to give you enough slack to line the sides of the pan without stretching the dough.

2. Trim the overhanging dough to 1 inch from the edge of the pan. Roll the dough under itself into a cylinder that rests on the edge of the pan.

3. To crimp the edge, have one hand on the inside of the edge and one hand on the outside, and use the index finger of the inside hand to push the dough between the thumb and index finger of the outside hand to form a U or V shape. Repeat around the edge of the pie plate, creating a crimped edge whose individual flutes are about an inch apart. As you are going along, if you notice that the edge is not perfectly symmetrical and that the amount of dough you'll have to crimp seems sparse in places, take a bit of trimmed scrap, wet it with a drop or two of water, and attach it to the sparse area by pressing it firmly into place.

4. Prick the sides and bottom of the crust all over with a fork. Refrigerate until firm, about 1 hour or overnight. This will relax the dough and help prevent the edges from caving in.

how to blind-bake a piecrust

Position a rack in the center of the oven and heat the oven to 425°F. Line the chilled piecrust with foil and fill it with dried beans or pie weights. Bake for 15 minutes; remove the foil and the beans or weights. Reduce the oven temperature to 375°F.

Bake until the bottom looks dry but is not quite done and the edges are light golden, 5 to 7 minutes more. Let cool on a rack.

sour cream pound cake

**YIELDS 1 LARGE BUNDT CAKE;
SERVES 8 TO 10**

11¼	**oz. (2½ cups) unbleached all-purpose flour**
2	**tsp. baking powder**
½	**tsp. table salt**
8	**oz. (1 cup) unsalted butter, slightly soft (70°F)**
2½	**cups sugar**
5	**large eggs, at room temperature**
1	**tsp. pure vanilla extract**
2	**tsp. almond extract**
½	**tsp. coconut extract**
1	**cup sour cream**
½	**cup golden raisins or currants (optional)**

The three extracts used here create an intriguingly delicious flavor. You can make this cake with only the vanilla, but try the recipe first as written.

1. Position a rack in the center of the oven and heat the oven to 300°F. Spray a large (10- to 12-cup) bundt pan with a nonstick coating and dust with flour.

2. Whisk together the flour, baking powder, and salt until well blended. With an electric mixer (I use the paddle attachment on my stand), beat the butter until it's very pale and little tails have formed. Sprinkle in the sugar and beat well until slightly fluffy. Scrape the sides of the bowl well. Add the eggs one at a time, beating until blended before adding the next. Add the extracts and sour cream; mix well. With the mixer on low, add the flour and mix until it's almost but not quite incorporated. Switch from the mixer to a stiff rubber spatula and fold until the batter is well blended and smooth, taking care to scrape the bowl's bottom and sides. Gently fold in the raisins or currants, if using.

3. Scrape the batter into the prepared pan and bake until the cake is golden brown and a toothpick comes out with just a few crumbs clinging to it when inserted in the center, 60 to 75 minutes. Baking time will vary depending on pan size and depth, so start checking at about 50 minutes. Let the cake cool for about 15 minutes and then invert it onto a large plate or platter, tapping the pan to release the cake. Slide the cake onto a rack and cool completely before serving. —*Carolyn Weil*

PER SERVING: 560 CALORIES I 7G PROTEIN I 76G CARB I 26G TOTAL FAT I 15G SAT FAT I 8G MONO FAT I 1G POLY FAT I 165MG CHOL I 210MG SODIUM I 1G FIBER

real chocolate mousse

SERVES 4

- **6** oz. semisweet or bittersweet chocolate, preferably 60% to 62% cacao, chopped
- **2** Tbs. unsalted butter, cut into 8 pieces
- **3** large egg whites

  Pinch of table salt
- **3** Tbs. granulated sugar
- **¾** cup cold heavy cream

  Chocolate shavings, for garnish (optional)

Serve the mousse right away for a slightly looser texture or chill it for a firmer result. This recipe calls for raw egg whites, and while the risk of salmonella infection is low, substitute pasteurized egg whites to be completely safe.

1. Put the chopped chocolate in a medium heatproof bowl and set the bowl in a skillet of barely simmering water. Stir the chocolate with a heatproof spatula just until it is melted. Remove the bowl from the skillet, add the butter to the chocolate, and stir until the butter is completely melted and the mixture is smooth.

2. In a medium bowl with an electric hand mixer on medium-high speed (or by hand with a balloon whisk), whip the egg whites and salt until they barely hold soft peaks. While whipping, gradually sprinkle in the sugar—go slowly, as adding it too fast may cause the whites to fall. Continue whipping until the whites just start to hold stiff peaks. Don't overbeat or the dissolved sugar may weep out of the whites.

3. Wipe the beaters (or whisk) clean and then whip the cream in a large bowl until it's fairly thick and holds a soft peak when the beaters are lifted.

4. With a large spatula, gently fold about one-third of the egg whites into the chocolate until the mixture is no longer streaky. Fold in the remaining whites, then scrape the chocolate mixture into the whipped cream.

5. Divide among 4 dessert dishes and serve immediately, or refrigerate for at least 30 minutes for a slightly firmer texture. Garnish with chocolate shavings, if using. —*Dabney Gough*

PER SERVING: 470 CALORIES | 6G PROTEIN | 39G CARB | 33G TOTAL FAT | 20G SAT FAT | 10G MONO FAT | 1G POLY FAT | 75MG CHOL | 135MG SODIUM | 3G FIBER

classic apple pie

YIELDS ONE 9-INCH DOUBLE-
CRUST PIE; SERVES 8 TO 10

1½ to 1¾ lb. Cortland apples (about 4 medium)

1 lb. Granny Smith apples (about 2½ medium)

2 tsp. freshly squeezed lemon juice

⅔ cup packed light brown sugar

¼ cup plus 1 Tbs. granulated sugar

3 Tbs. cornstarch

½ tsp. ground cinnamon

¼ tsp. kosher salt

⅛ tsp. ground nutmeg

1 large egg white

2 tsp. unsalted butter, softened, plus 1 Tbs. cold unsalted butter cut into small (¼-inch) cubes

4 to 6 Tbs. unbleached all-purpose flour

1 recipe Flaky Piecrust (recipe p. 238)

The filling in this classic version of apple pie is a blend of sweet Cortlands and tangy Granny Smiths, laced with just enough sugar and spice to make the apples' flavors sing. But as you'll discover when you try the recipe, it's the crust that makes this pie so special. Delicate, light, and exceptionally flaky, it's everything a piecrust should be. For best results, bake this pie at least a few hours before you plan to cut into it; otherwise, the filling may be soupy. With time, the fruit reabsorbs the juices, and the pie will cut like a charm.

Position two oven racks in the lower third of the oven and heat the oven to 400°F.

MAKE THE FILLING

1. Peel the apples, cut each in half from top to bottom, remove the cores with a melon baller, and trim the ends with a paring knife. Lay the apples, cut side down, on a cutting board. Cut the Cortland apples crosswise into ¾-inch pieces, and then halve each piece diagonally. Cut the Granny Smith apples crosswise into ¼-inch slices, leaving them whole. Put the apples in a large bowl and toss with the lemon juice.

2. Combine the brown sugar, ¼ cup of the granulated sugar, cornstarch, cinnamon, salt, and nutmeg in a small bowl. (Don't add this to the fruit yet.)

3. In a small dish, lightly beat the egg white with 1 tsp. water. Set aside.

ASSEMBLE THE PIE

1. Butter a 9-inch ovenproof glass (Pyrex) pie plate, including the rim, with the 2 tsp. of softened butter.

2. Rub 2 to 3 Tbs. of flour into the surface of a pastry cloth, forming a circle about 15 inches across, and also into a rolling pin stocking. If you don't have a pastry cloth, rub the flour into a large, smooth-weave, cotton kitchen towel and use a floured rolling pin. Roll one of the disks of dough into a circle that's ⅛ inch thick and about 15 inches across.

3. Lay the rolling pin across the upper third of the dough circle; lift the pastry cloth to gently drape the dough over the pin and then roll the pin toward you, wrapping the remaining dough loosely around it. Hold the rolling pin over the near edge of the pie plate. Allowing for about a 1-inch overhang, unroll the dough away from you, easing it into the contours of the pan. If the dough isn't centered in the pan, gently adjust it and then lightly press it into the pan. Take care not to stretch the dough. If it tears, simply press it back together—the dough is quite forgiving.

4. Brush the bottom and sides of the dough with a light coating of the egg-white wash (you won't need all of it). Leaving a ¼-inch overhang, cut around the edge of the dough with kitchen shears.

5. Combine the sugar mixture with the apples and toss to coat well. Mound the apples in the pie plate, rearranging the fruit as needed to make the pile compact. Dot the apples with the 1 Tbs. cold butter cubes.

6. Rub another 2 to 3 Tbs. flour into the surface of the pastry cloth and stocking. Roll the remaining dough into a circle that's ⅛ inch thick and about 15 inches across. Use the rolling pin to move the dough. As you unroll the dough, center it on top of the apples. Place your hands on either side of the top crust of the pie and ease the dough toward the center, giving the dough plenty of slack. Leaving a ¾-inch overhang, trim the top layer of dough around the rim of the pie plate. Fold the top layer of dough under the bottom layer, tucking the two layers of dough together. Press a lightly floured fork around the edge of the dough to seal it, or flute the edge of the dough with lightly floured fingers.

7. Lightly brush the top with cold water and sprinkle the surface with the remaining 1 Tbs. granulated sugar. Make steam vents in the dough by poking the tip of a paring knife through it in a few places; it's important to vent well so that the steam from the cooking apples won't build up and crack the top of the crust.

BAKE THE PIE

1. Cover the rim of the pie with aluminum foil bands. This will prevent the edge of the crust from overbrowning.

2. Place a rimmed baking sheet or an aluminum foil drip pan on the oven rack below the pie to catch any juices that overflow during baking. Set the pie on the rack above.

3. Bake until the top and bottom crusts are golden brown and the juices are bubbling, 60 to 75 minutes; to thicken, the juices must boil, so look for the bubbles through the steam vents or through cracks near the edges of the pie and listen for the sound of bubbling juices. During the last 5 minutes of baking, remove the foil bands from the edges of the pie. Cool the pie for at least 3 hours and up to overnight before serving.

4. Store the pie at room temperature for up to 1 day. For longer storage, cover with aluminum foil and refrigerate for up to 5 days; reheat before serving in a 325°F oven until warmed through, about 20 minutes. —*Carole Walter*

PER SERVING: 460 CALORIES | 4G PROTEIN | 60G CARB | 23G TOTAL FAT | 10G SAT FAT | 7G MONO FAT | 3.5G POLY FAT | 30MG CHOL | 230MG SODIUM | 2G FIBER

tips for assembling the pie

- Cortland and Granny Smith apples have different textures. To help them cook evenly and retain their shape, cut the Cortlands into ¾-inch-thick chunks and the Granny Smiths into ¼-inch-thick slices.

- Use a pastry cloth and pin stocking to roll the dough into a circle. Roll from the center out and avoid rolling the pin off the edge of the dough until the final stages of shaping.

- Use the pin to move the dough. Allow for about a 1-inch overhang when you unroll the dough on top of the apples.

- Make aluminum foil bands to prevent the edge from burning. Cut two 2- to 3-inch-wide strips of 18-inch heavy-duty foil and carefully cover the edge of the pie with the strips. Fasten the strips together with masking tape to keep them from falling off the pie.

continued on p. 238 ➤

continued from p. 237

flaky piecrust

YIELDS ENOUGH DOUGH FOR ONE 9-INCH DOUBLE-CRUST PIE

- **10½ oz. (2⅓ cups) unbleached all-purpose flour**
- **1 Tbs. granulated sugar**
- **¾ tsp. table salt**
- **½ tsp. baking powder**
- **4 oz. (½ cup) chilled unsalted butter, cut into ½-inch cubes**
- **4 oz. (½ cup) chilled vegetable shortening, cut into ½-inch pieces**
- **5 to 6 Tbs. ice water; more as needed**

Make Ahead

You can make the dough ahead and refrigerate it for up to 3 days or freeze it for up to 4 months (thaw it overnight in the fridge before using). Before rolling, let the dough sit at room temperature until pliable.

This recipe calls for a food processor to cut in the fat. If you're mixing the dough by hand, follow the instructions in the box below, noting the slight increase in flour needed.

1. Put the flour, sugar, salt, and baking powder in the bowl of a food processor fitted with the steel blade. Chill for 20 to 30 minutes.

2. Pulse the dry ingredients together for a few seconds to blend. With the processor off, add half of the butter and half of the vegetable shortening. Pulse 5 times, then process for 5 seconds. Add the remaining butter and shortening and pulse again 5 times, then process for 5 seconds. You should have a mixture of both large and small crumbs. Empty the mixture into a large mixing bowl.

3. Drizzle 1 Tbs. of the ice water around the edge of the bowl, letting it trickle into the crumbs. Flick the moistened crumbs toward the center with a table fork, rotating the bowl as you work. Repeat with 4 more Tbs. ice water, 1 Tbs. at a time. As you add the water, the crumbs should begin to form larger clusters. Once you've added 5 Tbs. water total, take a handful of crumbs and squeeze them gently—they should hold together. If they easily break apart, the mixture needs more water—add the remaining tablespoon, a teaspoon at a time, checking the consistency after each addition. If the crumbs still fail to hold together, you can add additional water, but do so sparingly.

4. Gather a handful of the crumbly dough and press it against the side of the bowl to form a small mass, flouring your hand as needed to prevent excessive sticking. Increase the size of this mass by pressing it into more of the crumbly mixture until you've used up about half of the total mixture in the bowl. Make a second mass of dough with the remaining crumbs. If some of the crumbs on the bottom of the bowl need more moistening, add a few drops of water.

5. Form the two masses of dough into balls, dust them with flour, and flatten them into 4- to 5-inch disks. Pat the disks to release any excess flour. Score the tops lightly with the side of your hand to create a tic-tac-toe pattern. With cupped hands, rotate each disk on the work surface to smooth the edges of the disks. Wrap each in plastic wrap. Chill for at least 30 minutes before using.

Making the Dough without a Food Processor

You can make this dough without a food processor, but you must use a bit more flour—11¼ oz. total—and sift it first; you should have 2½ cups after sifting. Also the butter shouldn't be rock hard, so take it out of the fridge for a few minutes before you start. Your finger should leave a slight imprint when you press the butter.

To cut in the fats by hand, whisk the dry ingredients together in a large mixing bowl.

Add the cubed butter and vegetable shortening and mix briefly with a fork to coat the fats with flour. Cut the fats into the dry ingredients with a pastry blender or two dinner knives, working the mixture until the particles have a coarse, mealy texture similar to that of fresh bread crumbs with some larger pea-size pieces. From there, continue with the recipe above to add the water and finish the dough.

classic rice pudding

SERVES 4

4 cups whole milk

½ cup raw medium-grain white rice

Pinch of table salt

1 vanilla bean, split, or 1½ tsp. pure vanilla extract

2 large egg yolks

⅓ cup granulated sugar

When using a vanilla bean, leave it in the pudding and then scrape out the seeds after the pudding has cooled. The seeds scrape out more easily from the softened bean, and the pudding gets an additional boost from the extra time the bean sits in it.

1. Put the milk, rice, salt, and split vanilla bean into a large, heavy saucepan (if you're using vanilla extract, don't add it yet). Bring to a boil over high heat, stirring constantly. Reduce the heat to low, cover, and simmer gently, stirring occasionally, for 15 minutes. Uncover and continue simmering, stirring frequently, until the rice is tender and the pudding is reduced to about 3½ cups, about 8 minutes. It's important to let the pudding simmer gently, not boil, and you'll need to stir constantly toward the end of cooking to prevent scorching.

2. In a medium bowl, whisk the egg yolks, sugar, and vanilla extract (if using). Slowly add the cooked rice mixture, whisking constantly. Pour the mixture back into the saucepan, making sure to scrape the bowl. Set the pan over medium-low heat and cook, stirring and scraping the sides and bottom of the pan constantly with a wooden spoon, until the mixture has thickened and coats the back of the spoon, about 1 minute. Remove the pan from the heat. Transfer the pudding to a bowl or serving dish and lay a sheet of plastic wrap right on the pudding's surface to prevent a skin from forming. If you've used a vanilla bean, fish it out when the pudding has cooled, scrape out the seeds, and stir the scrapings into the pudding. Discard the empty bean. Serve warm, at room temperature, or chilled. —*Abigail Johnson Dodge*

PER SERVING: 330 CALORIES | 11G PROTEIN | 47G CARB | 11G TOTAL FAT | 6G SAT FAT | 3G MONO FAT | 1G POLY FAT | 140MG CHOL | 200MG SODIUM | 0G FIBER

triple chocolate ice cream pie

SERVES 8 TO 12

- 5 Tbs. unsalted butter, melted; more for greasing the pan
- 6 oz. (about 30) chocolate wafer cookies
- 2 pints chocolate ice cream, slightly softened

  Quick Hot Fudge Sauce (recipe below), at room temperature
- 1 pint coffee ice cream, slightly softened
- 1 pint vanilla ice cream, slightly softened

This pie features a chocolate crust, chocolate ice cream, and chocolate sauce, with a few scoops of coffee and vanilla added for contrast.

1. Position a rack in the middle of the oven and heat the oven to 350°F. Butter a 9-inch Pyrex or metal pie plate.

2. Put the cookies in a zip-top bag and crush them with a rolling pin (or process in a food processor) until you have fine crumbs. Measure 1½ cups of crumbs (crush more cookies, if necessary) and put them in a bowl. Add the melted butter and stir until the crumbs are evenly moistened. Transfer to the pie plate and, using your fingers, press the mixture evenly into the bottom and sides (but not on the rim). Bake for 10 minutes. Let cool completely on a wire rack.

3. Scoop 1 pint of the chocolate ice cream into the cooled crust and spread it evenly with a rubber spatula. Place in the freezer to firm up for about 30 minutes. Remove the pie from the freezer and, working quickly, drizzle ½ cup of room-temperature fudge sauce over the ice cream. Using a small ice cream scoop (1½-inch diameter), scoop round balls of the chocolate, coffee, and vanilla ice creams and arrange them over the fudge sauce layer (you may not need all of the ice cream). Drizzle with about ¼ cup of the remaining fudge sauce, using a squirt bottle if you have one. Freeze until the ice cream is firm, about 2 hours. If not serving right away, loosely cover the pie with waxed paper and then wrap with aluminum foil. Freeze for up to 2 weeks.

4. To serve, let the pie soften in the refrigerator for 15 to 30 minutes (premium ice cream brands need more time to soften). Meanwhile, gently reheat the remaining fudge sauce in a small saucepan over medium-low heat. Pry the pie out of the pan with a thin metal spatula. (If the pie doesn't pop out, set the pan in a shallow amount of hot water for a minute or two to help the crust release.) Set the pie on a board, cut into wedges, and serve drizzled with more hot fudge sauce, if you like. *—Lori Longbotham*

PER SERVING: 495 CALORIES I 7G PROTEIN I 48G CARB I 34G TOTAL FAT I 20G SAT FAT I 6G MONO FAT I 1G POLY FAT I 90MG CHOL I 190MG SODIUM I 3G FIBER

quick hot fudge sauce

YIELDS 1½ CUPS

- 1 cup heavy cream
- 2 Tbs. light corn syrup

  Pinch of table salt
- 8 oz. bittersweet chocolate, finely chopped (to yield about 1⅓ cups)

This sauce will keep for at least 2 weeks in the refrigerator and for several months in the freezer.

Bring the cream, corn syrup, and salt just to a boil in a medium-size heavy saucepan over medium-high heat, whisking until combined. Remove the pan from the heat, add the chocolate, and whisk until smooth. Let cool to a bit warmer than room temperature before using in the ice cream pie. The sauce thickens as it cools; you want it warm enough to drizzle but not so warm that it melts the ice cream.

fudgy brownies

YIELDS SIXTEEN 2-INCH
SQUARES

- 5 oz. (10 Tbs.) unsalted butter, at room temperature; more for the pan
- 2 oz. unsweetened chocolate
- 5 oz. bittersweet chocolate
- 1 cup sugar
- 2 tsp. pure vanilla extract
- Pinch of table salt
- 2 large eggs, at room temperature
- 1 large egg yolk, at room temperature
- 3 oz. (⅔ cup) unbleached all-purpose flour

Using both bittersweet and unsweetened chocolate gives these brownies deep, sophisticated chocolate flavor. The consistency is fudgy but not gooey or underdone.

Position a rack in the center of the oven and heat the oven to 350°F. Butter an 8-inch square pan, line the pan bottom with parchment (or waxed paper), and then butter the parchment.
In a double boiler over simmering water, melt the butter and both chocolates. Remove the pan from the heat; cool slightly. Whisk in the sugar and then the vanilla and salt. The mixture will be somewhat grainy; this is OK. Whisk in the eggs and egg yolk, one at a time, stirring each time until blended. Add the flour, beating until thickened and smooth, 30 to 60 seconds. Pour into the prepared pan and bake until a toothpick inserted in the middle comes out with moist crumbs (not wet batter) clinging to it, 35 to 45 minutes. Set the pan on a rack until cool enough to handle. Run a paring knife around the inside edge of the pan and then invert the pan onto a flat surface and peel off the parchment. Flip the baked brownie back onto the rack to cool completely. Cut into 16 squares with a sharp knife. —*Cindy Mitchell*

PER BROWNIE: 210 CALORIES | 3G PROTEIN | 22G CARB | 13G TOTAL FAT | 8G SAT FAT | 3G MONO FAT | 1G POLY FAT | 60MG CHOL | 30MG SODIUM | 1G FIBER

how to get brownies out of the pan

For the neatest squares, flip the whole brownie out of the pan.

Run a sharp paring knife around the edge of the pan. This helps to ease the whole baked brownie out of the pan.

Flip out the whole brownie when the pan is cool enough to handle and then peel off the parchment.

Now invert the whole brownie on a rack to cool completely before cutting.

Cut with a sharp knife and wipe the knife after each pass.

creamy chocolate fudge

YIELDS TWENTY-FIVE
1½-INCH PIECES

3 Tbs. cold unsalted butter; more at room temperature for buttering the thermometer and pan

3¾ cups granulated sugar

1½ cups heavy cream

4 oz. unsweetened chocolate, coarsely chopped

3 Tbs. light corn syrup

1 tsp. table salt

The fudge will keep for up to 10 days stored in an airtight container at room temperature.

1. Lightly butter a candy thermometer and set aside.

2. Put the sugar, cream, chocolate, corn syrup, and salt in a large (4-quart) heavy-duty saucepan and stir with a spoon or heatproof spatula until the ingredients are moistened and combined. Stirring gently and constantly, bring the mixture to a boil over medium heat, 7 to 12 minutes. Cover the saucepan and let the steam clean the sides of the pan for 2 minutes.

3. Clip the candy thermometer to the pot, being careful not to let the tip of the thermometer touch the bottom of the pot, or you might get a false reading. Let the mixture boil without stirring until it reaches 236° to 238°F, 2 to 5 minutes. Take the pan off the heat and add the butter, but do not stir it into the mixture. Set the pan on a rack in a cool part of the kitchen. Don't disturb the pan in any way until the mixture has cooled to 110°F, 1 to 1½ hours.

4. Meanwhile, line the bottom and sides of an 8x8-inch baking pan with foil, leaving a 2-inch overhang on two opposite sides of the pan. Butter the foil. Set the pan aside.

5. Remove the thermometer from the fudge mixture. Using a hand mixer, beat the mixture on high speed until it is a few shades lighter in color and thickens enough that the beaters form trails that briefly expose the bottom of the pan as they pass through, 10 to 20 minutes. Pour the thickened fudge into the prepared pan, using a rubber spatula to help nudge it out of the pot. You can scrape the bottom of the pot but not the sides; any crystals that stick to the pot stay in the pot. Smooth the top of the fudge with the spatula. Set the pan on a rack and let the fudge cool completely, about 2 hours. The fudge will be slightly soft the day it's made but will firm up overnight.

6. Turn the fudge out onto a clean cutting board and peel off the foil. Turn the slab of fudge right side up and cut it into 25 equal pieces.
—*Bonnie Gorder-Hinchey*

PER PIECE: 190 CALORIES I 1G PROTEIN I 30G CARB I 9G TOTAL FAT I 6G SAT FAT I 2.5G MONO FAT I 0G POLY FAT I 25MG CHOL I 100MG SODIUM I 1G FIBER

secrets to smooth fudge

Making melt-in-your-mouth chocolate fudge is simple: You boil sugar, heavy cream, and chocolate, let the mixture cool, and then beat it to the right consistency. As the mixture boils, the sugar crystals dissolve, and the sugar concentration gradually increases. Then, once beating starts, the sugar begins to recrystallize. If the crystals stay small, the result is a smooth fudge. But if larger crystals form, the fudge will be grainy. Because large crystals can form at any time during fudge making, you need to be vigilant. Here's what to do every step of the way for perfect results.

USE CORN SYRUP AND BUTTER Both interfere with sugar crystallization, so adding them to the fudge prevents the crystals from growing too large. Butter should be added only after the boiling is done. If added before boiling, it coats the crystals and keeps them from dissolving, resulting in grainy fudge.

CLEAN THE PAN SIDES It's important to keep the boiling mixture from coming in contact with sugar crystals on the sides of the pan; otherwise, the sugar will start to recrystallize too soon, causing large crystals to form. To prevent this, cover the pot with a lid for 2 minutes after it starts boiling—the steam will wash the crystals down the sides.

BRING THE MIXTURE TO THE RIGHT TEMPERATURE Boiling the mixture to 236°F to 238°F (known as the soft-ball stage) results in the correct concentration of sugar, so the fudge sets up to the proper firmness after beating. Fudge boiled below this temperature is too soft to hold its shape, and fudge boiled above this point becomes too firm.

DON'T STIR THE FUDGE Shaking or stirring the fudge mixture while it's boiling or cooling causes premature crystal growth. If the crystals form too early, they continue to grow and become too large.

LET IT COOL Start beating the fudge only when it has cooled down to 110°F. It will be glossy and dark brown. If it's hotter, the crystals will form too fast and the fudge will be grainy. If the fudge is too cool, it will set up and be difficult to beat.

KNOW WHEN TO STOP BEATING Beat the fudge vigorously to form many small crystals and create a smooth texture; stop beating when it turns a lighter brown and becomes more opaque, and when the ripples made by the beaters hold their shape long enough to briefly expose the bottom of the pan.

METRIC EQUIVALENTS

LIQUID/DRY MEASURES	
U.S.	**METRIC**
¼ teaspoon	1.25 milliliters
½ teaspoon	2.5 milliliters
1 teaspoon	5 milliliters
1 tablespoon (3 teaspoons)	15 milliliters
1 fluid ounce (2 tablespoons)	30 milliliters
¼ cup	60 milliliters
⅓ cup	80 milliliters
½ cup	120 milliliters
1 cup	240 milliliters
1 pint (2 cups)	480 milliliters
1 quart (4 cups; 32 ounces)	960 milliliters
1 gallon (4 quarts)	3.84 liters
1 ounce (by weight)	28 grams
1 pound	454 grams
2.2 pounds	1 kilogram

OVEN TEMPERATURES		
°F	**GAS MARK**	**°C**
250	½	120
275	1	140
300	2	150
325	3	165
350	4	180
375	5	190
400	6	200
425	7	220
450	8	230
475	9	240
500	10	260
550	Broil	290

CONTRIBUTORS

Bruce Aidells is the author of 10 cookbooks, including *The Complete Meat Cookbook.*

Pam Anderson is a contributing editor to *Fine Cooking* and the author of several books, including her latest, *Perfect One-Dish Dinners: All You Need For Easy Get-Togethers.* She blogs weekly about food and life with daughters Maggy and Sharon on their Web site, www. threemanycooks.com.

Jennifer Armentrout is senior food editor at *Fine Cooking.*

John Ash is the founder and chef of John Ash & Co., in Santa Rosa, California. He teaches at the Culinary Institute of America at Greystone and is a cookbook author. His latest, *John Ash: Cooking One on One,* won a James Beard award.

Jessica Bard is a food stylist, food writer, and recipe tester who teaches cooking classes at Warren Kitchen and Cutlery in Rhinebeck, New York.

Karen Barker is a pastry chef and cookbook author. She co-owns Magnolia Grill in Durham, North Carolina, with her husband, Ben. She won the James Beard Outstanding Pastry Chef Award in 2003.

Ben Berryhill is the chef/owner of Red Drum in Charleston, South Carolina.

Paul Bertolli is a writer, artisan food producer, and award-winning chef in the San Francisco Bay area of California.

Eugenia Bone is a veteran food writer and author of *At Mesa's Edge, Italian Family Dining,* and *Well-Preserved.*

Julie Grimes Bottcher is a recipe developer and food writer.

Joanne Chang is the pastry chef and owner of Flour Bakery + Café, which has two locations in Boston.

Lauren Chattman has written 12 cookbooks. Her latest are *Simply Great Breads* and *Cookie Swap.*

Dina Cheney is a freelance writer, recipe developer, and tasting host based in Connecticut. She is the author of *Tasting Club* and *New Flavors for Salads.*

Scott Conant is the chef at Scarpetta restaurants in New York City, Miami, Toronto, and Beverly Hills. His latest cookbook is *Bold Italian.*

Robert Del Grande is chef and partner in the Schiller Del Grande Restaurant Group, whose restaurants include Cafe Annie, Rio Ranch, and The Grove.

Erica De Mane is a chef, food writer, and teacher specializing in Southern Italian cooking. She is the author of *The Flavors of Southern Italy* and *Pasta Improvvisata.*

Tasha DeSerio is a cooking teacher and food writer, and the co-owner of Olive Green Catering in Berkeley, California. She is also the co-author of *Cooking from the Farmer's Market.*

Paula Disbrowe was the chef at Hart & Hind Fitness Ranch in Rio Frio, Texas. Her latest cookbook is *Cowgirl Cuisine: Rustic Recipes and Cowgirl Adventures from a Texas Ranch.*

Abigail Johnson Dodge, a former pastry chef, is a food writer and instructor. She studied in Paris at La Varenne and is the author of seven cookbooks, including *Desserts 4 Today.*

Beth Dooley is the restaurant critic for *Minneapolis/St. Paul Magazine,* a columnist for the *Minneapolis StarTribune,* and a reporter for the NBC affiliate KARE-11 TV, covering farmers markets and the local food scene.

Rebecca Fasten is the sous-chef at Liberty Café in San Francisco.

Allison Fishman is co-host of Lifetime TV's *Cook Yourself Thin,* as well as a food writer and recipe developer.

Roy Finamore is the James Beard award-winning author of *Tasty: Get Great Food on the Table Every Day* and co-author with Rick Moonen of *Fish Without a Doubt* and with Molly Stevens of *One Potato, Two Potato.*

Melissa Gaman is a recipe developer and food stylist in the New York City area.

Joyce Goldstein is one of the foremost experts on Italian cooking in the United States. She is an award–winning chef, prolific cookbook author, and cooking teacher.

Dabney Gough is a frequent contributor to FineCooking.com and a former recipe tester for the magazine.

Alexandra Guarnaschelli is executive chef at Butter Restaurant and a chef-instructor at New York's Institute of Culinary Education.

David Guas is the chef/owner of DamGoodSweet, a pastry consulting company, the owner of Bayou Bakery, and author of *DamGoodSweet*.

Kate Hays is the chef-owner of Dish Catering in Shelburne, Vermont. She is also a recipe tester, recipe developer, and food stylist.

Bonnie Gorder-Hinchey has over 25 years of experience as a food scientist developing products and recipes for companies including General Mills, Nestle, and Starbucks to name a few. She owns Creative Cuisine and is an adjunct professor at The Art Institute of Seattle, where she teaches culinary classes as well as classes in nutrition and general science.

Martha Holmberg is the former editor in chief of *Fine Cooking* and a food writer and cookbook author.

Jill Hough is a cookbook author, food writer, recipe developer, and culinary instructor from Napa, California. Her first cookbook is *100 Perfect Pairings: Small Plates to Enjoy with Wines You Love*.

Arlene Jacobs is a former chef at Bette restaurant in New York City.

Cheryl Alters Jamison and **Bill Jamison** are authors of more than a dozen cookbooks, including *Around the World in 80 Dinners*.

Sarah Jay is a former executive editor of *Fine Cooking* and the proprietor of www.paellapans.com.

Eva Katz has worked as a chef, caterer, teacher, recipe developer and tester, food stylist, and food writer. She is a member of the Program Advisory Committee at the Cambridge School of Culinary Arts in Massachusetts.

Hubert Keller is the award-winning chef at Fleur de Lys and The Burger Bar and SLeeK Steakhouse and Lounge. He was awarded the James Beard Foundation's lifetime achievement for "Who's Who" in the industry.

Loretta Keller is chef-owner of Coco500 and partner with Charles Phan of the California Academy of Sciences in San Francisco.

Allison Ehri Kreitler is a *Fine Cooking* contributing editor. She has also worked as a freelance food stylist, recipe tester and developer, and writer for several national food magazines and the Food Network.

Ris Lacoste has been an award-winning chef for 25 years, including 10 years as the executive chef at 1789 Restaurant in Washington, D.C.

Eileen Yin-Fei Lo is a chef and author of 11 cookbooks, including *Mastering the Art of Chinese Cooking*.

Lori Longbotham is a recipe developer and cookbook author whose books include *Luscious Coconut Desserts* and *Luscious Creamy Desserts*.

Deborah Madison is a cookbook author, cooking teacher, and consultant. Her most recent book is *Seasonal Fruit Desserts from Orchard, Farm, and Market*.

Ivy Manning is a cooking teacher, food writer, and cookbook author; her most recent book is *The Farm to Table Cookbook*.

Nancie McDermott is a cooking teacher and cookbook author specializing in the cuisines of Southeast Asia.

Perla Meyers teaches cooking at workshops around the country and has cooked in restaurants throughout Italy, France, and Spain.

Denise Mickelsen is associate editor at *Fine Cooking*.

Susie Middleton is the former editor and current editor at large for *Fine Cooking* magazine. She is also Consulting Editor, writer, and photographer for *Edible Vineyard* magazine, as well as a cookbook author.

Cindy Mitchell and her husband, Glenn, own Grace Baking, an award-winning bakery in the San Francisco Bay area.

Diane Morgan is an award-winning cookbook author, food writer, culinary instructor, and restaurant consultant.

Maria and Lorant Nagyszalanczy are former contributors to *Fine Cooking*.

David Norman is a former *Fine Cooking* contributor.

Liz Pearson is a food writer and recipe developer based in Austin, Texas.

Melissa Pellegrino is an assistant food editor at *Fine Cooking* and author of *The Italian Farmer's Table*.

James Peterson worked in a number of restaurants in France and owned a restaurant in New York. He has published 14 books and has been the winner of six James Beard Awards.

Mai Pham is chef/owner of Lemon Grass Restaurant in Sacramento, California. A respected expert on Southeast Asian Cuisine, she writes for national publications, conducts cooking classes and seminars, and serves as a consultant to various food organizations throughout the United States.

Mary Pult is the chef at Liberty Café in San Francisco.

Nicole Rees, author of *Baking Unplugged* and co-author of *The Baker's Manual* and *Understanding Baking,* is a food scientist and professional baker.

Paige Retus is the pastry chef at Olives in Boston.

Juli Roberts works in the test kitchen at *Fine Cooking.*

Tony Rosenfeld, a *Fine Cooking* contributing editor, is also a food writer and restaurant owner based in the Boston area. His second cookbook, *Sear, Sauce, and Serve,* on high-heat cooking, will be out next spring.

Suvir Saran, owner/chef at Devi in New York City and American Masala restaurants, is a chef, consultant, and cookbook author. His books include *American Masala* and *Indian Home Cooking.*

Samantha Seneviratne is associate food editor and food stylist at *Fine Cooking.*

Tania Sigal is a food writer and chef/restaurant owner/caterer in Miami.

Maria Helm Sinskey is a noted chef, cookbook author, and Culinary Director at her family's winery, Robert Sinskey Vineyards, in Napa Valley, California. Her most recent cookbook, *Family Meals: Creating Traditions in the Kitchen,* was a 2010 IACP Cookbook Award Winner.

Irving Shelby Smith is a contributor to *Fine Cooking.*

Molly Stevens is a contributing editor to *Fine Cooking.* She won the IACP Cooking Teacher of the Year Award in 2006; her book *All About Braising* won James Beard and IACP Awards.

Kathleen Stewart runs the Downtown Bakery in Healdsburg, California.

Adeena Sussman is a food writer, recipe developer, chef, and cooking instructor in New York City.

David Tanis is head chef at Chez Panisse, as well as the author of *A Platter of Figs and Other Recipes.*

Alan Tardi began his cooking career at Chanterelle and Lafayette, with Jean-Georges Vongerichten. He was chef-owner of Follonico for almost 10 years. His latest book is *Romancing the Vine.*

Suzette Gresham-Tognetti is the chef at Acquerello in San Francisco. She was also the first female Chef's Apprentice to accompany the U.S. Culinary Olympic Team to Frankfurt, Germany, in 1980.

Julia Usher is a pastry chef, writer, and stylist whose work has appeared in *Vera Wang on Weddings, Bon Appétit, Better Homes and Gardens,* and more. She is a contributing editor at *Dessert Professional* as well as a director of the IACP.

Suneeta Vaswani has been teacing Indian cooking for close to 30 years and is the author of *Easy Indian Cooking.*

Carole Walter is a master baker, cooking instructor, and cookbook author; her most recent cookbook is *Great Coffee Cakes, Sticky Buns, Muffins & More.*

Alice Waters is the founder and proprietor of Chez Panisse in Berkeley, California.

Bruce Weinstein and **Mark Scarbrough** are the award-winning authors of 19 cookbooks, contributing editors to *Eating Well,* and columnists for www.weightwatchers.com.

Robert Wemischner teaches professional baking at Los Angeles Trade Technical College.

Anne Willan is an internationally renowned authority on the cooking of France and its culinary history. She has written over a dozen cookbooks and has served as president of the International Association of Culinary Professionals.

Clifford Wright is an award-winning cookbook author and is a contributor to www.zesterdaily.com. He has written for many cooking magazines, including *Bon Appetit, Food and Wine,* and *Saveur.*

Dawn Yanagihara is a former editor at *Cook's Illustrated.*

PHOTO CREDITS

Amy Albert, © The Taunton Press: p. 168

© Maren Caruso: pp. iii, iv, 9, 82, 158, 169, 171, 173, 174, 176, 182, 204, 227, 230

© Grey Crawford: p. 34,

© Mark Ferri: p. 85

© Brian Hagiwara: p. 30

© Christopher Hirsheimer: p. 215

Martha Holmberg, © The Taunton Press: pp. 43, 49, 234

© Alan Richardson: pp. 26 (top), 130

Scott Phillips, © The Taunton Press: pp. i, 2, 4-8, 10-25, 26 (bottom), 27, 29, 33, 35, 37, 40-41, 44-48, 50-63, 66-69, 72-80, 83, 84, 86-128, 132-138, 141-146, 148-156, 160-166, 170, 177-181, 184-202, 205-212, 214-224, 228, 229, 231-233, 235-243

© Laurie Smith: pp. 70-71

© Mark Thomas: pp. 38, 65, 139, 147

INDEX

TRY THESE OTHER DELICIOUS RECIPE COLLECTIONS FROM FINE COOKING.

Fine Cooking Fresh
Product #071261
ISBN 978-1-60085-109-4
$19.95

Fine Cooking Appetizers
Product #071323
ISBN 978-1-60085-330-2
$19.95

Fine Cooking Cookies
Product #071338
ISBN 978-1-60085-369-2
$19.95

Fine Cooking Italian
Product #071370
ISBN 978-1-60085-430-9
$19.95

To order, visit www.taunton.com.

For more information about Fine Cooking, go to finecooking.com.